THE EXECUTIVE'S COMPLETE GUIDE TO BUSINESS TAXES

ROBERT W. WOOD

DOW JONES-IRWIN
Homewood, Illinois 60430

Dow Jones-Irwin is a trademark of Dow Jones & Company, Inc.

Sponsoring editor: Jim Childs
Project editor: Jean Roberts
Production manager: Carma W. Fazio
Cover design: Tim Kaage
Compositor: Publication Services, Inc.
Typeface: 11/13 Century Schoolbook
Printer: Arcata Graphics/Kingsport

LIBRARY OF CONGRESS
Library of Congress Cataloging-in-Publication Data

Wood, Robert W.
The executive's complete guide to business taxes / Robert W. Wood
    p. cm.
  Includes index.
  ISBN 1-556-23116-4
  1. Business-enterprises–Taxation–United States. I. Title.
KF46450.Z9W66 1988
343.7306'8–dc19
[347.30368]
         88–20950
         CIP

Printed in the United States of America
2 3 4 5 6 7 8 0 K 5 4 3 2 1 0 9

PREFACE

Businesspeople have long been intimidated by our federal income tax system. A good part of this is due to the vagaries of the system itself. To a far greater extent than ever before, the federal tax laws are changing at a staggering pace.

Legislators have showered us with a major tax bill virtually every year for the last seven years. And far from just tinkering with the system, they have enacted sweeping changes going to the very underpinnings of the tax. With tax professionals staggering under the weight of these changes, it is no wonder that businesspeople have not been able even to hope to understand enough of the federal tax system to apply it effectively to their businesses.

The second reason for the intimidation felt by most businesspeople toward taxes and tax planning is the responsibility of tax advisers. Tax advisers have failed to adequately explain and demystify much of the gobbledygook that Congress has foisted upon us. This is certainly an understandable and even justifiable failing given the complexity of the tax law, the rapidity with which it is changing, and the danger of trying to summarize rules to which there are normally exceptions and even exceptions to the exceptions.

Yet this book attempts to do just that: to explain and demystify. It does so in a question and answer format to make reading—in the language of computers—more user friendly. Key tax terms used in the text are highlighted in bold face and defined in the glossary.

Armed with the material contained in this book, business people can do some tax planning of their own. Perhaps more importantly, they have an interpreter to a language that all too often seems foreign—and even extraterrestrial.

Robert W. Wood

For Bea and Bryce

CONTENTS

on the Dividends Received Deduction? Does
the Amount of the Dividend Have Any Bearing
on the Restrictions? What about Other
Special Corporate Tax Items? Are
Corporations Subject to Additional Taxes
over and above the Regular Corporate Income
Tax? How Is the Accumulated Earnings Tax
Applied? What Constitutes the "Reasonable
Needs of the Business"? If an Accumulation
Is Justified Based on a Planned Acquisition,
Must the Acquisition Actually Take Place?
Are Some Grounds for an Accumulation of
Earnings Considered "Unreasonable"? Who
Has the Burden of Proof in an Accumulated
Earnings Tax Case? Can't You Accumulate
Anything without Having to Show Reasonable
Needs of the Business? Are There Any
Other Corporate-Level Taxes? What Is
Personal Holding Company Income? How
Can All These Complex Income Items Be
Monitored? What Is the Tax Cost upon
Formation of a Corporation? Is It Difficult
to Go from a Corporation Back to a
Partnership or Proprietorship? Must All
Businesses (Partnerships and Corporations)
Now Operate on a Calendar Year? Is
This Kind of Fiscal-Year Tax Planning Gone?

When Can Purchases Be Written Off during One
Year? How Do You Tell What Items Are
Deductible? What Expenses Are Likely to Be
Treated as Nondeductible? What Are the
Restrictions Applicable to Automobile Expenses?
Aren't Some Automobile Expenses Deductible
Even If the Car Is Not Used Predominantly
for Business? What Other Auto Deductions
May Be Taken? What Items Can Be

Under Current Rules, over What Periods Can Assets
Be Written Off? Is Accelerated Depreciation
Still Available? What If You Don't Elect
Straight-Line Depreciation?

CHAPTER 4 Inventories, Accounting Methods, and Installment Sales 77

Who Is Subject to Inventory Rules? What Is the
Purpose of Measuring Inventory? What Must Be
Included in Inventory? How Is Inventory Valued?
What Is Considered a Cost of Inventory? Can Any
Expenses of Inventory Be Currently Deducted? Do
Interest Costs Have to Be Included in This
Inventory Computation? Can Interest Incurred to
Purchase Inventory Be Deducted? How Does One
Identify Which Inventory Items Have Been Sold?
Are These the Only Methods of Inventory
Identification? Which Method Applies to Most
Businesses? How Do Inventories Influence
Accounting Methods? Of the Cash and Accrual
Methods of Accounting, Which Is Better? Who
Is Entitled to Use the Cash Method? Can You
Switch Back and Forth between the Cash and
Accrual Methods? What Is the Installment
Method? Is the Installment Method Mandatory?
Does Every Sale Qualify for Installment
Sale Treatment? Can Dealers Who Sell Property
Report Their Gain on the Installment Method?
What about Dealer Sales of Real or Personal
Property That Occurred Prior to 1988? Are There
Any Exceptions That Allow Dealers to Report on
the Installment Basis? How Is the Gain on
an Installment Sale Computed? Is It Possible
under an Installment Sale to Be Taxed on More
Than the Amount of Cash Received? How Can the
Tax Be Greater Than the Cash Received? What Is
Considered Payments in the Year of Sale? Are
Some Installment Sales Disallowed If the Taxpayer
Has Outstanding Debt? Can Installment Obligations
Be Pledged? What Happens When an Installment

Note Is Sold? What If Interest Is Not Stated on
an Installment Obligation? When Does This Imputed
Interest Apply? Are There Any Exceptions from This
Imputed Interest Treatment? How Can the Imputed
Interest Rules Be Avoided? Doesn't a Special 9
Percent Test Rate Apply to Certain Sales? How
Often Is the Interest Tested?

How Are Sales of Inventory Assets Taxed? How
Are Sales of Capital Assets Taxed? Are Sales of
Capital Assets Taxed Just like Sales of Ordinary
Income Assets Now? Is It More Advantageous
Now to Have Capital Gains/Losses or Ordinary
Gains/Losses? Can You Plan to Avoid the
Capital Loss Problem? Is the Distinction
between Capital Gains and Ordinary Income of
Significance to Corporations? How Does a
Corporate Carryover or Carryback Work? Can
Corporations Engage in the Same Kind of Planning
That Individuals Do to Generate Capital Gains
to Offset Capital Losses? What Assets Are
Considered Capital Assets in the Business
Context? When Does Depreciation Recapture
Occur? What Kind of Property Is Subject to
Recapture? Is Depreciation Taken on Real
Property Subject to Recapture? What Is
Straight-Line Depreciation? Is Straight Line
or Accelerated Depreciation Better for Real
Estate? Would an Installment Sale of the Asset
Spread out the Recapture Tax? Is It Possible to
Exchange or "Swap" Property Tax-Free? What
Kind of Assets Must Be Received in a Tax-Free
Exchange? Are There Any Other Requirements
for a Successful Tax-Free Exchange? What Is a
Three-Party Exchange? Does This Kind of
Three-Party Exchange Really Work? What Happens
if Cash Is Also Transferred in a Like-Kind
Exchange? Can the Tax on the Cash Be Avoided
by Transferring Other Property? What Happens

Can Have "Constructive Receipt," How Can
Income Be Deferred?   What about an Annual
Bonus?   Must the Agreement to Defer Compensation
Be Entered into Prior to the Time *Any* Services Are
Performed?   Is It Ever Possible to Defer the
Income *after* the Services Are Rendered?   What
If the Employee Who Defers the Income Needs to
Get It Before It Comes Due under the Deferral
Agreement?   Is It Possible to Keep Rolling
Over a Deferral?   What about Getting Security
for the Deferred Payment from the Employer?   Is
There Any Way to Obtain Security for a Deferred
Compensation Obligation without Incurring Tax?
What Is a Rabbi Trust?   Are There Any Other
Methods of Securing an Employee's Interest in
Deferred Compensation Benefits?

What Types of Stock Options Are Available?   How
Are Recipients of Nonqualified Options Taxed?   How
Are Recipients of Incentive Stock Options Taxed?
Which Is Better for the Recipient, Nonqualified
Stock Options or Incentive Stock Options?   Which
Is More Popular, Incentive Stock Options or
Nonqualified Options?   What Other Stock
Compensation Methods Are There besides Stock
Options?   What Are the Advantages of a
Restricted Stock Plan?   What If the Employee
Pays Something for the Shares?   How Do
Restricted Stock Purchase and Restricted Stock
Bonus Plans Compare to Incentive Stock Option
and Nonqualified Option Plans?   What Is a
Phantom Stock Plan?   How Is a Participant in
a Phantom Stock Plan or Stock Appreciation
Rights Plan Taxed?   When Should These Plans
Be Used?   What Type of Compensation for Martin
Would Be Appropriate?   What If Martin Really
Wants "Real" Stock?   What Kind of Plan Is
Appropriate Here?   Is One Plan Better for

Employees Than Others from a Tax Standpoint?
What Is Good about the Stock Bonus Program?
What about the Company's Tax Planning?   Would
the Restricted Stock or Stock Option Plan Be
More Favorable?   Is an Incentive Stock Option
Plan More Restricted?   What Are the Other
Disadvantages of Incentive Stock Options?
Would a Phantom Stock Plan Be Desirable?
Charlene Opens the Board Meeting by Asking:
What Considerations Should Play a Part in
Choosing among These Alternatives?   What
Else Makes the Stock Plans Attractive Here?
What Tax Considerations Are There in the
Decision?

CHAPTER 8 Deferred Compensation Plans   148

What Is a Qualified Retirement Plan? What Types
of Qualified Retirement Plans Are There?   How
Can the Employer Promise to Provide a Particular
Benefit on Retirement?   Why Would Anyone Use a
Defined Benefit Plan?   What Requirements Apply
to Qualified Plans?   How Fast Must a Plan
Participant's Benefits Vest?   Aren't There
Different Types of Retirement Plans?   What Is
an ESOP?   What Is a 401(k) Plan?   Can More
Than $7,000 a Year Be Put into a 401(k) Plan?
With All These Types of Defined Contribution
Plans, When Are Defined Benefit Plans Used?
Isn't Making Large Contributions for the Owners
and Small Contributions for Most Employees
Discrimination?   What Are the Limits on
Contributions to Defined Contribution Plans?
What Is the Effect of a Plan's Integration with
Social Security?   Can Loans Still Be Made
from Qualified Retirement Plans?   When Does
a Plan Loan Have to Be Repaid?   How Are
Benefits Taxed from a Qualified Retirement Plan?
Can the Large Tax on the Lump-Sum Distribution
Be Reduced?   How Do You Qualify for Five-Year
Averaging on a Plan Distribution?   Does It Make

Stock?   Are There Any Tax Reasons to Prefer
an Assets Purchase?   How Is an Asset Purchase/
Sale Taxed?   Are the Sales Proceeds Taxed in
the Hands of the Shareholders as Well?   How
Is the Shareholder Tax Calculated?   When Are
Tax-Free Reorganizations Considered?   What
Are the Types of Tax-Free Reorganizations?
What Is a Stock-for-Stock Acquisition?   Could
This Also Qualify as a Statutory Merger?   What
Is a Stock-for-Assets Acquisition?   What Is
an Assets-for-Stock Acquisition?   What Is
Recapitalization?   Why Would a Recapitalization
Be Undertaken for Estate Planning Purposes?
Does This Procedure Work?   What Is a Leveraged
Buyout?   How Can a Company Be Acquired with
Funds Borrowed against That Same Company's Assets?
When Is a Leveraged Buyout Attractive?   What Are
the Disadvantages of a Leveraged Buyout?   Are
There Any Other Disadvantages to Leveraged
Buyouts?   What Are the Tax Implications of a
Leveraged Buyout?   What Form Can a Leveraged
Buyout Take?   How Can an Employee Stock Ownership
Plan Be Used in an Acquisition?   How Does an
ESOP Acquisition Work?   Does This Type of
Transaction Really Work?   Why Do the Sellers of
Stock Want to Sell an ESOP?   What Are the Tax
Benefits to the Seller in an ESOP Sale?   What
Requirements Must Be Met in Order for This
Reinvestment to Be Available?   But What
Constitutes a Qualified Security Eligible for
Reinvestment?   What Are the Income Tests?   Can
All of the Reinvestment Occur Prior to the Sale
of the ESOP?   Are There Any Other Requirements
That Apply to This Kind of ESOP Sale?   Are There
Any Drawbacks to the ESOP Buyout Method?

CHAPTER 10 Corporate Divisions and Partial Liquidations   195

What Is the Basic Goal of a Corporate Division?
What Would Happen If One of the Businesses Were
Sold?   What Are the Basic Requirements of a

CHAPTER 11 Planning for Troubled Businesses   **218**

From a Tax Perspective, What Happens When a
Business Files for Bankruptcy?   Can the IRS
Persist in Tax Collection Efforts against a
Company in Bankruptcy?   Is a Corporation's
Liability for Taxes Discharged in Bankruptcy?
Then Does It Make Sense to Declare Bankruptcy?
If a Business Is Reorganized in a Bankruptcy
Proceeding, Are There Any Tax Consequences?
What Options Are There Apart from Bankruptcy?
Does This Income Arise Whenever Debt Is Discharged?
Does This Mean That If the Corporation Is Insolvent
or in Bankruptcy, the Debt Can Be Forgiven
without Any Tax Consequences?   What Tax
Considerations Apply When the Business Will Not
Be Continued?   How Can a Net Operating Loss Be
Preserved?   How Can Another Corporation's Net
Operating Loss Be Acquired?   How Does This
Limitation Work?   What Is an Ownership Shift?
What Happens If an Ownership Shift Occurs?   If
an Ownership Shift Occurs, Can an NOL Still Be
Used?   What If This Continuity of Business
Enterprise Test Is Satisfied?   How Does This
Formula Work?   How Is This Multiplication
Performed?   If This NOL Percentage Test Is
Satisfied, Will the Net Operating Loss Be Usable?
Can a Company with an NOL Acquire a Profitable
Company to Offset Its Own Loss? What Happens to
the Shareholder's Investment When a Corporation
Goes Bankrupt?   How Much Is the Deduction Worth?
Why Are Capital Losses Worth Less Than Ordinary
Losses?   Is It Possible for a Worthless Stock
Loss to Produce Ordinary Loss Rather than Capital
Loss?   What Is Section 1244 Stock? What If
a Shareholder Also Holds Securities in the
Corporation? Does the Worthless Security Loss
Rule Apply?   What about Loans to the Corporation
That Are Not Paid?   What Is the Difference between
Business and Nonbusiness Bad Debts?   What
If the Company Is Owed Money That Is Not Paid?

CHAPTER 1

CHOOSING THE BUSINESS ENTITY

INTRODUCTION

Choosing the appropriate form of business entity is a critical factor in achieving virtually any business goal. Our tax laws distinguish in a variety of important ways between partnerships, proprietorships, corporations, and S corporations. As a result, substantial tax consequences (as well as business and state law consequences) will flow from the decision. Unfortunately, all too often the tax consequences are not fully considered until it is too late to make a change without a significant tax cost.

The importance of the decision is not limited to the inception of the business. Even after a business has been operating for a significant period, it may be profitable to reevaluate structural issues. A properly planned midstream change in form can save substantial dollars down the road.

Q: WHAT IS THE MOST APPROPRIATE FORM IN WHICH TO CONDUCT BUSINESS?

A: The appropriate form of business depends upon a variety of factors, including business goals and the desired tax treatment. There are three basic types of business organizations: corporations, partnerships, and proprietorships. Partnerships and corporations each have various subtypes.

A partnership may be either a limited partnership or a general partnership. For tax purposes, limited and general partnerships are treated almost identically. The only difference relates to the manner in which partners of each type of partnership may gain additional basis from partnership liabilities. A partner's basis is important for purposes of determining allowable loss deductions and calculating gain or loss on disposition.

A corporation may be either an S corporation or a C corporation. The tax treatment of C and S corporations is radically different.

Q: WHAT ARE THE TAX CONSIDERATIONS OF EACH TYPE OF BUSINESS ORGANIZATION?

A: A proprietorship is, by definition, owned by an individual. There is no separate taxpayer, and the proprietor's business income or loss is combined with the proprietor's income or loss from all other sources.

With a partnership, an unlimited number of partners can participate. Each partner receives a share of the income or loss of the partnership determined in accordance with the partnership agreement. The partner's income or loss from the partnership will be combined with the income or loss of each partner from all other activities. Like a proprietorship, a partnership is not a taxable entity for tax purposes. Unlike a proprietorship, however, a partnership is a separate entity for purposes of state and federal law.

A corporation is a separate entity both for tax purposes and under state and federal law. The income or loss of a corporation (other than an **S Corporation**, which is discussed below) does not flow through directly to the shareholders as would be the case with a partnership. Instead, the corporation is a separate taxpayer that is taxable on its income and may itself claim deductions.

When distributions are made to shareholders, the shareholders themselves will have income or loss. Thus, there is a double tax on corporate income: one on income earned by the corporation and one on distributions to shareholders. Like a partnership, a corporation may have an unlimited number of owners. However, it is more customary for a business with a large number of owners to be conducted in the corporate rather than the partnership form. Basic partnership and corporate tax rules are discussed in Chapter 2.

One type of corporation entitled to vastly different treatment is the S corporation. For most purposes, the S corporation is taxed like a partnership. Individual items of income and loss flow through to the shareholders as if they were partners in a partnership. The S corporation, discussed in more detail below, can have only 35 shareholders and one class of stock, and is subject to certain other limits.

PROPRIETORSHIPS

Q: WHEN CAN A PROPRIETORSHIP BE USED?

A: By definition, a proprietorship will be considered only where there is one owner of the business. However, a proprietorship can be conducted by a taxpayer and his or her spouse if they file joint returns, since for tax purposes they are treated as one person. The advantage of a proprietorship is that, like a partnership, deductions flow through directly to the proprietor. If the business incurs deductions resulting in a loss for one of its years of operation, for example, the proprietor individually will claim the loss.

If the business were conducted in corporate form, on the other hand, the loss would remain locked in the corporation and be usable only against the corporation's (but not the shareholders') income from previous or subsequent years. The corporate loss can be carried forward or carried back to other tax years only by the corporation, and thus be used to offset gain generated in those earlier or later tax years. Consequently, a proprietorship is advantageous when losses in the early years of operation are anticipated that would not be deductible in the corporate context.

Q: WHEN IS A PROPRIETORSHIP ADVANTAGEOUS?

A: Traditionally, a proprietorship was not viewed as the best form in which to operate a business if that business was expected to generate taxable income from its inception. In other words, if no initial loss period was anticipated, flow-through tax treatment was not needed. A lower tax cost might be achieved by leaving some money in a corporation (which would be taxable at the lower corporate tax rates) and not paying it out to the shareholders. This flexibility does not exist with a proprietorship, as all income is earned by the proprietor and not by a separate entity.

However, the traditional thinking has changed in recent years. With the higher tax costs now borne by corporations (after 1987, a top 34 percent rate applies for corporations compared with a top marginal 28 percent rate for individuals), the individual considering conducting business through a proprietorship or corporation will most frequently choose to conduct it as a proprietorship when taxes are the only consideration. Of course, corporations may still be preferred for reasons of limiting liability under state law. In this event, the person may wish to conduct business as an S corporation.

DJI Planning Guide

Proprietorships are the simplest and least expensive of any business form and can be ideal for a business start-up with only one owner (or an owner and spouse). A partnership, corporation, or S corporation can be formed later, normally with no tax cost. The need for limited liability from creditors and tort claims (which a proprietorship does not afford) may be solved by insurance. In any case, too often a proprietorship is not considered at all in view of the more sophisticated alternatives.

S CORPORATIONS

Q: WHAT ARE THE LIMITS AND RESTRICTIONS APPLICABLE TO S CORPORATIONS?

A: S corporations were first brought into the law in the late 1950s and have become extremely popular in recent years. An S corporation is a normal corporation under state law (virtually all states now have legislation paralleling the federal legislation governing S corporations). For tax purposes, however, an S corporation is treated much the same as a partnership. Individual items of income or loss pass through pro rata to the shareholders of the S corporation in relation to their percentage of stock in the corporation.

Q: WHO QUALIFIES TO USE AN S CORPORATION?

A: Even one individual can use an S corporation. Consequently, it represents an alternative to conducting business through a proprietorship. In fact, an S corporation can have up to 35 shareholders. A husband and wife (and their estates) are counted as a single shareholder for this purpose without regard to the manner in which they hold title to their shares under state law, so the actual number of shareholders may approach 70.

The eligibility of shareholders is also restricted. The shareholders must all be individuals or estates (and certain types of trusts), but no shareholder may be a nonresident alien. A nonresident alien is a non–U.S. citizen who does not reside in the United States.

Even an individual in bankruptcy may be an S corporation shareholder; the bankruptcy proceedings do not terminate the election. The types of trusts that may qualify include a grantor trust (a trust where the trust's income is taxable to the grantor of the trust), a voting trust (the beneficiaries of the trust being treated as shareholders), and, for a limited period of time, a testamentary trust.

A **qualified subchapter S trust** may also hold stock in an S corporation. This is a trust whose individual beneficiaries elect to be treated as the owner of the S corporation stock owned in the trust. In effect, the qualified subchapter S trust involves an election by a beneficiary to have the portion of the trust consisting of S corporation stock treated as a grantor trust. A grantor trust's income is taxable to the person who sets up or benefits from the trust.

Example

Mom & Pop, Inc. has four shareholders: Mom, Pop, Junior, and a long-term trust set up for the benefit of their other child, Spendthrift. In order for Mom & Pop, Inc. to qualify to make an S election, Spendthrift will have to elect to be taxable on the portion of the trust's income that is attributable to the stock.

DJI Planning Guide

In a situation like the above example, the benefits of the S election must be compared with the tax cost (if any) of having trust income taxable to the beneficiary instead of to the trust. It really requires an examination of the tax to be borne by the beneficiary of the trust in comparison to the tax to be borne by the corporation (and ultimately by the shareholders as a group) as a result of not making the S election.

Q: WHAT ARE THE OTHER RESTRICTIONS APPLICABLE TO S CORPORATIONS?

A: A corporation with more than one class of stock cannot qualify as an S corporation. Accordingly, each share in the corporation must be entitled to the same proportion of the corporation's profits and assets (all stock must be common stock). However, differences in voting rights may be maintained among the shares of common stock without resulting in the corporation's being treated as having two classes of stock (two classes of stock would disqualify S corporation treatment).

Traditionally, there has also been some concern that debt instruments issued by an S corporation would be recharacterized as stock (sometimes referred to as *equity*). If a debt instrument such as a promissory note is treated as a second class of stock, it will disqualify S corporation treatment.

Example

Entrepreneur, Ltd., an S corporation with three shareholders, issues a 10-year promissory note to one of its shareholders in exchange for cash. If the note is recharacterized considered a second class of stock, and S corporation treatment would no longer be applicable.

This recharacterization is less of a concern now than it once was. If an instrument such as a promissory note meets certain minimal requirements, it will not be treated as stock and therefore will not be considered a second class of stock.

Debt will not be recharacterized as equity (and treated as a second class of stock) if it is a written, unconditional promise to pay on demand or on a specified date a specified sum of money and if the following three requirements are met:

- The interest rate and payment date must not be contingent on profits, the borrower's discretion, or similar factors.
- The debt cannot be convertible into stock.
- The creditor must be an individual (other than a nonresident alien) or an estate or trust that would qualify to be an S corporation shareholder.

DJI Planning Guide

This "safe harbor" for debt instruments removes most of the concern for their being recharacterized as a second class of stock. Loans to the corporation should follow these safe harbor provisions whenever possible.

Q: HOW IS THE S CORPORATION ELECTION MADE?

A: The S election is made on a simple one-page form (IRS Form 2553). Each shareholder must sign the form, indicating his or her consent to the election. The election must be filed with the Internal Revenue Service Center where the corporation will file its tax returns on or before the 15th day of the third month of its tax year (i.e., March 15).

- If the election is filed before this March 15 deadline, the election will be effective for the entire taxable year (i.e., it will be retroactive to January 1).
- If it is filed after this deadline, it will be effective only for the following year (commencing January 1 of the next year).

Note

An S corporation is generally a calendar-year taxpayer, apart from certain limited cases. That is why the normal deadline for filing an S election is March 15.

Q: WHEN DOES AN S ELECTION TERMINATE?

A: An S election terminates involuntarily whenever the corporation is no longer eligible to be an S corporation. For example, if one of the shareholders of the S corporation sells stock to a nonresident alien or to a domestic or foreign corporation, the S corporation election terminates upon this disqualifying transfer.

Another way that an S corporation election can terminate is when the corporation has excessive **passive investment income** and was formerly a regular C corporation. If, for three consecutive years, a corporation has both (1) accumulated **earnings and profits** (accumulated from years in which the S corporation was a C corporation, when no election was in effect), and (2) passive investment income exceeding 25 percent of its gross receipts, then the election will terminate beginning with the following tax year. Passive investment income includes dividends, interest, royalties, and other passive income.

Example

Zyborg, Ltd. operated for years as a C corporation and filed its S election in 1986. For 1986, 1987, and 1988, the corporation's gross receipts consisted of 60 percent service income, and the other 40 percent of its gross receipts were from interest and dividends. The corporation has significant accumulated earnings and profits from its C corporation years (1985 and earlier), which are held in reserve during the S years. Effective at the beginning of 1989, the election will terminate because the corporation has for three consecutive years (1) accumulated earnings and profits from years in which it was a C corporation, and (2) passive investment income exceeding 25 percent of its gross receipts in each year.

Q: HOW CAN AN S ELECTION BE TERMINATED VOLUNTARILY?

A: An S election may be revoked intentionally only with the consent of shareholders holding more than one-half of the corporation's stock. The revocation of the election can specify an effective date for the revocation in the future. When no date is specified in the revocation, it will be effective retroactively to the beginning of the taxable year as long as the revocation is made on or before the 15th day of the third month of the corporation's tax year (the first 75 days of the year). If the revocation is filed after this deadline, it will be effective for the following taxable year. Note that this effective date parallels that of an S election.

Example

IPO Ltd., on a calendar year, revokes its S election on March 1 by filing a properly signed revocation form. The election is revoked effective January 1. But if the form were filed March 16 (more than 75 days after the beginning of the tax year), the revocation would not be effective until January 1 of the next year.

Q: ISN'T THERE AN EASIER WAY TO REVOKE AN S ELECTION THAT DOESN'T REQUIRE CONSENT?

A: If a shareholder of an S corporation desperately desires to have the election terminated but cannot muster the necessary 50 percent of the shareholders to revoke the election, the shareholder could transfer all or part of his shares to a disqualifying person (a nonresident alien or a corporate shareholder). In this way the election would be terminated even without the consent of the other shareholders. However, the shares of an S corporation are frequently subject to buyback restrictions and shareholder agreements to prevent this kind of manipulation.

DJI Planning Guide _____

It is frequently a good idea to restrict the ability of shareholders to terminate an election in this way. Buyback and first option restrictions in a shareholders' agreement will help to ensure that a disgruntled shareholder does not terminate the election either to achieve his own tax goals or merely as an act of spite.

Q: CAN THE S ELECTION BE MADE AND REVOKED FROM YEAR TO YEAR DEPENDING ON WHETHER IT IS DESIRABLE EACH YEAR?

A: No. Once an election has been terminated or revoked, a new election may not be made for five years unless the IRS consents. The IRS is likely to consent where the election is inadvertently terminated (i.e., by means of a very small transfer for a brief period of time to a corporate shareholder) but is not likely to consent where the election is terminated because of some perceived tax advantage on the part of the shareholders, who later determine there was no advantage.

Q: HOW ARE S CORPORATION SHAREHOLDERS TAXED?

A: Each S corporation shareholder reports his pro rata share of items of income, deduction, loss, and credit of the corporation on his individual return. When the shareholder has held shares for less than the entire year, the shareholder's portion of each item is computed on a daily basis according to the number of shares held on each day. The shareholders pay all of the corporation's tax, or claim all of its loss, on their own tax returns.

Notably, no special allocation of income or loss items is possible with an S corporation. All income or loss must be reported by shareholders strictly in accordance with their percentage interests in the stock of the S corporation. This restriction represents a significant disadvantage as compared with a partnership, in which special allocations of income, loss, deductions, or tax credits are permitted.

When a shareholder receives a distribution from an S corporation, if the corporation does not have any accumulated earnings and profits, the entire distribution is tax-free up to the extent of the shareholder's *basis* in the stock (the amount paid for the stock). If the distribution exceeds the taxpayer's basis in his stock, any excess distribution is treated as a *capital gain*. Of course, **ordinary income** and capital gain are currently taxed at the same rates.

Q: HOW DOES AN S CORPORATION HAVE EARNINGS AND PROFITS?

A: **Earnings and profits** are a corporation's profits accumulated over the years. An S corporation will have earnings and profits *only* if it was previously a C (or "regular") corporation.

It need not have been a C corporation for long. If a corporation is in existence for even one year (or a portion of a year) in which no S election was in effect, it was a C corporation during this period. If the corporation had accumulated earnings during that "C" period and these earnings were not reduced by dividend or other distributions by the C corporation, then the corporation would be considered to have "accumulated earnings and profits" when an S election is filed.

One way to be sure there are no earnings and profits is if the corporation was always an S corporation or if any period of operation as a C corporation resulted in earnings deficits.

DJI Planning Guide

One guide to determining whether there are earnings and profits is the corporation's **retained earnings** entry from its balance sheet. Although the two terms are not synonymous, there is a rough correlation between them. Many people use retained earnings as a gauge of earnings and profits. A true earnings and profits analysis will require the services of an accountant.

Q: WHAT HAPPENS IF THERE ARE ACCUMULATED EARNINGS AND PROFITS?

A: If the S corporation has accumulated earnings and profits, shareholders receive tax-free treatment on distributions only up to the amount of the corporation's **accumulated adjustments account**. This account is essentially the corporation's post-1982 accumulated gross income, less its deductible expenses. After this tax-free treatment up to the extent of the corporation's accumulated adjustments account, the excess is treated as a dividend to the shareholder up to the amount of the corporation's accumulated earnings and profits. Any balance of a distribution over the accumulated earnings and profits reduces the shareholder's basis in his stock until it is reduced to zero. Finally, any additional amounts are treated as a capital gain.

As can be seen from this description, the taxation of shareholders on distributions from S corporations is straightforward when there are no accumulated earnings and profits, but it can be quite complex when the corporation does have earnings and profits.

Q: BECAUSE OF THE PASS-THROUGH NATURE OF S CORPORATIONS, AREN'T S CORPORATIONS DESIRABLE WHERE LOSSES WILL BE REALIZED?

A: As with proprietorships and partnerships, the S election is frequently a good choice when initial losses are anticipated from the conduct of a business. If the S election is made, the losses will be available to the shareholders of the S corporation to offset other income. Losses would not be available if the corporation were a C corporation.

There is an important limitation, however, on the ability of a shareholder to claim losses from an S corporation. The shareholder's share of the corporation's loss is limited to the sum of the following:

- The shareholder's adjusted basis in his stock (basically, the price he paid for the stock).
- The shareholder's adjusted basis in any debt the corporation owes to him (what he loaned to the corporation).

Q: HOW DO THE LOSS DEDUCTIONS WORK?

A: Any loss the shareholder claims first reduces his basis in his stock and then his basis in his debt.

Example

Barbara owns 100 shares in Capital Ltd., an S corporation with a total of 1,000 shares that had a $50,000 loss this year. Barbara paid $200 a share for the stock (a total of $20,000 for her 100 shares). In addition, Barbara loaned $5,000 to the corporation this year under a promissory note. Barbara's share of the $50,000 loss is $5,000 (10 percent). Because Barbara has a $20,000 basis in her stock and a $5,000 basis in the debt to the company, she can deduct the entire $5,000 loss. This reduces her stock basis to $15,000 (her debt basis of $5,000 remains the same). If the corporation has losses in succeeding years, Barbara's basis in her stock will continue to go down. If her stock basis were reduced to zero, then her basis in her debt would go down. When her stock basis and debt basis both reach zero, she will be unable to deduct any more losses from the corporation until that basis is restored.

As should be clear from the above example, an S corporation may not be a better option than a proprietorship or partnership when losses are anticipated, particularly when the losses in the first year will more than use up the shareholder's stock basis.

Q: HOW CAN A SHAREHOLDER'S BASIS IN HIS STOCK OR DEBT BE RESTORED?

A: By making a contribution to the corporation's capital (giving the corporation money) or by making a loan to the corporation.

DJI Planning Guide ⎯⎯⎯⎯⎯⎯⎯⎯⎯⎯⎯⎯⎯⎯⎯⎯⎯⎯⎯⎯

If it becomes apparent in any year that an S corporation shareholder's share of losses will exceed his basis, there is an easy solution to make sure all the loss can be claimed by the individual. The shareholder can make a loan (or another loan if there are already loans outstanding) to the corporation. A $20,000 loan to the corporation will provide another $20,000 in basis against which losses can be deducted.

Q: WHAT ADJUSTMENTS ARE MADE TO A SHAREHOLDER'S BASIS IN HIS STOCK?

A: A shareholder's basis (purchase price) in stock in an S corporation is adjusted due to various events. During the period an S election is in effect, each shareholder's basis in his stock is increased by his share of income items that are passed through to him (whether the income is taxable or not, so that tax-exempt income also increases the shareholder's basis in his stock). Although it is not of great consequence, the shareholder's basis is also increased by the excess of the corporation's deductions for depletion over the basis of the property on which the depletion is taken.

The shareholder's basis is decreased to the extent he receives nontaxable distributions from the corporation (not in excess of his basis), together with all loss and deduction items attributable to his percentage interest in the company. The shareholder's basis is also reduced in two other ways: (1) by expenses of the corporation that are not deductible in computing taxable income and are not properly chargeable to capital account, and (2) by the shareholder's deduction for depletion on oil and gas wells to the extent not in excess of the shareholder's proportionate share of the adjusted basis of that property.

Q: CAN THESE ADJUSTMENTS REDUCE THE SHAREHOLDER'S BASIS IN HIS SHARES BELOW ZERO?

A: No, the shareholder's basis in his stock cannot go below zero. When it reaches zero, the shareholder's basis in any debt the corporation owes him is reduced until it also reaches zero.

Q: HOW DOES A SHAREHOLDER'S BASIS GO BACK UP AFTER IT HAS BEEN REDUCED?

A: When the shareholder's basis in both his stock and his debt has been reduced through one of the above reductions, it is "restored" when an addition is made to the basis. This "restoration" is simply an addition to the shareholder's basis when there was previously a reduction in that basis. The restoration is made first to the corporation's debt to the shareholder (if that debt basis was reduced) and thereafter to increase the basis of the shareholder's stock.

Example

Barbara has now claimed a $25,000 loss on her shares in Capital Ltd., an S corporation, reducing her basis in her stock and her debt to zero. She then receives a $5,000 distribution together with a $5,000 allocation of income, which first restores her basis in her debt. Additional income distributions and allocations will restore her basis in her stock until the full $20,000 (the amount of her original basis) has been restored.

Q: IS AN S CORPORATION ITSELF TAXED?

A: Since the S corporation is a pass-through entity, the shareholders pay tax on the corporation's income items. The S corporation itself is not taxed. But there are several exceptions to this general proposition that an S corporation is not itself subject to tax. Which of the exceptions applies depends upon when the corporation first elected S status.

For corporations electing S status after 1986, the corporation itself is subject to a tax on its **built-in gain** recognized on the disposition of any of its property within ten years after the S election. The built-in gain is defined as any gain (basically, any appreciation in the corporation's assets) that arose *before* the corporation became an S corporation. In other words, the built-in gain applies only in cases where a C corporation converts to S status after 1986.

If the built-in gain tax is applicable, the tax is imposed on the built-in gain (the appreciation in corporate assets that occurred while the corporation was a C corporation). Once the S election is effective, any further appreciation in the corporation's assets can no longer give rise to built-in gain. But the amount of appreciation that arose during the corporation's taxable years as a C corporation continues to be subject to the built-in gain tax to the extent those assets are disposed of within 10 years after the S election is first made.

Note

As a ceiling, the built-in gain tax cannot be more than the tax that would be imposed if the corporation were a regular C corporation instead of an S corporation.

Example

Capital Holdings, a C corporation, has assets worth $2 million, and its basis in the assets is only $500,000. It elects S in 1989. There is $1.5 million in built-in gain. If the corporation sells any of these assets within 10 years after the S election, the built-in gain tax (at the 34 percent rate) will apply.

DJI Planning Guide _____

In several circumstances you do not need to worry about the built-in gain tax at all. If a corporation comes into existence and elects S status after 1986, it *cannot* have any built-in gain and so would not be subject to this tax. In addition, the built-in gain tax does not apply if the corporation has always, from its inception, been an S corporation and has never been taxed as a C corporation (even if it has been in existence for many years prior to 1987).

Q: DO ANY OTHER TAXES APPLY TO AN S CORPORATION?

A: Yes. The second type of tax to which an S corporation may be subject is the Section 1374 capital gain tax. This tax is imposed only on corporations that first elect S status prior to 1987. Once again, this tax does not apply at all to an S corporation that was always an S corporation (one that did not convert from a C corporation). It imposes a special capital gain tax at the corporate level on any disposition of capital assets by the S corporation within three years of the S election.

This capital gain tax applies only if all of the following are true:

- A corporation elects S status and within three years sells capital assets.
- The capital gain generated is more than $25,000.
- The capital gain is more than 50 percent of the corporation's taxable income for the year.
- The taxable income exceeds $25,000.

With these substantial qualifications, the S corporation capital gain tax is actually of very limited application.

There is also a special **passive investment income tax** applicable to S corporations.

Q: WHAT IS THE PASSIVE INVESTMENT INCOME TAX?

A: This tax applies, as its name would suggest, only to passive investment income, such as dividends and interest. Moreover, the tax is imposed only on an S corporation that has earnings and profits from years during which the S corporation was a C corporation. (Recall that an S corporation that has been an S corporation from its inception *cannot* have earnings and profits.) Even for such S corporations with subchapter C earnings and profits, the tax is imposed only on passive investment income totaling more than 25 percent of the corporation's gross receipts.

The concept of passive investment income includes not only interest and dividends but also royalties, rents, annuities, and gains from sales or exchanges of stock or securities. Deductions directly attributable to the production of this passive income (e.g., brokerage fees or costs of producing rental income) are allowable and therefore reduce the amount that could potentially be subject to the passive income tax.

Q: DOES THE TAX APPLY TO ALL PASSIVE INCOME?

A: No. The tax applies only to the S corporation's passive investment income in excess of 25 percent of its gross receipts. Actually, even this is not entirely accurate. The tax is imposed on "excess net passive income," meaning the portion of the S corporation's passive investment income determined under the following formula:

$$\text{Net Passive investment income for the year} \times \frac{\text{Passive investment income in excess of 25\% of gross receipts}}{\text{Passive investment income for the year}} = \text{Excess net passive income}$$

Any gain subject to the passive income tax will not also be subject to the built-in gain tax.

Q: ARE THERE ANY OTHER RESTRICTIONS APPLICABLE TO S CORPORATIONS?

A: Yes. An S corporation may deduct as business expenses only the fringe benefits that it pays for employee-shareholders owning 2 percent or less of its stock. Examples of fringe benefits are accident and health insurance plans. Employee-shareholders owning more than 2 percent of the S corporation's stock are treated as if they were partners in a partnership. In other words, they are not entitled to the more favorable fringe benefits applicable to corporations.

Although this denial of corporate-level fringe benefits is a disadvantage compared with operating as a regular C corporation, the S corporation's advantages of basic partnership tax treatment may outweigh the disadvantage of partnership fringe benefit treatment.

Q: WHAT IS AN OVERALL COMPARISON OF PROPIETORSHIPS, PARTNERSHIPS AND CORPORATIONS?

A: Table 1–1 compares the choices of entities.

TABLE 1–1
Summary of Entity Options

	Proprietorship	Partnership	Corporation	S Corporation
Who is eligible	1 person (and spouse)	No limit	No limit	Up to 35 (70 with spouses). No non-resident alien or corporate shareholders.
Tax on income	Taxed along with proprietor's other income	Taxed to partners according to percentage of interest	Corporation pays tax; shareholders pay tax on dividends	Taxed to shareholders according to percentage of interest
Tax on sale or liquidation	Taxed along with proprietor's other income	Taxed to partners according to percentage of interest	Corporation taxed on gain; shareholders taxed again	S Corporations taxable on their gain if previously a C corporation. Gain taxed to shareholders according to percentage of interest
Permitted tax years	Calendar	Generally must be calendar	Any year OK except for personal service corporations	Generally must be calendar
Losses	Offset proprietor's other income	Offset each partner's income up to amount at risk	Offset only corporate income; may be carried back or forward	Offset shareholders' income up to basis in stock and debt
Fringe Benefits	Not available	Not available	Available	Not available

CHAPTER 2

PARTNERSHIP AND
CORPORATE TAX TREATMENT

INTRODUCTION

The two most popular and prevalent forms of business organization are partnerships and corporations. Although the tax treatment of the two is radically different, each has advantages depending on the situation. Most businesses of even moderate size have long been conducted as corporations. This is true for a number of reasons, not the least of which is the availability of limited liability to the owners of the business from creditors and tort claims.

Partnerships have become more popular in recent years than ever before because of their flow-through tax treatment (similar to that of S corporations). Determining which vehicle to select for the operation of a business requires a basic understanding of both the partnership and the corporate tax rules. For a chart comparing alternatives, see p. 20.

PARTNERSHIPS

Q: ARE PARTNERSHIPS TAXED JUST LIKE S CORPORATIONS?

A: Basically yes, although normally one thinks of S corporations being taxed like partnerships rather than the reverse. Partnerships are flow-through entities, so each partner receives his or her pro rata share of every item of income, deduction, or credit, which is then combined with that partner's other income or loss from other sources. The partnership actually files a return itself (on Form 1065), and each partner receives a schedule from the partnership (*Schedule K-1*), which is then attached to that partner's tax return. The various limitations applicable to S corporations—such as the limitation to 35 shareholders, one class of stock, and so on—do not apply to partnerships.

One other significant difference is that partnerships may employ special allocations of income, loss, deductions, and/or tax credits to particular partners if certain technical rules are complied with, while S corporation income, loss, deductions, and credits must be allocated among shareholders strictly on the basis of their percentage of stockholdings in the corporation.

Q: ARE LIMITED PARTNERSHIPS TAXED THE SAME WAY?

A: Basically any partnership from a two-man handshake partnership up to a partnership with thousands of partners qualifies for this flow-through tax treatment. Limited partnerships and general partnerships are taxed identically. The only tax difference between general partnerships and limited partnerships relates to the manner in which limited partners as opposed to general partners may acquire additional basis in their partnership interest by reason of partnership indebtedness. This difference is discussed thoroughly below.

Q: ARE ALL PARTNERSHIPS ELIGIBLE FOR THIS FLOW-THROUGH TAX TREATMENT?

A: Not really. Under case law and IRS Regulations, certain partnerships may be taxed as corporations. This is obviously a bad situation. The partnership has to pay tax itself, and the partners must then also pay tax on their distributions. The IRS has invoked this doctrine to attempt to tax certain publicly traded limited partnerships as corporations where it believes the partnership flow-through device has been used to avoid paying taxes.

Virtually every offering circular on limited partnership interests offered to the public includes a discussion of this so-called **association taxable as a corporation** doctrine. Whether a partnership is eligible for partnership tax treatment or will be taxed as a corporation depends on whether the partnership has these four characteristics of a corporation:

- Centralized management (a limited number of control persons like a corporation).
- Continuity of life (perpetual existence like a corporation).
- Free transferability of interests (partnership interests that are readily transferable like stock certificates).
- Limited liability (a limited partnership achieving limited liability like a corporation).

Most partnerships can be structured to avoid a majority of these characteristics and therefore avoid corporate tax treatment.

DJI Planning Guide

These "corporate" characteristics are fairly easy to avoid.

Examples
- Limit the partnership's life to a specific period like 40 years—thus negating "continuity of existence."
- Limit the transferability of partnership interests with partner qualification and buy-back provisions—thus negating "free transferability of interests."
- Maintain management control in a broad class of partners—thus negating "centralization of management."

Q: IS IT UNLIKELY, THEN, THAT A PROPERLY ADVISED PARTNERSHIP WILL BE TAXED AS A CORPORATION?

A: No, that is not correct. Although a properly advised partnership has traditionally been able to avoid being taxed as a corporation, the Revenue Act of 1987 imposes corporate tax treatment on certain **publicly traded partnerships**. A publicly traded partnership for purposes of this new statute clearly encompasses the so-called "master limited partnerships" that have received wide publicity in recent years. A publicly traded partnership also includes any partnership whose interests are traded on an established securities market (such as a national securities exchange) or are readily tradable on a secondary market or the substantial equivalent of a secondary market (any market that provides the kind of liquidity one obtains on an exchange).

Although the legislative history of the 1987 Revenue Act includes a substantial discussion of established securities markets and secondary markets, basically any security that is tradeable over a national exchange or for which there is a ready secondary market providing equivalent liquidity will be treated as publicly traded. This new law applies to partnerships formed after the 1987 Act was passed (December 22, 1987). For partnerships existing prior to the 1987 Act's enactment, however, the new provision does not begin to apply until tax years beginning after 1997 (there is a 10-year phase-in).

Q: IS A PARTNER LIMITED IN THE AMOUNT OF LOSSES HE MAY CLAIM FROM A PARTNERSHIP?

A: Yes, although the limitation is different from the limit applicable to S corporation shareholders. Recall that an S corporation shareholder can claim a loss up to his basis in his stock plus his basis in debt the corporation owes him. A partner in a partnership may claim losses on his partnership interest up to the amount of money contributed to the partnership and on amounts for which the partner is "at risk" (the amount he stands to lose). This amount is sometimes called the partner's basis.

With a general partnership interest, this basis is the amount the partner has invested in cash or property plus the amount for which that general partner is liable. The general partner is liable for his pro rata share of the partnership's liabilities. This is so whether the liabilities are recourse or nonrecourse liabilities, a distinction discussed below.

Q: DOES THE SAME LIMITATION ON LOSSES APPLY TO LIMITED PARTNERS?

A: A limited partner is also subject to the same general rule that losses may be claimed up to the limited partner's cash investment plus amount at risk. In determining the amount a limited partner has at risk, however, recourse and nonrecourse liabilities of the partnership must be separated. **Recourse liabilities** are those for which the partnership may be pursued, and **nonrecourse liabilities** are those that do not extend beyond particular property (such as a typical real estate loan).

With respect to recourse liabilities of the partnership, a limited partner is treated as having a share of those liabilities (giving the limited partner additional basis against which to deduct loss) only if that limited partner has agreed to contribute to the partnership the amount of any deficit in his **capital account** upon dissolution of the partnership. A deficit in a partner's capital account (an amount below zero) may occur because of loss deductions taken from the partnership in excess of the partner's basis.

Q: BUT AREN'T LIMITED PARTNERS SHIELDED FROM THESE LIABILITIES?

A: Yes. Under state law, a limited partner cannot be held liable for any amount beyond his initial capital contribution. To get an additional amount "at risk," however, a limited partner may actually agree to bear a share of the liabilities. Basically, this kind of agreement means that despite state law (under which a limited partner could not be held liable for any amount in excess of the amount of cash he invested), the limited partner would actually owe the balance of any deficit in his capital account to the partnership.

For nonrecourse liabilities, it is not necessary for the limited partner to agree to such a liability. Instead, the limited partner will be deemed to have **"at risk"** his percentage share of the partnership's nonrecourse debt as long as the partnership agreement includes certain provisions. These technical partnership provisions are known as "minimum gain charge-back" and "qualified income offset" provisions.

Example

Specu-lative, Ltd., a limited partnership, has 1 general partner (owning 5 percent) and 19 limited partners (each also owning 5 percent). The partnership owns a building on which there is a $1 million nonrecourse loan (secured by the building but no personal liability to the partnership). The partnership also has a $200,000 debt under its line of credit with a bank for which the partnership is personally liable (recourse).

To be treated as at risk for the $200,000 debt, the limited partners would have to agree to a share of the liability. But even without such an agreement, they will be treated as owning their percentage share (5 percent each) of the $1 million loan as long as the partnership agreement is properly drafted.

Q: HOW IS A PARTNER'S BASIS IN HIS INTEREST ADJUSTED?

A: A partner's basis in his partnership interest begins with the amount of cash he paid for the partnership interest and, as discussed above, with a share of liabilities for purposes of computing allowable loss deductions. If the partner contributed property to the partnership, his basis would be increased by the adjusted basis (basically his cost in the property, less any **depreciation** already taken) on the property at the time of its contribution.

Note

A partner's basis in his partnership interest is not increased by the market value of the property contributed but only by its adjusted basis.

During the operation of the partnership, a partner's basis in his interest is constantly moving. It is increased by his distributive share of partnership taxable income, his distributive share of partnership tax exempt income, and his distributive share of the excess of the partnership deductions for depletion over the basis to the partnership of the depletable property.

There are also decreases to a partner's basis in his interest. His basis is decreased (but not reduced below zero) by distributions to him and by the sum of his share of partnership losses, his share of nondeductible partnership expenditures not chargeable to capital account, and, if applicable, his depletion deduction for oil and gas wells.

Example

Penelope Partner buys her partnership interest for $10,000. During the first year, her share of the partnership's taxable income is $4,000, and her share of the partnership's tax-exempt municipal bond interest is $500. Accordingly, the partnership distributes $4,500 to Penelope. Penelope's basis in her interest goes up by $4,500 (because that is her distributive share), and then goes down by $4,500 upon the actual distribution. Penelope's basis in her interest therefore remains at $10,000.

As can be seen from the above example, a partner's basis in his interest will go up when his distributive share of partnership income is not actually distributed to him.

Q: WHAT OTHER RELEVANCE DOES A PARTNER'S BASIS IN HIS INTEREST HAVE?

A: For one thing, the partner's basis in his interest will be used to determine the amount of gain or loss he will recognize when he sells the interest. Note that although a failure by the partnership to distribute income to its partners will affect the basis of the partner's interest in the partnership, it will not affect whether the income is taxable to the partners.

Example

Penelope contributes $50,000 to the capital of a partnership in exchange for a partnership interest. During year one, her share of partnership taxable income is $20,000, but only $10,000 is distributed to her. The $20,000 in taxable income increases her basis to $70,000, and the $10,000 distribution decreases it to $60,000. However, the entire $20,000 is taxable to her.

DJI Planning Guide

Because of the importance of a partner's basis in his partnership, it is advisable to keep a timely and accurate record of the partner's adjusted basis according to the adjustments described above.

Q: WHAT HAPPENS WHEN A PARTNER RECEIVES A DISTRIBUTION FROM THE PARTNERSHIP IN EXCESS OF HIS BASIS IN HIS INTEREST?

A: When a distribution of money exceeds a partner's basis in his interest, the partner realizes gain as though he had sold or exchanged his partnership interest. This is the case whether the distribution is from ongoing partnership operations or is in liquidation of the partnership.

If property is distributed in kind (instead of in cash), regardless of the value of the property, the partner will not recognize any gain until he disposes of the property. (In some circumstances, a nonliquidating partnership distribution of property subject to liabilities may cause income to the recipient partner.)

Q: WHAT HAPPENS WHEN A PARTNER SELLS HIS PARTNERSHIP INTEREST?

A: In many respects, the transaction is treated as if the partner had sold stock in a corporation. The gain or loss is computed to the selling partner with reference to the sales price in comparison to the partner's basis in his partnership interest.

Example

Paul Partner paid $20,000 for his partnership interest in Positively Profitable, and sells his interest two years later for $30,000. He has a $10,000 gain. Although the gain would generally be capital gain, there are limits on this treatment. These limits are designed to prohibit a selling partner from applying capital gain treatment to profits on his share of inventory items or on his share of uncollected and untaxed partnership income which *would* have been ordinary income had Paul received these profits through the partnership.

There are special limitations to prevent all of the gain being taxed as a capital gain in some circumstances. Basically, these rules prevent a partner from applying capital gain treatment to profits on his share of inventoriable items or his share of uncollected and untaxed partnership income. The theory is that this would have been ordinary income had the profits been received by the partner through the partnership. Of course, these rules are of considerably less importance with the current lack of tax rate distinction between ordinary income and capital gain.

Q: WHAT ABOUT PAYMENTS TO RETIRING PARTNERS?

A: Here again, special rules govern the extent to which capital gain versus ordinary income treatment is available. Typically, however, capital gain treatment will be available for payments to a retired partner. Again, the distinctions are significantly less important now than they were when there was still a favorable capital gains rate. But there are many indications that a favorable capital gains rate (or perhaps an increased ordinary income rate) will be brought back into the law in the not-too-distant future.

Q: WHEN A PARTNERSHIP DISSOLVES, DOES THE PARTNERSHIP RECOGNIZE GAIN OR LOSS?

A: No, individual partners may have gain or loss on distributions in liquidation, but the partnership itself does not bear a tax burden. This makes the partnership form compare favorably to a corporation in terms of the tax burden borne by the entity on a liquidation or a sale of control.

Commencing in 1987 for most corporations and in 1989 for all others, liquidating corporations will no longer be able to sell their assets and allow the shareholders to pay only a single level tax on the sales price. Now both the corporation and the shareholders will pay a tax on the sale, making corporations (all other things being equal) unattractive to those interested in building up a business and then selling it.

A partnership will be treated as a flow-through entity even on dissolution, so that individual partners will merely compare the proceeds they receive (and any other partnership income to which their interest is entitled) with the amount they paid for their partnership interest.

When a partner receives property instead of cash in a distribution from the partnership, no gain will be recognized to a partner on the liquidating distribution of the noncash property. When property is distributed in some other context, as in ongoing partnership operations, again the partner recognizes no gain and will take a basis in the asset equal to the basis that the asset had in the partnership's hands immediately prior to the distribution.

CORPORATIONS

Q: WHEN DOES IT MAKE SENSE TO OPERATE A BUSINESS THROUGH A CORPORATION RATHER THAN A PARTNERSHIP?

A: This is a complex determination. To begin with, the incentives have changed considerably in recent years. After the 1986 Tax Reform Act, for the first time in many years the highest marginal corporate tax rate is higher than the highest marginal individual tax rate. The highest corporate rate is now 34 percent compared to a top individual rate of 28 percent.

Note:

> Although some individual income may be subjected to a 33 percent rate, this is only to take away the benefits of the lower 15 percent rate for higher bracket taxpayers. In other words, the 33 percent rate can apply only to a limited amount of income; the maximum total average rate to which any individual can be subjected is still 28 percent. So the relevant corporate/individual tax rate comparison is between 34 and 28 percent rather than between 34 and 33 percent.

The higher corporate rate means that any unincorporated business such as a partnership or proprietorship is paying a lower effective tax rate (28 percent) than a corporation (34 percent). Just how striking a development this is must be placed in a historical perspective.

It was once almost rote that corporate tax rates were (and indeed should be) lower than individual tax rates. The 1986 Tax Act really destroyed this myth and with it generations of traditional tax planning notions. Add to this the fact that once the income is taxed at the corporate tax rate, it will be subjected to taxation again at the shareholder level upon distribution (at up to the individual 28 percent rate), and the comparison between these tax rates is even more dramatic.

Q: ARE THESE TAX RATES RELEVANT WHEN ALL INCOME WILL BE DISTRIBUTED?

A: It depends. In many businesses, such as professional businesses, it is customary to drain all of the cash out of the corporation in the form of salary payments. When this practice is followed, the corporation will have no (or very little) corporate taxable income to be taxed at this higher 34 percent rate. Instead, the individual shareholder/employees will pay tax at their own individual rates (up to 28 percent).

This practice places the unincorporated and the incorporated business on an even footing. But generally speaking, in the absence of draining all the income out of the corporation every year (which, depending on the amount of income may or may not be possible), the unincorporated business has at least this tax rate advantage over the incorporated one.

DJI Planning Guide

In order to effectively reduce the corporate tax, the monies must be paid out on a deductible basis. They can be paid out as compensation to employee/shareholders (see Chapter 6), typically as salary and bonuses. If the amounts are paid out as dividends, they will not be deductible to the corporation and will thus be taxable to both the corporation and shareholders—a true double tax.

Moreover, beginning in 1988, **personal service corporations** are ineligible for the graduated corporate income tax rates and instead are taxable at a flat rate of 34 percent no matter how small or large their income. A personal service corporation is one that engages in activities involving the performance of services in the fields of health, law, engineering, architecture, actuarial science, performing arts or consulting.

Q: IS THERE ANYTHING APART FROM TAX RATES THAT NOW FAVORS OPERATING IN A FLOW-THROUGH ENTITY?

A: Yes. Another recent development that heavily favors proprietorships, partnerships, and S corporations over regular C corporations is the repeal of the so called "General Utilities" doctrine, which was repealed in the 1986 Tax Reform Act. The General Utilities doctrine, named after the *General Utilities* case, existed in the law for nearly 50 years.

Under *General Utilities*, corporations could liquidate and distribute their assets out to shareholders without recognizing gain on the appreciation in the corporate assets. Alternatively, the assets could be sold at the corporate level, and the entire sales proceeds (unreduced by income taxes) could be distributed out to shareholders. The shareholders paid a single level tax at the shareholder level. However large this shareholder tax might be, it was infinitely better than paying a "double tax" (at the corporate and again at the shareholder level) on the liquidation.

With the repeal of this doctrine, corporations now must pay a corporate-level tax followed by a shareholder-level tax, making the effective tax rate nearly 52.5 percent!

Example

Samuel Shareholder started ABC Company by paying $10,000 for its stock. The company purchased equipment with the $10,000 and commenced business. The equipment has been fully depreciated, so it has a zero basis in the hands of the corporation. Over the years, however, the equipment has appreciated in value and is now worth $30,000. From earnings, the corporation also acquired additional property that has depreciated, and its property now has a total market value of $50,000. Its combined basis in all its property is $10,000. If the corporation liquidates, it will have a $40,000 corporate level gain taxable at up to the maximum 34 percent tax rate. Once the corporation pays its tax and distributes the remainder to the shareholder, the shareholder will pay tax on the difference between the $10,000 he paid for his shares and the amount of cash he actually receives. If he receives $30,000 he will also have a $20,000 gain.

Q: DOES THIS MEAN IT IS INADVISABLE TO OPERATE A BUSINESS AS A CORPORATION NOW?

A: No, it does not. By number, most businesses will probably still be operated as corporations because of the need for limited liability from creditors and tort claims and for other reasons. A corporation can obviously achieve limited liability under state law even as an S corporation, but the S corporation restrictions (such as the limit to 35 shareholders, one class of stock, no nonresident alien or corporate shareholders, and so on) are quite limiting.

Moreover, even if a large and diversified business could be operated as a partnership (some have tried as so-called "master limited partnerships"), partnerships with readily tradable partnership interests are treated as corporations for tax purposes and are taxed as such. The initially avoided corporate tax treatment therefore comes back to roost. In any case, the main area in which significant choices will be exercised in determining how the business will be conducted is in the closely held business context.

DJI Planning Guide ————————————————

Since for must purposes flow-through treatment is desirable, an initial plan for most situations should probably be to establish an S corporation for a manufacturing or sales business, a partnership for a real estate business, and a C corporation for a service business in which all income can be paid out as compensation.

Q: ARE CORPORATIONS ENTITLED TO ALL THE SAME DEDUCTIONS AND CREDITS THAT INDIVIDUALS CAN CLAIM?

A: No, corporations are not entitled to some of the deductions that may be claimed by individuals. For example, there are no personal exemptions for a corporation; a corporation cannot deduct medical expenses, moving expenses, and so on. On the other hand, corporations are entitled to some deductions and special rules to which individuals are not. Probably most important is the **dividends received deduction**, which enables corporations to deduct all or part of the dividends they receive from other corporations.

Q: HOW DOES THE DIVIDENDS RECEIVED DEDUCTION WORK?

A: The dividends received deduction breaks into three parts.

1. If a corporation owns 80 percent or more of the stock of the dividend paying corporation, any dividend received from it will be 100 percent deductible to the corporate recipient.
2. If the corporation receiving the dividend owns 20 percent or more of the stock of the dividend paying corporation (but less than 80 percent), the dividend received will be 80 percent deductible by the corporate recipient.
3. If the corporate recipient owns less than 20 percent of the stock of the dividend paying corporation, it will still be able to deduct 70 percent of the amount of dividends received.

Example

Capital, Ltd. owns 50 percent of the stock in an affiliated entity, ABC, Inc., plus 90 percent of the stock in a subsidiary called Capital II, and a variety of shares in public companies, in none of which it owns more than 10 percent of the stock. Capital, Ltd.

will be able to deduct 100 percent of any dividends it receives from Capital II, 80 percent of any dividends it receives from ABC, Inc., and 70 percent of any dividends it receives from any of the public companies.

Q: IS THE DIVIDENDS RECEIVED DEDUCTION AVAILABLE EVEN IF THE STOCK WAS PURCHASED WITH BORROWED FUNDS?

A: No. In recent years, the dividends received deduction—precisely because it is of such enormous benefit—has been cut back substantially. If any stock is deemed to be **debt-financed portfolio stock**, the dividends received deduction is cut back. Basically, "debt-financed portfolio stock" is stock whose purchase or maintenance has been financed through the company's borrowing.

The reason for this restriction is that it would not seem equitable for a corporation to incur indebtedness, deduct interest payments made on the indebtedness, and use the borrowed money to buy stock on which it will receive dividends eligible for the dividends received deduction. "Debt-financed portfolio stock" restrictions prevent this kind of double dipping.

Q: ARE THERE ANY OTHER RESTRICTIONS ON THE DIVIDENDS RECEIVED DEDUCTION?

A: Yes. The restrictions on the dividends received deduction applicable to debt-financed portfolio stock do not apply to dividends eligible for the 100 percent dividends received deduction (dividends received from members of the taxpayer's **affiliated group**).

There are a few other restrictions on the dividends-received deduction, too. For example, dividends received on preferred stock of public utilities do not qualify for the deduction unless the public utility paying the dividend is entitled to a dividends paid deduction under special rules. Even when the deduction to the recipient of such dividends is allowed, it can be limited. Furthermore, no deduction is allowed for dividends received from certain distributions that qualify for U.S. possessions tax credits.

Another limitation on the dividends received deduction relates to the recipient corporation's holding period for the stock. No deduction is allowable for stock held less than 45 days. Moreover, if the stock is cumulative preferred stock with dividend arrearages, it must be held at least 91 days if the recipient receives more than 366 days' worth of dividends. These holding period requirements seem easy to meet, but any period of time is excluded during which the corporation's risk of loss from the stock is diminished because of any of the following circumstances.

- The corporation has an option to sell, is under an obligation to sell, or has made (and not closed) a short sale of substantially identical stock or securities.
- The corporation has granted an option to purchase substantially identical stock or securities.
- The corporation has reduced its risk by holding one or more other positions with respect to substantially similar or related property.

Q: DOES THE AMOUNT OF THE DIVIDEND HAVE ANY BEARING ON THE RESTRICTIONS?

A: Yes. Certain types of dividends that are eligible for the dividends received deduction may require the corporate taxpayer to reduce its basis in its stock by the nontaxed portion of the dividend. The nontaxed portion of the dividend is the 70 or 80 percent portion that was deducted (depending on how much of the paying corporation's stock the recipient corporation held).

This rule generally applies to "extraordinary dividends," generally defined as dividends exceeding 10 percent of the taxpayer's adjusted basis in the stock or the fair market value of the stock just before the "ex-dividend date." This is the cut-off

date after which transferees of stock will acquire it without a
right to receive accrued dividends. This extraordinary-dividend
rule applies only when the taxpayer has not held the stock for
more than two years before the day the dividends are declared,
agreed to or announced.

Example

XYZ Corp. owns 18 percent of the stock of TipTop, Inc. XYZ paid
$10,000 for the stock. TipTop now declares a $4,000 dividend on
the stock. If XYZ has not held the stock for more than two years
before the date the dividend is declared, agreed to or announced,
XYZ will be able to take the dividends received deduction,
deducting 70 percent of the $4,000 dividend it receives. However,
XYZ would have to reduce its $10,000 basis by $2,800 (70 percent
× $4,000). Accordingly, after the receipt of the dividend and the
use of the dividends received deduction, XYZ's basis in its Tip-
Top stock will be $7,200. When it sells the TipTop stock, it will
therefore have a larger gain. If it had received a loss on its disposition of the TipTop stock, this rule would reduce the amount
of the allowable loss.

Q: WHAT ABOUT OTHER SPECIAL CORPORATE TAX ITEMS?

A: A corporation's organizational expenditures may not be
deducted. Instead, the most favorable treatment they are entitled to is **amortization** over 60 months beginning with the
first month the corporation is actively involved in its business.
Amortization of organizational expenditures allows them to be
deducted in equal parts over the 60 months.

Organizational expenditures (such as lawyers' and accountants' fees to establish the corporation, state law filing fees, and
the like) may not be terribly significant, but stock issuance fees
typically are.

Example

Newly organized corporation Newco spends $500,000 in a public
stock issuance. These expenditures would have to be amortized

over 60 months. Consequently, they would be deductible at the rate of $100,000 a year ($8,333 a month) for five years.

Most commonly, the incorporation and organization of a corporation with its initial stock issuance does not involve a public issuance; therefore, the costs that must be amortized are not too staggering.

DJI Planning Guide

Because stock issuance costs in a public or semipublic offering can be substantial, it is normally advisable for such offerings to take place after (and not as part of) the initial organization of the corporation. The goal is to avoid the 60-month amortization and to write off as much of the costs as possible immediately.

Another special corporate item (actually several items) is special corporate taxes over and above the regular corporate income tax.

Q: ARE CORPORATIONS SUBJECT TO ADDITIONAL TAXES OVER AND ABOVE THE REGULAR CORPORATE INCOME TAX?

A: Yes, although such taxes apply primarily to closely held corporations. These additional corporate level taxes have, at least in part, been responsible for some of the perceived complexity of our corporate tax system.

Accumulated Earnings Tax

The first special tax is the **accumulated earnings tax**. Basically, it seeks to penalize corporations for retaining earnings (on which tax has already been paid at the corporate level) and failing to distribute them to shareholders. Since the government prefers to see monies distributed to shareholders so they can be taxed again at the shareholder level, the accumulated earnings tax looks for circumstances in which there are sufficient earnings at the corporate level upon which this penalty can be imposed.

Note that the incentive to fail to distribute corporate earnings was strongest when the individual marginal tax rates reached as high as 50 percent. (Prior to the 1981 Economic Recovery Tax Act, the rates rose as high as 70 percent!) Yet there is still considerable incentive not to distribute corporate earnings. If $50,000 of corporate income incurs a corporate tax of 34 percent and is then distributed to shareholders who are taxed at a 28 percent individual tax rate on top of that, there is a double tax. When the controlling shareholders can feel secure that it is "their" money whether it is distributed from the corporation or not, it is understandable that they may wish to leave it in the corporation. At least the funds not paid in taxes can generate additional income for the shareholders.

Q: HOW IS THE ACCUMULATED EARNINGS TAX APPLIED?

A: The accumulated earnings tax is imposed at the rate of 27.5 percent on the first $100,000 of "accumulated taxable income" and at 38.5 percent on any excess above $100,000. The accumulated taxable income to which this tax applies is the corporation's taxable income with certain adjustments and certain deductions. These deductions include taxes, charitable contributions (with an unlimited amount of charitable deductions allowed for this purpose), current capital losses, and even current capital gains. However, no net operating loss or capital loss carryback or carryover may be deducted.

The accumulated earnings tax is imposed only when the shareholders fail to distribute the earnings to avoid paying taxes on them.

DJI Planning Guide _____

Tax avoidance intent may be determined from corporate minutes, correspondence, actions, and so on. Avoid even referring to the accumulated earnings tax in any documentation.

Unfortunately, the law presumes that an accumulation of earnings beyond the "reasonable needs of the business" constitutes tax avoidance. Consequently, most of the disputes in a case where the accumulated earnings tax may be applicable focus on whether the corporation is accumulating earnings beyond the reasonable needs of the business. Although shareholder tax avoidance is relevant, the law explicitly states that the accumulated earnings tax applies regardless of the size of the corporation, and the government has occasionally attempted to impose it on large publicly held corporations. Obviously, however, it has its primary application to closely held entities.

Q: WHAT CONSTITUTES THE "REASONABLE NEEDS OF THE BUSINESS"?

A: What constitutes the reasonable needs of the business is inherently factual. What is reasonable for one business may not be for another. However, there are clear criteria that may justify an accumulation if the corporation and its shareholders can show that they have feasible, definite, and reasonable plans to accomplish one of these goals. Examples are

- To provide for expansion of the business or replacement of plant or equipment.
- To acquire a business enterprise through purchasing stock or assets.
- To provide for the retirement of indebtedness created in connection with the trade or business.
- To provide necessary working capital for the business (i.e., to purchase inventory).
- To provide for investments or loans to suppliers or customers if necessary in order to maintain the business of the company.
- To provide for the payment of reasonably anticipated product liability losses.

Although this is by no means an exclusive list, it illustrates that there are many reasons that may justify an accumulation.

DJI Planning Guide

One of the most difficult grounds on which to justify an accumulation is to provide for the corporation's "working capital." To determine the working capital needed for most businesses, the IRS and the courts have developed a formula that depends primarily on the number of days it typically takes for the inventory of the business to turn over and on the number of days it typically takes for the accounts receivable of the business to be collected. Most of the other grounds, however, depend primarily on what the corporation and its controlling shareholders intend. So keep good records in the corporate minutes of intended expansion, acquisitions, and so on.

A plan to accumulate several million dollars in earnings by a widget-making business in order to expand into retail car sales may be perfectly justifiable. The key is whether the plan is reasonably definite, feasible, and genuine, and whether the amount accumulated does not exceed the amount reasonably called for under the plan.

Q: IF AN ACCUMULATION IS JUSTIFIED BASED ON A PLANNED ACQUISITION, MUST THE ACQUISITION ACTUALLY TAKE PLACE?

A: No. Although it will certainly be helpful if at some point in the future the new business is in fact acquired (giving some ratification to the reasonableness of the prior plan), this is not a necessity. The plan can be abandoned for a variety of reasons, and the abandonment would not give rise to an accumulated earnings attack for the prior years.

However, once the need for the accumulation no longer exists, it will be necessary either to seek another ground for the accumulation, to distribute earnings (such as in the form of dividends to shareholders), or to face a possible accumulated earnings attack.

DJI Planning Guide _____

Good recordkeeping is a must, especially when a plan—used previously to justify an accumulation—is abandoned.

Q: ARE SOME GROUNDS FOR AN ACCUMULATION OF EARNINGS CONSIDERED "UNREASONABLE"?

A: Yes. There are some reasons that have been advanced to justify an accumulation that clearly will not constitute a reasonable need of the business. Examples are

- Loans to shareholders or the expenditure of corporate funds for the personal benefit of shareholders.
- Loans having no reasonable relation to the conduct of the business that are made to relatives, friends of shareholders, and/or other persons.
- Loans to another corporation having a business unrelated to the taxpayer corporation if the shareholders of the other corporation are also in control of the taxpayer corporation.
- Investment in properties or securities that are unrelated to the business of the taxpayer corporation.
- The retention of earnings and profits to provide against unrealistic hazards.

A common theme can be seen from the above list: the personal goals of shareholders are unlikely to be treated as a reasonable need of the business. However, the last item, retention of earnings and profits to provide against unrealistic hazards, really calls for a case-by-case determination of what is reasonable and what is not.

Q: WHO HAS THE BURDEN OF PROOF IN AN ACCUMULATED EARNINGS TAX CASE?

A: The government bears the burden of proof on the accumulated earnings tax if it fails to notify the corporation in advance of a formal deficiency notice that it intends to assess the accumulated earnings tax. (In other words, a special advance warning must be given to corporate taxpayers regarding the proposed assessment of the accumulated earnings tax, or the government will have to prove the existence of an *un*reasonable accumulation.)

The government also bears the burden of proof on the issue even if it does give this formal notice to the taxpayer but the taxpayer responds within 60 days stating the grounds on which it can establish that its accumulation was reasonable. These two "government burden" situations apply only in the U.S. Tax Court.

In all other circumstances in the Tax Court, and in any other court (such as the U.S. District Court or Court of Claims), the taxpayer must bear the burden of proof in showing that its accumulation was reasonable.

DJI Planning Guide

The burden of proof is not a mere formality. It often spells the difference between winning and losing your case with the IRS. As a result, if the IRS issues an advance notice that the accumulated earnings tax will be the subject of a proposed adjustment, it is critical that the corporation respond in writing within 60 days with a well-thought-out set of reasons for any accumulation. Professional advice here is almost always a good idea.

Q: CAN'T YOU ACCUMULATE ANYTHING WITHOUT HAVING TO SHOW REASONABLE NEEDS OF THE BUSINESS?

A: Yes, but this rule is quite limited. You may accumulate up to $250,000 (from past and present earnings combined) without fear of your accumulation being considered unreasonable. Certain personal service corporations (such as those in the fields of health, law, engineering, etc.) may accumulate only $125,000.

Q: ARE THERE ANY OTHER CORPORATE-LEVEL TAXES?

A: Yes. The most important is the **personal holding company tax**. In addition to the regular corporate tax, the personal holding company tax is a 38.5 percent tax imposed on the "undistributed personal holding company income" of a "personal holding company."

Basically, a personal holding company is any corporation that has "personal holding company income" equal to at least 60 percent of its income and for which more than 50 percent by value of its outstanding stock is owned (directly or indirectly) by five individuals at any time during the last half of the tax year. In other words, there are two requirements: a stock ownership requirement and a percentage-of-income requirement. If both are met, the corporation is a "personal holding company."

The personal holding company tax was enacted at a time when the tax rates applicable to individuals were substantially higher than those applicable to corporations. The personal holding company tax was designed primarily to prevent nonbusiness activity (such as passive investments) that a few individuals were conducting in corporate form to take advantage of the lower corporate tax rates. Since the behavior the government sought to prevent was the earning of such income in a corporation without distributing it to shareholders (if it were distributed to shareholders as dividends, the income would be taxed at the individual shareholder's tax rate, too), the tax is imposed only on undistributed personal holding company income.

Note

Even though the corporate income tax rate is now *higher* than the individual tax rate (and thus there would seem to be no reason for the personal holding company tax), the tax can still be imposed.

Q: WHAT IS PERSONAL HOLDING COMPANY INCOME?

A: The definition of **personal holding company income** is set out below, but basically the five-shareholder rule makes personal holding company problems apply only to closely held businesses. The definition of personal holding company income makes the tax apply principally to corporations holding primarily passive investments and generating dividends, interest, and the like (sometimes called "incorporated pocketbooks"), and to corporations receiving their income as a result of the services of one individual (sometimes called "incorporated talents").

More specifically, personal holding company income means corporate income consisting of any of the following:

- Dividends, interest, royalties, and annuities.
- Rents (unless the rents are 50 percent or more of the corporation's income and the dividends paid by the corporation exceed the amount by which the personal holding company income exceeds 10 percent of the income).
- Mineral, oil, and gas royalties (unless they constitute 50 percent or more of the corporation's income and certain percentage tests are met).
- Copyright royalties (unless copyright royalties derived from works of nonshareholders make up 50 percent or more of the corporation's income and certain percentage tests are met).
- Rents from the distribution and exhibition of produced films (a film interest acquired before the film production was substantially complete) unless the rents are 50 percent or more of the corporation's ordinary gross income.
- Amounts received as compensation for the use of tangible property where 25 percent or more by value of the outstanding stock is owned by a person entitled to use the property and the corporation's other personal holding company income is more than 10 percent of its ordinary gross income.
- Amounts received from contracts for personal services if a person other than the corporation can designate the individual to perform the services (or the contract designates him) and if at some time during the year, 25 percent or more by value of the corporation's stock is owned by that designated person.
- Income required to be reported by a corporate beneficiary under the estate and trust income tax rules.

Q: HOW CAN ALL THESE COMPLEX INCOME ITEMS BE MONITORED?

A: As can be seen from this list, what constitutes personal holding company income is extremely complex and requires many fine determinations. Personal holding company income problems are most frequently discerned only by tax experts. However, any time a closely held corporation's passive income (such as dividends, interest, royalties, rents, etc.) is 60 percent or more of the corporation's total income, the problem should be examined very carefully.

DJI Planning Guide ───────────────────────────

This tax is imposed not on the corporation's personal holding company income but on its *undistributed* personal holding company income. Thus, it is perfectly all right to have a corporation generate 100 percent of its receipts from dividends or interest as long as these amounts are paid out as dividends to shareholders. Taking care that regular dividend distributions are made can alleviate much of the concern over personal holding company problems.

Note

The accumulated earnings tax (discussed above) is *not* imposed on personal holding companies, so *both* an accumulated earnings tax *and* a personal holding company tax will not be imposed.

Q: WHAT IS THE TAX COST UPON FORMATION OF A CORPORATION?

A: There is generally no tax to pay upon incorporation. Even if the business has previously been conducted as a proprietorship or partnership and has a long history and many assets, incorporation is generally tax-free. The owners of the business exchange the various assets they own for stock in the corporation, which, in turn, will now own the assets and operate the business.

DJI Planning Guide _____

Note that this rule is in contrast to the situation presented when the owners of a business wish to get *out* of the corporate form and, for example, go back to being partners or proprietors. From this perspective, the choice whether to incorporate appears deceptively simple. Going into a corporation is always tax-free, but coming out is not. Going back to our theme at the beginning of Chapter 1, the entire picture of conducting a business, including the result when the business is liquidated, should be factored into the decision of what form in which to conduct the business from the outset. In particular, it is generally not advisable to incorporate a business while expecting to liquidate a relatively short time later.

Q: IS IT DIFFICULT TO GO FROM A CORPORATION BACK TO A PARTNERSHIP OR PROPRIETORSHIP?

A: Yes, it can be, and it usually involves some tax cost. Generally speaking, prior to 1987 this decision could be made and accomplished with little tax cost. For many corporations entitled to transition relief under the 1986 Tax Reform Act, this was the case through the end of 1988. However, for even these corporations after 1988 (and for all other corporations after 1986), going from an incorporated to an unincorporated form of business generally involves paying a substantial tax.

Note

This tax is measured by the difference between the corporation's basis in its assets and their respective fair market values. Since business assets are frequently depreciated (thus reducing their basis for tax purposes), this difference between fair market value and tax basis may be substantial.

The types of corporations that qualify for transitional relief through the end of 1988 and that thus may be able to "disincorporate" prior to 1989 without this big tax cost are corporations that have both of the following:

- Ten or fewer shareholders owning at least 50 percent of the stock and who have owned their shares for at least five years (or, if shorter, the period of the corporation's existence).
- A total value of $5 million or less. If the corporation has a value between $5 million and $10 million, partial relief of the tax (but not complete relief) may be available. For a corporate value of $10 million or more, no relief from the new double-level tax on liquidation has been provided.

Q: MUST ALL BUSINESSES (PARTNERSHIPS AND CORPORATIONS) NOW OPERATE ON A CALENDAR YEAR?

A: No, not quite, although this certainly is the direction Congress is heading. Generally speaking, as a result of the Tax Reform Act of 1986, all businesses (with only a few exceptions) are required to operate on a calendar year. The demon Congress has sought to eliminate is a **fiscal year** that could end with any month and might allow taxpayers to shift their personal income into a subsequent taxable year.

Traditionally, for example, a fiscal year ending January 31st has allowed a corporation to distribute its earnings through bonuses to shareholder/employees in the last month of its tax year. This way, the corporate income was reduced to zero, and the shareholders who received the bonuses did not have to pay tax on them for another full year. Because the bonuses were paid in January and almost all individuals report and pay tax on a calendar year, the individuals did not include the bonuses in their income until they filed their returns on April 15 more than one year later.

Q: IS THIS KIND OF FISCAL-YEAR TAX PLANNING GONE?

A: Not entirely. A fiscal year may still be allowed, but its use has been drastically cut back. Effective for taxable years after 1986, all S corporations, partnerships, and personal service corporations may elect to use a taxable year other than the calendar year. Such entities may elect the same year as their 1986 year (if they had a fiscal year) or may generally elect a year with no more than a three-month deferral. (This means that they could elect a tax year ending on September 30, October 31, or November 30.)

Significantly, however, effective for tax years beginning after 1987, S corporations and partnerships must make a required tax payment for each taxable year for which this fiscal year election is in effect. For a taxable year for which this election is in effect, the required payment is an amount determined by a mathematical formula. Basically, the formula is designed to obtain for the government a tax equal to the amount of deferral benefit which the fiscal year generates. The tax is phased in over several years commencing in 1987, so that it does not grow to its full extent until 1990 and subsequent years.

For a chart comparing a few of the characteristics of partnerships, corporations, S corporations, and proprietorships, see p. 20.

CHAPTER 3

BUSINESS EXPENSES, CAPITAL INVESTMENTS, AND DEPRECIATION

INTRODUCTION

An understanding of the rules governing business expense deductions is essential to operating any business. For every dollar spent, the *tax* objective of most businesses is to obtain the largest deduction as soon as possible. Generally speaking, deducting in full the cost of the item at an early date (sometimes called "expensing" the item) is better than depreciating it over several years. Depreciation involves writing off the cost of the asset over a number of years depending on the asset's useful life. Expensing results in an immediate benefit.

Every business makes purchases of property that it does not intend to resell but that will be used in the business. Property that will be resold (such as by a wholesaler who buys assets only to distribute them to a broader market) is usually referred to as **inventory**. The tax treatment of inventory transactions and sales in the course of business is discussed fully in Chapter 4.

Here, however, we are concerned with assets that are *used* in the business, whether they be machinery, real property, contract rights, or goodwill. These items will have to be **capitalized**, the cost being written off in the form of depreciation over a number of years. The depreciation rules have become very complex, and an understanding of their provisions is necessary to making effective purchases.

If an asset cannot be expensed or depreciated, it may fall into the least desirable category of all—something for which no deduction is available.

BUSINESS EXPENSES

Q: WHEN CAN PURCHASES BE WRITTEN OFF DURING ONE YEAR?

A: One of the classic debates within our income tax system is whether something can be **expensed** or must be "capitalized." In a business context, expensing is simply writing off the cost of the asset entirely in one year. Supplies that are consumed, such as paper, pencils, typewriter ribbons, and so on, clearly fall within this category.

To "capitalize" an asset means to add the asset to the company's books at its cost. The asset is then "depreciated" over its useful life. The theory of depreciation is that the asset loses value every year, and an approximation of that decrease in value is deductible in each year. Examples of assets that must be capitalized include automobiles, trucks, buildings, machinery, and leasehold improvements.

Q: HOW DO YOU TELL WHAT ITEMS ARE DEDUCTIBLE?

A: The overwhelming number of deductions taken by any business are lumped into a general category known as "business expenses." Unfortunately, there is relatively little guidance in the tax law concerning what items are deductible and what are not. The law allows a deduction for all "ordinary and necessary" business expenses, and there are literally volumes and volumes of case law authority interpreting the words "ordinary and necessary."

There is no question that many expenses are ordinary and necessary. The IRS will rarely examine an expense—such as rent on new office space—and ask whether it was really "necessary" for the business to expand its office. Similarly, they are unlikely to question an expense deduction for typewriter ribbons and disks for word processors and computers, even if the business already has a storage room full of these items.

However, the personal expenses of a shareholder, such as a personal automobile or living expenses, are not ordinary and necessary and are therefore not deductible to any business.

Q: WHAT EXPENSES ARE LIKELY TO BE TREATED AS NONDEDUCTIBLE?

A: There are several areas in which deductions are more likely to be disallowed than in other areas. There are also several areas where detailed rules govern the allowability of the deduction. Examples of particularly sensitive deductions are those for automobile expenses and those for entertainment.

Q: WHAT ARE THE RESTRICTIONS APPLICABLE TO AUTOMOBILE EXPENSES?

A: Automobile deductions have become particularly confusing in the last few years. The major reason is Congress' concern that automobile expense deductions have been especially abused. Automobile expense deductions are now deductible only if the automobile is used 50 percent or more for business or for the **production of income.** The "production of income" includes investment activity such as investigating investment property, travel to and from a stock brokerage house, and so on. Personal usage, however, does not count toward satisfying this 50 percent test.

Q: AREN'T SOME AUTOMOBILE EXPENSES DEDUCTIBLE EVEN IF THE CAR IS NOT USED PREDOMINANTLY FOR BUSINESS?

A: Yes, although the deductions are rather limited. Interest paid on an installment purchase of a car to be used for personal purposes (or a car that has been financed) is no longer fully deductible since it is classified as **personal interest**. Forty percent of the interest is deductible in 1988, 20 percent in 1989, and 10 percent in 1990. After 1990, none of the interest is deductible..

License fees for the car are deductible if based on the value of the vehicle. If losses or damages are incurred, such as in an accident that is not compensated for by insurance, these may be deductible subject to limitations.

Q: WHAT OTHER AUTO DEDUCTIONS MAY BE TAKEN?

A: Other automobile deductions are available only if the 50 percent threshold is crossed: the car must be used 50 percent or more for business or for the production of income. If it is, the car may be depreciated; gasoline, oil, and lubrication, as well as insurance would be deductible. Note, however, that the 50 percent threshold is an initial qualification threshold. These deductions are available only if the car is used 50 percent or more (based on mileage) for business or the production of income, but the deductions are available only to the extent of the percentage of actual business or income producing use.

Example

J. P. Executive uses his car 60 percent for business, 10 percent in connection with his active stock trading activities, and 30 percent for personal use. Since only 70 percent of the use of the automobile is for business or the production of income, only 70 percent of the otherwise allowable depreciation will be deductible, 70 percent of oil and gasoline, 70 percent of insurance, etc. Note that the "personal use" of the automobile will include commuting to and from work in addition to other more purely personal trips. Commuting to and from work is not classified as business travel.

DJI Planning Guide _____

Although recordkeeping is always important and advisable, it is particularly critical with automobile expenses. A few years ago, the IRS adopted strict recordkeeping rules mandating contemporaneous logs of business travel. Although these rules no longer apply (they were revoked after great outcry), keeping a contemporaneous log of business travel is clearly still advisable. The record should include date, origin and destination of travel, and purpose.

Q: WHAT ITEMS CAN BE DEDUCTED FOR AUTOMOBILE USAGE?

A: Assuming the automobile is used 50 percent or more in business or for the production of income, the largest permissible deductions are for depreciation, gasoline, oil, and repairs. Other possibilities include:

- Automobile club memberships.
- Parking.
- License fees (even if not based on the value of the car).
- Bridge and highway tolls.
- Washing and waxing.
- Chauffeur costs.
- Judgment or settlement payments for damages due to negligent driving.

Q: WHAT IS THE DEPRECIATION DEDUCTION FOR AN AUTOMOBILE?

A: Automobiles are treated as five-year property under the current depreciation rules. This means that the cost of the automobile is recovered over five years. But the manner in which this five years is measured really results in recovery over six years. The reason for this six-year rule is that the property is treated as placed in service mid-year, so one-half a year's depreciation is allowable both in year one and in the last year (year six).

Example

J. P. Executive uses his automobile 100 percent for business purposes. The cost of the automobile was $12,000. Ten percent of this cost is deductible as depreciation in year one, 20 percent of the cost will be deductible in years two through five (each year), and the remaining 10 percent is deductible in year six.

Once the depreciation deduction is computed, it must be tested against an overall limit. Even though an automobile is used more than 50 percent for business purposes, further limits on the annual depreciation apply. The maximum deduction that may be claimed for depreciation on a car placed in service after 1986 is $2,560 for the first year, $4,100 for the second year, $2,450 for the third year, and $1,475 for the fourth and subsequent years.

DJI Planning Guide _____

These limits really stretch out the allowable deductions, particularly when the current cost of automobiles is considered. For example, a $20,000 automobile used exclusively for business ends up depreciated over 11 years! This harsh result applies because of the annual limits on the depreciation deduction.

Note

The rules regarding depreciation on automobiles have changed substantially over the last few years. Different limitations apply for automobiles placed in service before 1987.

Q: APART FROM AUTOMOBILES, WHAT OTHER SPECIAL LIMITATIONS ON DEDUCTIONS APPLY?

A: Technically, automobiles are part of a category of property known as **listed property**. Listed property includes automobiles, airplanes, trucks, and boats. It also includes entertainment, recreational and amusement property, and computers and peripheral equipment. The IRS can keep adding to the items that constitute listed property when abuses are perceived. All these types of property, like automobiles, are subject to special depreciation rules over and above the ordinary depreciation concepts that are discussed more fully below.

Q: WHAT ABOUT ENTERTAINMENT AND MEAL DEDUCTIONS?

A: Entertainment expenses and business meals have become very controversial in the last few years. The current rules provide that entertainment and business meal expenses may still be deducted, but various special limitations apply. It no longer follows that the entire cost of a business meal will be deductible.

Q: WHAT LIMITS APPLY TO BUSINESS MEAL DEDUCTIONS?

A: The limitations fall into several categories. First, as a threshold, a business meal will not be deductible at all unless the meal expense directly precedes or follows a "substantial and bona fide" business discussion. In other words, the business meal must either involve actual business discussion at the meal, immediately before it, or after it. This business discussion must be substantial, so that a brief reference to business is insufficient. Another general requirement is that the expense has to be substantiated (generally by receipts).

Several other requirements must be satisfied in order for a meal expense to be deductible. Meal expenses cannot be deducted if neither the taxpayer nor his employee is present at the meal. So no deduction is available if because you are unable to take an important customer to dinner when he is in town, you simply "buy him dinner."

Another restriction relates to the type of meal. No expense will be deductible to the extent that the meal is "lavish or extravagant" under the circumstances. This is obviously an amorphous standard to apply, but only the lavish or extravagant portion of the meal would be disallowed.

Q: ISN'T THERE AN 80 PERCENT LIMIT ON BUSINESS MEAL AND ENTERTAINMENT EXPENSES?

A: Yes. The final—and in some ways most painful—limitation on business meals is that only 80 percent of otherwise qualifying expenses are deductible. Even assuming the above requirements are met for a meal expense, only 80 percent of the amount will be deductible, and the balance will not be deductible.

Example

Charlie CEO takes his most important wholesale customer to lunch following a product demonstration meeting at Charlie's headquarters. Whether they discuss a business transaction during the meal or not, the meal expense should satisfy the required nexis to the business since it immediately followed a substantial business discussion. If the meal did not follow or precede a substantial discussion, Charlie and his customer would actually have to talk business during lunch for the meal cost to be deductible.

Charlie will need to produce a receipt to substantiate the cost of the lunch, but any portion that is "lavish or extravagant" will not be deductible. Generally speaking, the lavish and extravagant rule has not prohibited most businesses from deducting expensive business meals. However, if Charlie orders a $300 bottle of wine at lunch, he probably has a problem.

Finally, note that only 80 percent of the otherwise qualifying expenses are eligible for deduction. If Charlie spends $100 on lunch for the two of them, only $80 would qualify for the deduction. But suppose Charlie does buy the $300 bottle of wine? In that case, let's assume $250 of the wine cost is disallowed as lavish and extravagant. That means only $150 is deductible. Then the 80 percent limit is applied, and the deduction is really only $120.

Q: ARE ALL BUSINESS MEALS SUBJECT TO THE 80 PERCENT LIMIT?

A: No, there are a few exceptions. The cost of meals incurred by an employee and reimbursed by an employer are not subject to the 80 percent limit, but the *employer* is subject to the 80 percent limit on the reimbursement. In addition, food and beverages that are excludable from an employee's income are not subject to the 80 percent deduction limit.

Q: DOES THE SAME SET OF RULES APPLY FOR BUSINESS ENTERTAINMENT?

A: Not exactly, but the same basic principles apply. To begin with, special harsh restrictions apply to "entertainment facilities." Under these rules, *no* deduction is allowed for any expense paid or incurred for the use of certain entertainment facilities. Examples are hunting or fishing lodges, yachts, swimming pools, tennis courts, and bowling alleys. The same harsh rule applies to certain housing located in recreational areas.

Q: CAN ANY DEDUCTION BE TAKEN FOR ENTERTAINMENT FACILITIES?

A: Yes. The cost of dues and fees paid to social, athletic or sporting clubs or organizations may be deductible if the taxpayer establishes that the facility was used primarily for the furtherance of his or her trade or business, and that the cost deducted was directly related to that trade or business.

Q: WHAT RULES APPLY TO OTHER TYPES OF ENTERTAINMENT?

A: The entertainment rules arc very similar to the rules governing business meals. The basic entertainment expense rule is that no deduction is allowed for the cost of entertainment, amusement, or recreation unless it is directly related to the active conduct of a trade or business. The taxpayer must have more than a general expectation of deriving income from the entertainment at some indefinite future time. The taxpayer must engage in the active conduct of business with the person being entertained, or there must be a specific transaction or arrangement that the taxpayer is seeking to bring to fruition.

In other words, hoping someday to get some business from the person being entertained is too indefinite to support a deductible entertainment expense. And like business meals, generally speaking, the entertainment must either directly precede or follow a substantial business discussion.

Q: CAN "GOODWILL" ENTERTAINMENT EXPENSES BE DEDUCTED?

A: In some cases, entertainment expenses may be deductible notwithstanding the fact that they are more in the nature of "goodwill" expenditures. Expenses for the cost of entertainment that directly precedes or follows a substantial business discussion may be deductible even though the entertainment does not have a specific business goal other than to generally improve the taxpayer's business.

The test of this rule's applicability is purely one of remoteness. The deduction for entertainment will be allowed unless there is only a remote possibility that the entertainment will result in the production of income. But a real and substantial business discussion must either precede or follow the entertainment.

Example

Betty Broker has made commissions on real estate sales to Irving Investor several times in the past. She is currently trying to find a buyer for a large piece of industrial property and meets with Irving at his office for an hour to try to sell the property. At the end of the meeting, Irving says he is not interested, but as planned, Betty takes him out to a nightclub anyway. This type of "goodwill" expense would be a deductible entertainment expense, subject to the 80 percent limitation.

Note

The rule that an entertainment expense deduction will not be allowed when there is only a remote possibility of resulting income seems unlikely to prove a problem in all but the most unusual situations.

Q: DOES THE 80 PERCENT LIMITATION APPLY TO ENTERTAINMENT EXPENSES AS WELL?

A: Yes, with certain exceptions. Generally speaking, just as with business meals, only 80 percent of otherwise allowable entertainment expenses may be deducted. The eligibility tests are applied first; if the expense is otherwise deductible, the 80 percent limit is applied.

Q: ARE ALL ENTERTAINMENT EXPENSES SUBJECT TO THE 80 PERCENT RULE?

A: No. As with business meals, there are certain exceptions. The following meal and entertainment expenses are not subject to the 80 percent limit and are therefore fully deductible.

- Expenses for services, goods, and facilities that are treated as compensation and wages for withholding and income tax purposes.
- Reimbursed expenses to employees, if the employer does not treat the expenses as wages subject to withholding, or if the services are performed for a person other than an employer and the one who receives the reimbursement accounts to that person.
- Recreational expenses for employees such as company picnics or Christmas parties, unless the employees are certain highly compensated individuals.
- The costs of goods, services and facilities made available to the public.
- Entertainment sold to customers for adequate consideration.

- Certain food and beverage expenses that are excludable from the recipient's gross income under technical fringe benefit rules.

Q: ARE BUSINESS GIFTS TREATED LIKE ENTERTAINMENT EXPENSES?

A: No, special limitations apply to business gifts. Deductions for business gifts are limited to $25 per recipient each year. However, signs, display racks, and other promotional materials donated to a retailer for use on the retailer's business premises are not classified as gifts.

Example

Business Books, Inc. publishes books and sells them through retail bookstores. The company, without charge, gives display racks and placards for its books to the bookstores, which purchase certain minimum orders of its books. Business Books, Inc. can deduct the cost of these display racks, placards, and related materials even though it did not charge for them. They are not treated as business gifts and therefore are not subject to the $25-per-recipient rule. However, if Business Books also gives away leather calendars worth $35 to selected customers, only $25 per recipient will be deductible under the business-gift limit.

Note that the $25-per-recipient limit is computed on an aggregate basis (five $5 items would reach the limit). However, advertising items having a cost of $4 or less will not count toward the $25 limit. Binders or pens imprinted with the firm logo are two examples.

Q: WHAT OTHER TYPES OF BUSINESS DEDUCTIONS ARE AVAILABLE?

A: Compensation is deductible as a business expense if it is "reasonable." Chapter 6 discusses the deductibility of compensation as well as many other issues concerning compensating with cash. Chapter 7 discusses compensating with stock.

Subject to limits and technical rules, business expense deductions are also available for contributions to employee benefit plans, disability payments, and life insurance premiums. Deferred compensation plans are discussed in detail in Chapter 8.

Another type of deductible business expense is interest. Professional fees paid to attorneys, accountants, and other advisors are also deductible.

With all of these business expenses, however, keep in mind the recurring issue of capitalization. If attorneys' fees are paid in connection with ongoing operations, they are deductible. But if they are paid in connection with the acquisition of a building, they would have to be "capitalized" as a part of the cost of acquiring the building. The fees would then be recovered over the life of the building.

DJI Planning Guide

There are relatively few areas where special limitations apply to business expense deductions. In general, if something advances the interests of the business and is not a purchase of an asset that has to be capitalized, it will be a deductible business expense.

Q: WHAT KINDS OF TAXES ARE DEDUCTIBLE?

A: The following are among the most significant taxes that businesses are entitled to deduct:

- State, local, and foreign real property taxes.
- State or local personal property taxes.
- State, local, or foreign income, war profits, or excess profits taxes.
- The federal windfall profit tax.
- Any other state, local, or foreign tax paid or accrued within the tax year if it is directly attributable to a trade or business or to property from which rents or royalties are derived (but note that sales and use taxes are not deductible).

Note

As with other expenses, some taxes may have to be capitalized. For example, taxes paid during the production of property must be capitalized.

Example

Developco subdivides a large tract of land and begins building houses on the lots. The property taxes paid during construction cannot be deducted but must be capitalized and treated as a cost of producing the finished homes.

Q: ARE SOCIAL SECURITY TAXES DEDUCTIBLE?

A: Yes, although technically they are deductible as a business expense, not as a tax. The portion of the Social Security tax the employer pays is deductible, but the portion paid by the employee is nondeductible. The federal unemployment insurance tax (sometimes called "FUTA") is also deductible by the employer—again, technically as a business expense and not as a tax.

But if you are self-employed (i.e., as a proprietor), the self-employment tax is not deductible.

Q: ARE THERE PARTICULAR LIMITATIONS APPLICABLE TO EMPLOYEE BUSINESS EXPENSES?

A: Yes, a number of special rules apply to an employee's business expenses. To begin with, an employee's business expenses are generally not deductible except to the extent they exceed 2 percent of the employee's adjusted gross income. This means that unless the aggregate amount of these **miscellaneous deductions** exceeds 2 percent of the employee's adjusted gross income, *no* deduction may be taken.

The only significant exception to this 2 percent threshold is expenses paid by an employee under an employer reimbursement policy. That type of expense incurred by an employee is fully deductible by the employee, and the reimbursement by the employer offsets the employee's deduction.

Example

Sid Salesman incurs $8,000 of traveling expenses during the year and receives full reimbursement from his employer. Sid can deduct the $8,000 paid and includes the $8,000 reimbursement income. The net result is a wash.

DJI Planning Guide

An appropriate planning device in light of the 2 percent rule is for an employee who will have significant employee business expenses to have his or her employer reimburse all the expenses and, if necessary, to have the employee receive a correspondingly lower salary.

Q: ARE TRAVELING EXPENSES DEDUCTIBLE?

A: Yes. Ordinary and necessary traveling expenses incurred by a taxpayer away from home in the conduct of a trade or business are deductible. They are not even subject to the 2 percent floor if they are payments by an employer to reimburse the employee. Unreimbursed traveling expenses are deductible but are subject to the 2 percent miscellaneous deduction floor.

The key to determining deductible traveling expenses is whether the taxpayer is "away from home." Normally a person is considered away from home if his duties require him to be away from his home for longer than an ordinary work day and if he will need sleep or rest. The idea here is not to allow deductions for traveling expenses, including meals and lodging, for travel near the taxpayer's home.

Q: WHERE IS THE TAXPAYER'S HOME?

A: Occasionally it is difficult to tell where the taxpayer's home really is. Generally a taxpayer's home for this purpose is his regular or principal place of business, or, if he has no regular or principal place of business, his regular residence.

When there are multiple places of business, the principal place of business will serve. The time spent at each place of business, the amount of business in an area, and the amount of financial return will all be relevant in determining a principal place of business.

Q: ARE HOME OFFICE DEDUCTIONS STILL AVAILABLE?

A: The home office deduction has generated great controversy over the last few years. In their current form, the home office rules do allow the taxpayer to deduct expenses for using his or her home for business, but strict rules apply. The taxpayer cannot take any deduction unless the expenses are attributable to a portion of the home used *exclusively* and on a *regular* basis as one of the following:

- The principal place of any business carried on by the taxpayer.
- A place of business used by patients, clients, or customers in meeting or dealing with the taxpayer in the normal course of business.

Exclusive use of a portion of the home for business purposes means the taxpayer cannot use it for anything else. A family room or den where some personal activities take place will not suffice. The only exception to this rule is for wholesale or retail sellers whose dwelling unit is their sole fixed location of business. In that case, expenses allocable to space within the dwelling used for storing inventory can generate a deduction.

Q: WHAT OTHER LIMITS ARE THERE ON THE HOME OFFICE DEDUCTION?

A: Apart from the "exclusiveness" and "regular basis" requirements, one of the most significant limitations applies to employees. On top of the other requirements, in order for an employee to take the home office deduction, the use of the home office must be for the "convenience of the employer." The idea here is that the deduction is unavailable unless the employer requests the employee to perform work at home and generates the need for the home office.

DJI Planning Guide _____

The "convenience of the employer" requirement applicable to employees is difficult to satisfy. The employer must actually require that work be performed at home as opposed to on the employer's business premises. As a practical matter, this means that most employees cannot qualify for home office deductions unless they have a business of their own on the side.

There are also limitations imposed by the way the home office deduction is computed. To begin with, the home office deduction is limited to the taxpayer's gross income from the activity engaged in at the office. In other words, a home office deduction cannot shield income from other sources. It can only reduce the income from the activity engaged in at the home office.

Q: HOW IS A HOME OFFICE DEDUCTION COMPUTED?

A: In determining whether the taxpayer had a gain or loss from the business activity performed at the home office, otherwise deductible items (such as a mortgage interest and property taxes) must be deducted *first*. These otherwise allowable deductions are subtracted from the business income generated from the activity for which the home office is used. This procedure reduces the amount of business income and therefore reduces the allowable home office deduction.

Once this is done, the expenses allocable to the home office are deducted from the business income. Expenses that relate to the whole house are allocated for this purpose according to the ratio of the square footage in the home devoted to business use divided by the total square footage in the home.

Example

Elaine Entrepreneur is a Manager of High Technologies, Inc. and has started her own consulting company out of her home office to do other work. Last year, she generated $25,000 from her own consulting business. The portion of her home she uses for a home office is one-fifth of the square footage in the residence. Her property tax payment for her residence was $5,000 last year, and interest expense on the house was $25,000 for the year. In computing the allowable home office deduction, Elaine must subtract from the $25,000 she made one-fifth of the property tax payment ($1,000) and one-fifth of the interest payments ($5,000). Thus, the maximum home office deduction (for depreciation, utilities, etc.) that Elaine can take for the year is $19,000. The cost of utilities and depreciation would also be allocated at one-fifth of the total.

CAPITAL ASSETS AND DEPRECIATION

Q: WHAT COSTS AND PURCHASES MUST BE CAPITALIZED?

A: Once again, the distinction between deductible expenses and costs that must be capitalized is an inherently difficult one. Where assets have a useful life beyond the end of the year, their cost must generally be capitalized. The cost is then subject to depreciation, a subject discussed below.

There are also certain other costs that must be capitalized on the theory that they are attributable to producing property.

For example, although legal expenses are generally deductible as business expenses, legal expenses attributable to purchasing capital assets (such as a building or machinery) have to be capitalized as a cost of acquiring the capital asset. This principle applies not only to legal expenses but also to any direct cost of acquiring the property. Brokerage fees and other costs are similarly treated.

Q: WHAT IS A CAPITAL ASSET?

A: Although it is sometimes said that anything with a useful life longer than a year is a capital asset, technically a capital asset is defined in the negative. A capital asset is any property (whether or not it is connected with a trade or business) that does not fall within a certain category of property. Those items of property that cannot constitute a capital asset include, among other things, inventory; property held primarily for sale to customers; notes or accounts receivable; copyrights; and literary, musical, or artistic compositions.

Depreciable business property and real property used in a taxpayer's trade or business are technically not capital assets; they are **Section 1231 Assets**, which are treated just like capital assets for nearly all purposes except for determining the limits on the deduction for losses from their sale.

Q: IS DEPRECIATION ALLOWABLE ON ALL CAPITAL ASSETS?

A: No, depreciation is not allowable on property used for personal purposes. For property used partially for business and partially for personal purposes (such as an automobile), depreciation is allowable only on the business-related portion.

No depreciation is allowable on land apart from its improvements, nor for depletable natural resources (although depletion deductions may be available for them). Depreciation may be available for intangible assets, however. For example, depreciation is available for patents, copyrights, licenses, franchises, and certain contracts that have a limited useful life. Goodwill, however, is not depreciable.

**Q: HOW IS THE USEFUL LIFE OF
AN ASSET COMPUTED?**

A: Methods of calculating depreciation have changed substantially over the last ten years. Currently, the actual useful life of most assets is not directly relevant. What is relevant is the arbitrary category assigned by the IRS to the particular kind of asset.

For *tangible* property placed in service after 1986, the cost of the property is recovered over the "recovery period" for the asset. Some common recovery periods are listed below. See pp. 74-75. The same general principle applies for property placed in service between 1981 and 1987 under the **Accelerated Cost Recovery System**, sometimes called "ACRS." For property placed in service after 1987, the **Modified Accelerated Cost Recovery System**, sometimes called "MACRS," applies. As explained below, useful lives are still relevant for intangible assets.

**Q: DOES THE TAXPAYER HAVE
A CHOICE ABOUT WHICH
METHOD OF DEPRECIATION
TO USE?**

A: Yes, to some extent. However, most tangible property placed in service after 1986 must be depreciated according to the Modified Accelerated Cost Recovery System ("MACRS").

For tangible property placed in service after 1980 and before 1987, the Accelerated Cost Recovery System ("ACRS") applies. It is very similar to the Modified Accelerated Cost Recovery System effective for 1987 and beyond but generally allowed faster write-off schedules.

Q: WHAT ABOUT DEPRECIATING INTANGIBLE PROPERTY SUCH AS CONTRACTS, FRANCHISES, AND COPYRIGHTS?

A: For assets placed in service before 1981, and for assets such as intangible property that are excluded from the operation of ACRS and MACRS, the depreciation allowable is based on several factors. First, the remaining useful life of the property must be determined. (Under ACRS and MACRS, the life of the property is *assumed* to be a specified number of years for certain classes of property.)

Once the remaining useful life is determined, the salvage value of the property must be determined. The salvage value is the remaining value the asset can be expected to have upon the expiration of its useful life. The difference between the cost and salvage value is then spread over the useful life of the property, and the depreciation deductions are allowed accordingly.

Example

Copyslurp, Ltd., a company that specializes in exploiting copyrights purchased from struggling authors, has purchased a copyright for $5,000. Under copyright law, the term of the copyright (its useful life) is the life of the author plus 50 years. Although the author is still alive, Copyslurp calculates the remaining life expectancy of the author as 20 years, giving the copyright a useful life of 70 years. Copyslurp calculates the salvage value of the copyright upon its expiration as $100. The salvage value is subtracted from the $5,000 total. Accordingly, Copyslurp can deduct as depreciation one-seventieth of $4,900 ($70 per year).

Q: WHAT EFFECT DOES A PURCHASE MADE EARLY, MID, OR LATE IN THE YEAR HAVE ON THE DEPRECIATION DEDUCTION?

A: A purchase during the tax year will require a proration of the depreciation deduction. Under the depreciation rules applicable to intangibles (such as patents, copyrights, licenses, franchises, etc.) and to tangible assets placed in service before 1981, this proration was determined according to the number of months the property was actually used.

If the asset was purchased during a given tax year, only part of a full year's depreciation was allowed for the first year. The expected full-year depreciation allowance was multiplied by the number of months the property was owned, then divided by 12.

Example

If $6,000 of depreciation were allowable annually on a piece of property, and if the property had been purchased on April 1 of the calendar tax year, only nine months of depreciation would be allowed. Thus, the depreciation deduction for the first year would be $4,500 instead of $6,000.

Q: WHAT ABOUT MID-YEAR PURCHASES OF OTHER PROPERTY?

A: For property qualifying for ACRS depreciation (basically, tangible property placed in service after 1980 and before 1987), a "half-year convention" was applied. Under this convention, one half-year's depreciation would be allowed for any mid-year purchase—even if the purchase occurred on the last day of the tax year. But by the same token, only one half-year's depreciation would be allowed even if the property had been purchased on the second or third day of the tax year. Any time that the property was not used during the entire tax year, the half-year convention would apply.

Q: DOES THIS HALF-YEAR CONVENTION APPLY TO PROPERTY UNDER THE CURRENT MACRS DEPRECIATION SYSTEM?

A: Yes. For tangible depreciable personal property placed in service after 1986 (under the Modified Accelerated Cost Recovery System), the half-year convention is still generally applied.

However, there are now several exceptions to the application of the half-year convention. Most importantly, a mid-month convention is applied for depreciable real property. Under this rule, property is treated as placed in service or disposed of during the middle of the month, and the depreciation deduction is based on the number of months the property was in service.

The other important exception for MACRS property concerns a "mid-quarter convention," under which all property placed in service during any quarter of a tax year (a three-month period) is treated as placed in service at the mid-point of the quarter. This mid-quarter convention applies to all property except real property that is covered by the mid-month convention if certain percentage tests are met. Otherwise, the mid-year convention would apply.

DJI Planning Guide

Note that these conventions, which in effect allow for more depreciation than the taxpayer is really entitled to for a portion of the year, encourage purchases late in the year. The taxpayer may generate a healthy depreciation deduction and thus reduce his taxes by purchasing depreciable property and putting it to use before year end. An advance calculation of the taxpayer's estimated tax liability before year end will help facilitate this kind of tax planning.

Q: IS IT POSSIBLE TO WRITE OFF THE ENTIRE COST OF AN ASSET DURING THE YEAR INSTEAD OF DEPRECIATING IT?

A: Yes, subject to limitations. It is possible to write off or "expense" the cost of property that would otherwise be subject to depreciation. This is accomplished by an election made on a form (IRS Form 4562) attached to the taxpayer's tax return for the year. The maximum amount that may be expensed is $10,000 ($5,000 for married persons filing separate returns). However, this $10,000 ceiling is reduced by the excess cost of certain property over $200,000 placed in service during the tax year.

Example

Corner Store, a corporation, purchases new counters for $5,000 in 1988. The corporation may elect to expense the cost of the counters rather than to depreciate them. However, if Corner Store were *also* to place $205,000 of depreciable property (counters, refrigerators, meat cutters, etc.) in its store during 1988, it would not be able to elect to expense the counters. The excess of the other depreciable property above $200,000 (in this case $5,000) would reduce the available expensing election to zero.

DJI Planning Guide

Generally speaking, the election to expense depreciable property is desirable; it removes the need to keep records of the property from year to year. Moreover, the expensing election is desirable in that it obviously results in a greater dollar amount deducted in earlier years. Note, too, that although the deduction limit is $10,000 per year, it can be applied on a partial basis to depreciable property having a greater value (e.g., $10,000 of a $15,000 machine could be expensed, and the remaining $5,000 could be depreciated over time).

Q: UNDER CURRENT RULES, OVER WHAT PERIODS CAN ASSETS BE WRITTEN OFF?

A: Under the Modified Accelerated Cost Recovery System (MACRS), which generally applies to tangible property put in service after 1986, assets are classified as either 3-year property, 5-year property, 7-year property, 10-year property, 15-year property, 20-year property, 27.5-year residential real property, or 31.5-year nonresidential real property. A few examples of the covered property are listed below.

- *3-year property*. Includes very little property.
- *5-year property*. Includes cars, light and heavy general-purpose trucks, technological and computer equipment, and office machinery.

- *7-year property.* Includes office furniture and fixtures and single-purpose agricultural or horticultural structures. Serves as a catch-all for other items of property that are not classified.
- *10-year property.* Includes vessels, barges, and tugs.
- *15-year property.* Includes municipal wastewater treatment plants and telephone distribution plants.
- *20-year property.* Includes municipal sewers and farm buildings.
- *27.5-year residential real property.* Includes buildings or structures producing predominantly rental income from dwelling units.
- *31.5-year nonresidential real property.* Includes buildings other than those constituting residential real property (office buildings, commercial and industrial buildings, etc.).

DJI Planning Guide

The 27.5-year and 31.5-year depreciation schedules for real property have proven a substantial blow to the real estate owner, particularly when compared with the 19-year depreciation schedule of the recent past. These depreciation schedules, along with the passive activity loss restrictions, clearly make real estate ownership less of a "tax haven" than it was prior to the Tax Reform Act of 1986.

Q: IS ACCELERATED DEPRECIATION STILL AVAILABLE?

A: Yes, for many assets. To begin with, property placed in service between 1981 and 1987 is still governed by the old ACRS system, which permitted **accelerated depreciation**. Moreover, under the new Modified Accelerated Cost Recovery System (MACRS), there is a choice as to the rate of depreciation. A taxpayer may elect to use the **straight-line** MACRS method, under which the depreciation deductions are ratable over the life of the asset.

Example

An asset costing $1,000 in the 10-year class of property would be depreciated at a rate of $100 a year. Note that salvage value is not considered in a straight-line MACRS deduction.

Q: WHAT IF YOU DON'T ELECT STRAIGHT-LINE DEPRECIATION?

A: If the taxpayer does not *elect* to have the straight-line MACRS method apply, an accelerated depreciation method applies automatically. Property in the 3, 5, 7, and 10-year classes is recovered using a "200 percent declining balance" method, with a switch to the straight-line method. Depreciation on 15- and 20-year property is recovered using a 150 percent declining balance method, with a switch to the straight-line method. Both the 200 percent and 150 percent declining balance methods involve rapid write-offs with greater deductions in the early years.

Under the Modified Accelerated Cost Recovery System, no accelerated depreciation is available for residential rental and nonresidential real property. It is recovered using a straight-line method.

CHAPTER 4

INVENTORIES, ACCOUNTING METHODS, AND INSTALLMENT SALES

INTRODUCTION

Apart from businesses that provide a service, most businesses maintain inventory of some type. Inventory may be purchased and then resold in the same condition or in an altered state. Alternatively, it may be constructed or manufactured and become inventory when it is completed. Complex tax rules govern the manner in which inventories are kept and the rate at which income is generated from sales.

Since inventory may obviously be purchased at different times and at different costs, the method of inventory accounting that is chosen by the taxpayer (**First In First Out, Last In First Out,** and their variations) may substantially affect the time at which taxes become payable. There is also a choice to be made concerning the valuation of inventory. It can be valued at either its cost or market value. A basic understanding of the sweeping impact of these inventory rules is critical to virtually all businesses.

The applicability of inventory rules also affects whether a taxpayer can use the cash or accrual method of accounting. The concepts of cash and accrual accounting and the rules governing who can still use the cash method are also discussed in this chapter.

Finally, the installment method of reporting gain can make a tremendous difference in the taxes payable by a business.

Since the installment method is elective, an understanding of its operation and use is a key to effective tax planning.

INVENTORIES

Q: WHO IS SUBJECT TO INVENTORY RULES?

A: Inventory rules apply in each case where the production, purchase, or sale of merchandise is an "income-producing factor" in a business. Basically, this means that the production, purchase, or sale of merchandise need not be the taxpayer's sole revenue source or even his primary revenue source. It must be only *one factor* in income production. Even a farmer who grows crops and later sells them is covered by inventory rules since the crops become inventory when they are grown.

Q: WHAT IS THE PURPOSE OF MEASURING INVENTORY?

A: The main purpose of measuring inventory is to determine taxable income. The gross profit from a business is calculated by deducting the "cost of goods sold" from total receipts. The cost of goods sold, in turn, is determined by adding the inventory at the beginning of the year to the cost of goods purchased or produced during the year, then deducting from this figure the inventory at the end of the year.

Since the items in inventory will influence the cost of goods sold and thus influence the company's income, what is included in inventory is obviously significant.

Q: WHAT MUST BE INCLUDED IN INVENTORY?

A: An inventory list should include partly finished goods as well as finished goods. Even raw materials and supplies that were purchased for resale as is, or that will become a part of the merchandise for sale should be included. However, merchandise is included in inventory (whether it is finished or unfinished) only if the taxpayer owns the merchandise.

Finished goods that the seller has already contracted to sell may still have to be included in inventory if these goods have not yet been segregated from the rest of the goods for pick-up or delivery, unless title to the goods has already passed to the buyer. Conversely, a buyer who has purchased goods but has not yet received them must include these purchased goods in *his* inventory as long as title to the goods has passed to him, even though delivery may occur later.

Q: HOW IS INVENTORY VALUED?

A: Inventory valuation is at least as important as the items that make up inventory. The valuation placed on inventory will affect the cost of goods sold and the company's income. There are two basic methods of valuing inventory:

- The cost method.
- The cost or market method, whichever is lower.

Whichever method is chosen, it must be used for valuing both opening and closing inventories (inventory at the beginning and at the end of each year).

The "cost" method of inventory valuation is straightforward: The taxpayer has kept a record of what the inventory cost him, and this figure is used for inventory valuation. With the "cost or market" approach, the taxpayer looks at each specific item of inventory, comparing the cost paid for the inventory to the current market value. For each item, the cost and market value are compared and the lower becomes the inventory value.

Note

If the "cost or market" approach is used, the comparison of which value is lower is made on an item-by-item basis. The taxpayer cannot value his entire stock under both methods (at cost and also at market) and then pick the lower value. Valuation must be determined on an item-by-item basis.

Example

A metals manufacturer has three classes of brass bars in stock at the end of the tax year. Their values are as follows:

Grade	Cost	Market Value
A	$30,000	$35,000
B	$15,000	$20,000
C	$10,000	$ 5,000

The cost and market value are compared on an item-by-item basis, so total inventory value at the end of the year totals $50,000 ($30,000 plus $15,000 plus $5,000).

Market value is ordinarily determined by the price the item would cost on the inventory valuation date. The cost of the item to the taxpayer is normally easy to determine since the taxpayer will have kept records of inventory purchases.

Q: WHAT IS CONSIDERED A COST OF INVENTORY?

A: Cost includes the amount actually paid for the item of inventory. The cost of the property also includes any costs incurred to produce the property. For example, suppose the taxpayer's inventory is not purchased and resold in the same condition but is something produced by the taxpayer? Examples are films, video tapes, books, and similar property. The amounts expended to produce these items will all go to make up its "cost."

All the costs of producing the property must be added together to arrive at the "cost" of the inventory. All such costs must be capitalized (i.e., they cannot be immediately deducted).

Q: CAN ANY EXPENSES OF INVENTORY BE CURRENTLY DEDUCTED?

A: Yes, there are a few exceptions to the normal rule that the cost of inventory must be capitalized. The following costs may currently be deducted:

- Marketing and selling expenses.
- General and administrative expenses that do not directly benefit the production or the acquisition of inventory.
- Deductible losses (including losses unreimbursed by insurance, casualty losses, and worthless securities losses).
- Income taxes attributable to sales.
- Costs of pension plans related to past service.
- Costs attributable to strikes.
- Depreciation on equipment and facilities that are temporarily not being used.

DJI Planning Guide _____

It is clearly more desirable to receive a current deduction for any item of cost than to be required to capitalize it as a cost of inventory. A few of the above listed items can provide the taxpayer with substantial flexibility in determining whether to capitalize or deduct. For example, when it is not clear whether general and administrative expenses directly benefit inventory items, the taxpayer should prefer to deduct those expenses.

Q: DO INTEREST COSTS HAVE TO BE INCLUDED IN THIS INVENTORY COMPUTATION?

A: Yes. Interest paid to finance the construction, building, installation, manufacture, development, or improvement of property produced by the taxpayer must be capitalized. This requirement is in contrast to the ordinary rule for interest expenses in the business context—that they are immediately deductible. The property that is subject to this interest capitalization requirement includes property produced by the taxpayer for use in a trade or business or in an activity for profit that has one of the following:

- A long, useful life (generally 20 years or more).
- An estimated production period exceeding two years.
- An estimated production period exceeding one year and a cost exceeding $1 million.

Q: CAN INTEREST INCURRED TO PURCHASE INVENTORY BE DEDUCTED?

A: Yes. The interest capitalization requirement focuses on the construction, manufacture, and improvement of property. If a dealer purchases inventory and then sells it, incurring interest costs, that interest is deductible.

To determine whether interest is allocable to the production of property, one should first look at interest on debt that directly financed production or construction costs. But if production or construction costs of an asset exceed the amount of direct debt, then interest on other loans can also be subject to capitalization. The assumption is that these other loans are indirectly financing the cost of construction.

Example

Irving Inventor incurs debt to produce 50,000 of his newest model widgets in his manufacturing plant. The interest cost is $30,000 for 1989. Irving also uses funds from his general operating account that were made available under a line of credit from his local bank. The additional interest cost for the amount drawn under the line of credit was $15,000. This $15,000, in addition to the $30,000, is subject to the interest capitalization rule.

Q: HOW DOES ONE IDENTIFY WHICH INVENTORY ITEMS HAVE BEEN SOLD?

A: A determination of which items of inventory have been sold is obviously relevant to determining the amount of gain recognized on the sale.

Example

Cyborg Company has five identical items of inventory this year. It purchased the first item three years ago for $10, and the other items ranged in cost between $20 and $60. If it sells one item for $100, how much gain must Cyborg report? The inventory identification methods explained below seek to provide the answer.

There are two basic methods of inventory identification, along with variations of each. The "Last In First Out" (LIFO) method assumes that the last item produced or acquired is the first item sold. The items in inventory at the beginning of the year (opening inventory) are treated as being first, and those acquired during the tax year are treated as being second.

The second major type of inventory identification is FIFO, "First In First Out." As the name implies, the First In First Out method looks to the earliest acquired inventory first and compares its cost with the sales price. This means that inventory with a lower cost is typically deemed sold first, thus producing larger gain.

Q: ARE THESE THE ONLY METHODS OF INVENTORY IDENTIFICATION?

A: No. One variation of the LIFO method that may be adopted is the "Dollar-Value LIFO" method. Under Dollar-Value LIFO, the total dollar values of the beginning and ending inventories in the first year are compared, and any dollar-value increase to current prices is determined by reference to an index. There is also a "Simplified Dollar-Value LIFO" method, which is a further variation of this procedure.

Q: WHICH METHOD APPLIES TO MOST BUSINESSES?

A: By number, probably FIFO. This is because FIFO applies unless the taxpayer elects otherwise.

DJI Planning Guide ⎯⎯⎯⎯⎯⎯⎯⎯⎯⎯⎯⎯⎯⎯⎯⎯⎯

An election must be made in order to use the LIFO method, but the election does not have to be approved by the IRS. An election to use the LIFO method may be particularly desirable where the cost of items fluctuates or has gone up substantially.

ACCOUNTING METHODS

Q: HOW DO INVENTORIES INFLUENCE ACCOUNTING METHODS?

A: Any business that maintains inventories must use the **accrual method of accounting** for purchases and sales. The **cash accounting method** measures income based on actual cash received and cash paid. Accrual accounting, on the other hand, determines income by *when* the right to receive income matures, even though it is paid at a later date. Deductions under the accrual method are thus determined according to when payment is due, even though payment might be made at a later date.

Example

Retail Sales Co., a retail furniture seller, receives a bill from one of its suppliers on December 20, payable immediately. Since the company is on the accrual method, it is entitled to deduct the payment to the supplier this year even if it does not actually make payment until January. Similarly, if Retail Sales is *owed* money, it will have to include it in income when payment is due, even though it may not actually collect the money until the following year.

Q: OF THE CASH AND ACCRUAL METHODS OF ACCOUNTING, WHICH IS BETTER?

A: There is really no answer to this question. To begin with, most individuals use the cash basis as their method of accounting and report income in the year it is actually or constructively received.

Constructive receipt is the deemed receipt of income when the taxpayer has a right to it and when there is no restriction on his ability to demand it. A classic example is demonstrated by someone telling an employer, "I don't want my check until next year." This practice does not prevent the income from being currently taxed. Deductions are taken in the year the payments are actually made. Because of this, the cash method of accounting allows somewhat more flexibility, particularly regarding the time of payment.

Under the accrual method, income is included when the right to receive it comes into being, even though payment may be made much later. This feature of the accrual method effectively obviates the constructive receipt doctrine. Similarly, expenses are deductible in the year the obligation for payment arises, even though payment may be made later. This rule eliminates the flexibility of payment that exists under the cash method.

Q: WHO IS ENTITLED TO USE THE CASH METHOD?

A: Many taxpayers are prohibited from using the cash method. The following taxpayers are generally required to use the accrual method and are therefore ineligible to use the cash method:

- C corporations (regular corporations that have not made an S election).
- Partnerships that have a C corporation as a partner.
- Charitable trusts if and to the extent that they have "unrelated trade or business income" (a special income tax

imposed on the business activity of the exempt organizations).

There · are certain exceptions to the above rules. For instance, a small business entity with average annual gross receipts of $5 million or less can still use the cash method of accounting. And certain personal service corporations such as medical, law and accounting businesses are treated as individuals, so they too can use the cash method of accounting.

DJI Planning Guide _____

Since accrual accounting is now required for most business taxpayers, it is sometimes assumed that the cash method should be used for those taxpayers who are still permitted to use it. Particularly for small businesses, for which the cash method has its primary continued application, the cash method offers greater simplicity.

Q: CAN YOU SWITCH BACK AND FORTH BETWEEN THE CASH AND ACCRUAL METHODS?

A: No. Even for taxpayers who can still use the cash method, it is not possible to change accounting methods without obtaining advance permission from the IRS.

INSTALLMENT SALES

Q: WHAT IS THE INSTALLMENT METHOD?

A: The installment method is a special method of taxing gains from the sale of property. In order to have an **installment sale,** all that is necessary is that at least one payment be received in a tax year other than the year of the sale. The gain on the sale is then spread over the number of years that payment is received.

Example

Company X paid $5,000 for a piece of machinery that it has depreciated to $3,000 and now chooses to sell. The sale is made for a cash payment this year for $3,000, with another payment due on January 2 of next year for the balance of $3,000 (for a total sale price of $6,000). The total profit is $3,000. Half the profit will be reported in the first year, and half the profit in the second year.

Q: IS THE INSTALLMENT METHOD MANDATORY?

A: No, it is the taxpayer's choice whether it applies. Under current rules, however, the installment method applies *unless* the taxpayer elects not to have it apply. In order for an election to be effective, it must be made on the tax return for the year in which the sale (which otherwise would be subject to the installment sales rules) will be reported. The election is made by reporting the entire gain in the year of the sale even though all of the sales proceeds have not yet been received.

DJI Planning Guide ————————————————

If a taxpayer desires to elect not to have the installment method apply, the tax return must be filed on time. The IRS generally will not permit untimely elections. Note, too, that the consequences of the election should be carefully considered before the election is made. Once an election is made not to have the installment sales rules apply, revocation of such an election can be made only with IRS consent.

Q: DOES EVERY SALE QUALIFY FOR INSTALLMENT SALE TREATMENT?

A: No, the installment method is available only for certain types of sales. The installment sale method may be used by persons who casually sell or dispose of personal or real property that does not constitute inventory.

Q: CAN DEALERS WHO SELL PROPERTY REPORT THEIR GAIN ON THE INSTALLMENT METHOD?

A: No, not after 1987. The Revenue Act of 1987 repealed the installment method for dealer sales of personal and real property. After 1987, even if a dealer in real or personal property does not receive the entire sales price on a purchase, the dealer will have to include the entire sales price in his income for the year of the sale.

Example

Salesco, Inc. is a retail typewriter seller. On October 1, Salesco sells a group of typewriters to an accounting firm with payment to be made in 12 monthly installments over the next year. If Salesco is a calendar-year taxpayer, under the traditional installment method, Salesco will have to report in its income only the three installments received for October, November, and December of the current year, with the remaining nine payments going into next year. Because dealer sales of personal property no longer qualify for installment sale treatment, however, Salesco will treat all payments as received in the first year.

Q: WHAT ABOUT DEALER SALES OF REAL OR PERSONAL PROPERTY THAT OCCURRED PRIOR TO 1988?

A: Although dealer sales of real or personal property no longer qualify for installment sale treatment after 1987, transitional rules govern the inclusion of income from dealer sales that occurred in prior years. The new rules do not apply to dealer installment sales made before March 1, 1986 (so installment sale treatment does apply to those sales). Sales made between March 1, 1986, and January 1, 1988, receive special treatment.

Q: ARE THERE ANY EXCEPTIONS THAT ALLOW DEALERS TO REPORT ON THE INSTALLMENT BASIS?

A: Yes, but the exceptions are quite limited. Farmers can still make dealer sales on the installment basis. Residential lots can also be sold by property dealers, as long as neither the seller nor any related person will make improvements on the lots. The sale of timeshare units can also still qualify for installment sale treatment if certain requirements are met.

Q: HOW IS THE GAIN ON AN INSTALLMENT SALE COMPUTED?

A: For the sales to which the installment method can now apply (casual sales of real and personal property that is not inventory), the basic concept of the installment sale provision is to tax only a proportionate amount of the gain on each installment. For example, in a sale of property with payment in two installments, in which the sales price is twice the cost of the item, it is easy to see that half of the gain would be reported upon receipt of each installment. When there are more than two installments, the computations can become more complex.

Example

Investment Partnership, Ltd., a calendar-year partnership, sells a piece of real estate for $1 million. Payment is to be made with $100,000 down and the balance in yearly installments of $100,000 plus interest at nine percent. The first installment is due on January 1 of next year. The partnership has a basis in the property of $300,000. Accordingly, apart from interest, the partnership has a profit of $700,000 on the sale. Of each $100,000 payment received in subsequent years, $70,000 (one-tenth of the total profit) must be declared in the partnership's income.

Q: IS IT POSSIBLE UNDER AN INSTALLMENT SALE TO BE TAXED ON MORE THAN THE AMOUNT OF CASH RECEIVED?

A: Yes, and this possibility should be considered before making any sale on the installment basis. One way this can happen is through "depreciation recapture."

Depreciation recapture treats sales proceeds on a disposition of depreciable property as ordinary income for which depreciation deductions have already been claimed. Basically, depreciation recapture seeks to convert what otherwise would be capital gain back into ordinary income. The rationalization is that since the taxpayer enjoyed depreciation deductions from ordinary income while he held the property, the amount of this depreciation should be recharacterized as ordinary income upon sale of the property. Depreciation recapture applies to all depreciation taken on personal property but only to the depreciation in excess of straight-line depreciation taken on real property.

Q: HOW CAN THE TAX BE GREATER THAN THE CASH RECEIVED?

A: The way depreciation recapture rules can result in a taxpayer being taxable on more cash than he actually gets in an installment sale is best illustrated through an example.

Example

Investment, Ltd., a calendar-year partnership, sells an office building for $1 million, with the first installment of $200,000 paid on closing and the other eight installments of $100,000 each due over the next eight years. Interest at 11 percent is added to each installment. If the partnership had a basis in the building of $200,000, it will receive a gain of $800,000 on full payment.

However, suppose the depreciation taken on the building were $400,000 under one of the accelerated methods of depreciation and that $200,000 were taxable as depreciation recapture. This $200,000, together with $180,000 of the $200,000 downpayment, will be taxable in the year of sale! [$180,000 of the downpayment is taxable gain because installments will be taxed as one-fifth basis ($200,000) and four-fifths gain ($1 million).] This means that the partnership is taxable on more cash than it actually receives in sales proceeds!

DJI Planning Guide ──────────────────────────

Because depreciation recapture overrides the installment sales provisions, any possible depreciation recapture must be considered *before* any installment sale is consummated. If the business terms of a sale call for payment to be stretched over a number of years, merely electing out of installment sale treatment will not solve the problem generated by depreciation recapture. Indeed, electing out of installment sale treatment will generally make the situation worse.

Electing out of installment sale treatment will generally result in having *all* gain (not just the recapture) taxed in the year of the sale. If depreciation recapture will apply to a sale, perhaps the sale simply should not be structured as an installment sale at all. At a minimum, sufficient cash should be generated in the form of a downpayment to pay any tax due by reason of depreciation recapture.

───

Another pitfall that can result in unanticipated taxes on an installment sale is if some of the obligations received by the seller are considered cash payments.

Q: WHAT IS CONSIDERED PAYMENTS IN THE YEAR OF SALE?

A: Obviously, the amount of cash received in the year of sale is treated as received by the seller. However, certain noncash items are also treated as payment. The following are among the more common types of debt instruments that will be considered payment:

• *A debt instrument issued by a person other than the purchaser.* For example, on a sale of property by Seller to Buyer, if Buyer tenders a cash-down payment plus a note by someone *other* than the Seller, Buyer will have received full payment, and installment treatment will not be available.

• *A debt instrument secured by cash or a cash equivalent such as a bank certificate or a treasury note.* If Seller sells property to Buyer and Buyer tenders a cash-down payment plus Buyer's note secured by a bank certificate of deposit, Seller may be treated as having received full payment in the year of sale.

• *A bond or other evidence of the buyer's indebtedness if it is payable on demand is readily tradable or is issued with coupons or in registered form.* If Seller receives from Buyer a downpayment plus readily tradable securities, Seller should obviously be treated as receiving all cash.

• *Indebtedness assumed or taken subject to by the Buyer to the extent that it exceeds the Seller's basis for the property adjusted to reflect selling expenses.* If Seller owes $100 on the property and has a basis of only $80, and if Buyer assumes the whole $100 debt, then the $20 excess is treated as cash to Seller.

• *Cancellation of Seller's indebtedness to the Buyer in consideration of the sale.* If Seller owes Buyer money prior to the sale and this debt is cancelled, then Seller is considered to have received an equivalent amount of cash.

Q: ARE SOME INSTALLMENT SALES DISALLOWED IF THE TAXPAYER HAS OUTSTANDING DEBT?

A: No, not any longer. The so-called "proportionate disallowance rules" enacted in the 1986 Tax Reform Act provided that certain installment sales would be disallowed (either entirely or in part) depending upon the amount of the outstanding debt a taxpayer owed. These extremely complex rules were repealed effective for transactions beginning in 1988.

In determining whether installment sale treatment is available, therefore, it is no longer necessary to determine the amount of debt the taxpayer has. The only exception is for certain dealer sales made between March 1, 1986, and January 1, 1988, unless an election is made.

Q: CAN INSTALLMENT OBLIGATIONS BE PLEDGED?

A: Yes, but in some cases this can accelerate the tax on the installment sale. If indebtedness is secured by a nondealer real property installment obligation to which certain rules apply, then the net proceeds of the secured debt will be treated as payment received on the installment obligation, generally when the taxpayer receives the proceeds. In these cases, in effect, the proceeds from the loan secured with the installment obligation are treated as payments on the installment obligation itself.

Q: WHAT HAPPENS WHEN AN INSTALLMENT NOTE IS SOLD?

A: Generally speaking, when an installment note is transferred, the person transferring the obligation can no longer report the transaction on the installment basis. Any gain inherent in the installment note is "accelerated" into the current year upon transfer of the installment note.

Example

Ed Executive sells a piece of investment real property for $1 million, receiving a $300,000 downpayment and a note for $700,000 plus interest payable over five years. Ed's basis in the building was $500,000, so his profit in the building was also $500,000. One half of every principal payment will be a return of his basis, and the other half will be profit. If Ed sells the installment note to his bank in the third year, then all the rest of his gain will be taxable in that year. Note, however, that Ed can take a loss deduction for any difference between the face amount of the note and the amount he actually gets for it. This amount represents the discount he takes on the sale to the bank.

DJI Planning Guide _____

Note that the transfer of an installment note will not necessarily produce cash—Ed was fortunate in the above example. Some transfers will not produce cash to the transferor but will still accelerate the tax! While there are several exceptions to the rule that a transfer or "disposition" of an installment obligation produces gain, it is best to proceed with extreme caution before making any transfer of an installment note.

Q: WHAT IF INTEREST IS NOT STATED ON AN INSTALLMENT OBLIGATION?

A: If interest is not stated on an obligation, **imputed interest** principles are applied to recharacterize a portion of the principal payments as interest. As a result, the buyer receives an interest deduction for a portion of the principal payments (since the assumption is that some portion of the principal he pays is really interest), and the seller is treated as receiving interest income for a portion of the principal payments.

Q: WHEN DOES THIS IMPUTED INTEREST APPLY?

A: The imputed interest rules apply to a sale of property if all of the following are true:

• A debt instrument is given in exchange for the property.
• At least one payment is due more than six months after the date of the sale or exchange.
• The amount payable at maturity of the note exceeds the principal amount of the note. If the note provides for adequate stated interest, the principal amount is determined from the face of the note. If the note does not provide for adequate stated interest, the principal amount is determined according to discount principles.

Whenever the imputed interest rules apply, if the stated interest rate is not "adequate," then an adequate rate will be imputed by the IRS. What is considered "adequate" is announced monthly by the IRS depending on market conditions.

Q: ARE THERE ANY EXCEPTIONS FROM THIS IMPUTED INTEREST TREATMENT?

A: Yes, there are a number of different exceptions. To begin with, no imputed interest will result if all payments are due within six months of the date of the sale. In addition, no imputed interest will result on

- The sale of a farm for $1 million or less if sold by an individual, an estate, a testamentary trust, a small business corporation, or certain partnerships.
- The sale of a principal residence.
- Any sale of property for $250,000 or less.
- Sales of publicly traded debt instruments or debt instruments issued for publicly traded property.
- Sales from patents or amounts that are contingent on the productivity, use, or disposition of the property transferred.
- Land transfers of $500,000 or less between family members.

Q: HOW CAN THE IMPUTED INTEREST RULES BE AVOIDED?

A: First, make sure one of the exceptions listed above does not apply. For example, the blanket $250,000 exception may cover the transaction. If no exception applies, then the only way to avoid the imputed interest rules is to insure that any note taken back in a sale provides for adequate stated interest. Interest rates that satisfy this requirement (called **applicable federal rates**) are announced monthly by the IRS. They can be obtained from IRS offices and from a variety of publishers of tax materials.

The applicable federal rates are divided into three categories, depending on the duration of the note that is being tested for adequate interest. If the note is less than three years in duration, then the "short-term rate" applies. If the note is three to nine years in duration, the "mid-term rate" applies; and if the note is over nine years, the "long-term rate" applies.

Q: DOESN'T A SPECIAL 9 PERCENT TEST RATE APPLY TO CERTAIN SALES?

A: Yes. A 9 percent rate applies to any debt instrument given for the sale or exchange of property if the principal amount of the obligation does not exceed $2.8 million.

Q: HOW OFTEN IS THE INTEREST TESTED?

A: Only once, when the note is signed and issued. At that time, depending on the stated term of the note, the short-term, mid-term, or long-term applicable federal rate would pose no imputed interest problem.

Example

Marvin Manufacturer sells two unneeded machines to a competitor, receiving 50 percent down and the balance in the form of a note for $300,000 paid over two years at eight-percent interest. The short-term applicable federal rate for the month of the sale would be compared to the eight-percent rate, and as long as eight percent was no lower than the short-term rate, there would be no imputed interest on the note. The note would never have to be tested again for below-market interest rates.

DJI Planning Guide ⎯⎯⎯⎯⎯⎯⎯⎯⎯⎯⎯⎯⎯⎯⎯⎯

Getting in the habit of checking the IRS' applicable federal rates prior to making any sales on time is advisable. Since applicable federal rates are pegged to government securities rates, however, transactions between unrelated parties dealing at arm's length are most likely to meet or exceed the announced interest rates. It is primarily in the context of related buyers and sellers that concern for imputed interest is present.

CHAPTER 5

SALES AND
EXCHANGES
OF PROPERTY

INTRODUCTION

Businesses of all types make sales and exchanges of property. The sales may be of inventory assets—the very core of producing income in the business—or they may be sales of assets that are used (as opposed to being held for resale) in the business. An example of the latter is the sale of machinery by a manufacturing business or the sale of one store by a multi-store retailer. The common occurrence of such sales in business makes it critical to understand the tax laws governing them.

Some problems associated with these sales, such as the effects of depreciation recapture, may make the sale unattractive from a tax perspective. The tax may be large either because of depreciation recapture (taxation of previously claimed depreciation deductions) or because of a low adjusted basis in the property (the point from which gain or loss is measured). Where the taxable gain that would be generated from a sale is unpalatable, it may be desirable to restructure the transaction as a tax-free exchange. A tax-free exchange of the property may avoid taxes altogether.

Occasionally, asset dispositions are not planned but are compelled by forces or events the taxpayer does not control. Losses of property due to fire, accident, theft, or even government condemnation are examples. Knowing the tax rules that govern these events can save a substantial amount of money down the road.

SALE OF ASSETS

Q: HOW ARE SALES OF INVENTORY ASSETS TAXED?

A: The treatment of inventory accounting and inventory methods is the subject of Chapter 4. These rules are used to determine the value of a company's inventory. The inventory accounting methods of Last In First Out (LIFO) and First In First Out (FIFO) are used to determine the amount of income generated on a sale. In other words, they account for which item of inventory out of many was sold.

Once these variables are filled in, the taxation of inventory assets is extremely simple. Such assets produce ordinary income to the business whether a corporation, individual, or partnership makes the sale.

Q: HOW ARE SALES OF CAPITAL ASSETS TAXED?

A: Sales of capital assets are taxed somewhat differently than inventory assets. Traditionally, there was a tremendous distinction between the sale of an inventory asset (sometimes called an "ordinary income asset") and the sale of a capital asset. The difference stems from the difference in tax rates applicable to ordinary income and capital gains. As late as 1987, there was still a difference between ordinary income and capital gain rates.

The 1986 Tax Reform Act phased out capital gain rates through the end of 1987. For 1988 and beyond, there is no difference in tax rates (either to an individual, a partnership, or a corporation) between ordinary income and capital gain.

**Q: ARE SALES OF CAPITAL ASSETS TAXED
JUST LIKE SALES OF ORDINARY INCOME
ASSETS NOW?**

A: Not quite. Although the tax rates applicable to capital
gains have been harmonized with the ordinary income rates,
capital gains and losses must still be computed separately from
gains or losses from the sale of ordinary income assets. **Long-
term** and **short-term** gains and losses are "netted" first. A long-
term asset is one held for more than one year, and a short-term
asset is one held for one year or less.

> **Note**
>
> Although the holding period for long-term capital gain sta-
> tus was previously more than six months, effective for assets
> acquired after 1987 it has gone back up to more than one year.

The separate netting of capital gains and losses is significant where there is a net loss. All short-term and long-term
gains and losses are grouped together. The losses (both long-
term and short-term losses) are deductible for individuals only
to the extent of the aggregate gains (both long-term and short-
term) plus up to $3,000 of ordinary income. This limitation for
individuals makes the distinction between capital assets and
ordinary income assets very much alive.

**Q: IS IT MORE ADVANTAGEOUS NOW
TO HAVE CAPITAL GAINS/LOSSES
OR ORDINARY GAINS/LOSSES?**

A: The different treatment of losses makes taxpayers prefer
to have losses on ordinary income assets since they will be
deductible in full against ordinary income. A loss on a capital
asset, depending on the existence of other capital gains, may or
may not be fully deductible against ordinary income.

> **Example**
>
> In the 1988 tax year, Irving Investor had ordinary income of
> $65,000, a net short-term capital loss of $8,000, and a net long-

term capital loss of $3,000. On his joint tax return, Irving's capital loss deduction is $11,000. However, Irving can use only $3,000 of the $11,000 loss against his $65,000 of ordinary income. The remaining $8,000 can be carried over until next year.

In contrast, taxpayers frequently do not care as much whether an asset sold at a *gain* is capital or ordinary. Of course, if the taxpayer also has a capital loss, the capital gain may be needed to offset the capital loss. (If the gain were treated as ordinary, only $3,000 of it could offset the loss).

Q: CAN YOU PLAN TO AVOID THE CAPITAL LOSS PROBLEM?

A: Yes, provided the taxpayer has other assets that can be disposed of. Some planning may clearly be engaged in by timing the dispositions of assets in order to generate sufficient capital gains to offset capital losses.

Example

Irving Investor sells a capital asset this year that generates a $30,000 capital loss. As the end of the year approaches, he has no capital gains to offset the loss, so he knows his loss will be limited to $3,000 this year. He may choose to sell one of his investments to produce a capital gain in an offsetting amount—such as stock that would bring a $27,000 capital gain. If he makes the sale before the end of the year, he will have avoided the problem of excess capital loss. The remaining $3,000 loss can be deducted against his ordinary income.

DJI Planning Guide

It is advisable for all taxpayers to review any capital gains and losses generated during the year—and to do it *before* it is too late to make other sales. December 1 or so of each year would be a good benchmark. If there are losses that need to be offset with capital gains, this will allow sufficient time to determine the amount of offsetting gain needed and, hopefully, time to sell the appropriate asset.

Q: IS THE DISTINCTION BETWEEN CAPITAL GAINS AND ORDINARY INCOME OF SIGNIFICANCE TO CORPORATIONS?

A: Yes. In fact, the significance of this distinction to corporations can be even greater than to individuals. While individuals may offset up to $3,000 of ordinary income with capital losses per year, corporations are not even given this allowance. A corporation can use capital losses for a tax year only to offset capital gains in the same year. The corporation's ordinary income cannot be reduced by corporate capital losses, regardless of their amount. The corporation must carry the loss over to future years or carry it back to prior years.

Q: HOW DOES A CORPORATE CARRYOVER OR CARRYBACK WORK?

A: A corporation can carry back a capital loss to each of the three tax years prior to the year in which the loss occurs. Basically, the corporation can look back to its three prior tax returns. If there were sufficient capital gains in the prior years to be offset by the carried back capital loss, it can obtain a refund of tax for the prior year.

The corporation can also carry over any excess forward into future years. A five-year carryover into future years is allowed. If the corporation carries losses back three years and forward five years and *still* has capital losses remaining unused, these capital losses will be lost as deductions.

Q: CAN CORPORATIONS ENGAGE IN THE SAME KIND OF PLANNING THAT INDIVIDUALS DO TO GENERATE CAPITAL GAINS TO OFFSET CAPITAL LOSSES?

A: Yes. Particularly when the three prior tax years (into which the current capital loss could be carried) do not contain sufficient capital gains to offset the capital losses in the current year, the corporation may choose to dispose of one or more capital assets or Section 1231 assets in order to generate offsetting capital gains.

Q: WHAT ASSETS ARE CONSIDERED CAPITAL ASSETS IN THE BUSINESS CONTEXT?

A: First of all, it is necessary to distinguish between true "capital assets" and so-called "Section 1231 assets." The technical definition of a "capital asset" excludes business real estate and depreciable business property. But these important categories of property are then included in a special category known as "Section 1231 assets." Basically, Section 1231 assets are treated like capital assets, but they are technically distinct throughout the tax law.

In determining what constitutes a capital asset or a Section 1231 asset, the main inquiry is whether the asset is held for sale in the business. If the asset is in the nature of inventory, it cannot be a capital asset or a Section 1231 asset. A capital asset is property (whether or not it is connected with a trade or business) that does not include inventory assets, property held primarily for sale to customers, notes or accounts receivable acquired in the ordinary course of business, and certain other assets. The corollary to capital assets—Section 1231 assets— includes property used in the taxpayer's trade or business that is depreciable, business real property, and certain other assets.

Q: WHEN DOES DEPRECIATION RECAPTURE OCCUR?

A: Depreciation recapture, by definition, arises only in a case where depreciation has previously been taken on an asset. There could be no depreciation recapture on a sale of inventory, since the inventory would not have been depreciated. Depreciation is covered in detail in Chapter 3.

On a sale or other disposition of depreciable personal property, the amount of any prior depreciation deductions taken on that property are "recaptured" as ordinary income. This does not mean that additional gain is generated but only that any recognized gain is characterized as ordinary income rather than as capital gain. The principle of "recapture" obtains because the depreciation deductions for the property are taken against ordinary income. Consequently, when the property is disposed of, these deductions are "recaptured" as ordinary income instead of as capital gain.

Example

Manufacturing, Inc. sells one of its tool and die machines for $10,000. It originally purchased the machine for $12,000, but the machine has been depreciated down to $5,000. (The depreciation deductions reduced the basis of the asset.) The entire gain of $5,000 (the difference between the $5,000 basis and the $10,000 sales price) is recaptured as ordinary income. Note that in this example, there is an additional $2,000 of depreciation that is *not* recaptured, since that gain is never realized.

Q: WHAT KIND OF PROPERTY IS SUBJECT TO RECAPTURE?

A: Virtually any business property (other than inventory) that is sold by the taxpayer is subject to recapture. However, the extent of the recapture depends on the type of property. As indicated above, for depreciable personal property, *all* the depreciation previously taken on the asset is recaptured.

Depreciable personal property includes items such as machinery, automobiles, and furniture. It also includes tangible personal property such as contract rights, franchises, and the like. It even includes livestock. Basically, any asset other than real property (not a building or its structural components) that is depreciable or subject to amortization is included.

Q: IS DEPRECIATION TAKEN ON REAL PROPERTY SUBJECT TO RECAPTURE?

A: Yes, but in a different fashion than on other property. First of all, depreciation is available only on real property such as buildings and their structural components. Structural components include separate parts of the building that are depreciable. No depreciation is allowable on the land itself.

On a disposition of real property (such as a building) on which depreciation has been taken, a much more favorable rule applies. Gain on the sale or other disposition of depreciable real property is treated as ordinary income only to the extent that depreciation has been taken on the property *in excess* of straight-line depreciation. In other words, if a taxpayer depreciates a building on the straight-line method of depreciation, *no* recapture results.

Q: WHAT IS STRAIGHT-LINE DEPRECIATION?

A: Straight-line depreciation is the method of depreciation under which the cost of the asset is written off ratably over the life of the asset. For example, under current rules, a building might be depreciated over 27.5 years. Straight-line depreciation would essentially divide the total allowable depreciation deductions (the total cost of the building) over 27.5 years, and equal depreciation deductions would be allowed in each year.

In contrast, there are various accelerated methods of depreciation that, as the name suggests, seek larger depreciation deductions in earlier years. The "150 percent declining balance method," the "200 percent declining balance method" and assorted other technical depreciation methods have in the past been used by the taxpayer to obtain larger depreciation deductions in the early years of the operation of a building. The accelerated methods for real estate are no longer generally available.

Q: IS STRAIGHT-LINE OR ACCELERATED DEPRECIATION BETTER FOR REAL ESTATE?

A: Obviously, accelerated depreciation will result in larger up-front deductions for real estate (such as a building). However, the possibility of depreciation recapture on a sale of the property must be borne in mind.

DJI Planning Guide _____

Traditionally, straight-line depreciation for real property was frequently a desirable choice in that the hazard of recapture could be avoided. However, as there is currently no distinction between the tax rates applying to ordinary income and those applying to capital gain, this traditional wisdom should be questioned. The benefits of larger initial depreciation deductions, which one of the accelerated methods provides, may be desirable. (Note that under the accelerated methods, the *total* amount of depreciation allowable is not different.)

To complicate things just a little further, however, keep in mind that it seems likely that at some point in the next few years, a capital gains rate will come back into the law. After all, 1988 is the first year we have been without a capital gains rate, and already Congressional leaders and the President have strongly advocated a return to an era of capital gains.

Q: WOULD AN INSTALLMENT SALE OF THE ASSET SPREAD OUT THE RECAPTURE TAX?

A: No. If an installment sale of property is made—even though all of the cash is not received in the year of the sale—any recapture due by application of the above rules is *fully* taxable in the year of the sale. This could mean that there is more tax to pay in the first year of the installment sale than the seller actually gets as downpayment!

DJI Planning Guide _____

Depreciation recapture should be considered in any installment sale *before* a deal is struck. It may not be economically feasible for a seller to get a relatively small downpayment and still face a large recapture tax.

TAX-FREE EXCHANGES

Q: IS IT POSSIBLE TO EXCHANGE OR "SWAP" PROPERTY TAX-FREE?

A: Yes. This possibility may be particularly attractive where a large recapture tax, or simply a large gain, is produced on a sale.

The kind of property that qualifies for a tax-free exchange is any property held for production or used in a trade or business or for investment. Basically, any property used in a business or for investment qualifies except the following: inventory assets or stock in trade, stocks, bonds, notes, partnership interests, securities, evidences of indebtedness, and trust certificates.

Example

Manufacturing, Inc. owns several buildings that it uses for manufacturing and office space. It also has several hundred large manufacturing machines, a fleet of commercial trucks, and a good deal of computer equipment. All of these assets are "held for productive use in a trade or business" and therefore could be exchanged tax-free.

Q: WHAT KIND OF ASSETS MUST BE RECEIVED IN A TAX-FREE EXCHANGE?

A: For an exchange to be tax-free, the trade, business, or investment assets transferred must be in exchange for other trade, business, or investment assets. A tax-free exchange is sometimes called a **like-kind exchange** for this reason. The assets received must be of "like-kind" to the assets transferred.

This "like-kind" principle does not require that the property be identical, although some similarities are necessary. For example, an exchange of real property for personal property is not considered like-kind. However, city real estate (such as a building) could be exchanged for country real estate (such as a farm).

Example

Manufacturing, Inc. exchanges one of its machines for a small office building. The exchange is not tax-free because this is an exchange of personal property for real property. However, if Manufacturing, Inc. exchanges one of its own office buildings for the other office building, the transaction could be tax-free.

Q: ARE THERE ANY OTHER REQUIREMENTS FOR A SUCCESSFUL TAX-FREE EXCHANGE?

A: Yes. Questions of timing and valuation must be addressed. As far as timing is concerned, there will be no problem present when the exchange is a true "swap," where one property is given for another. However, creative tax planners long ago discovered that the tax-free exchange principle can be used where there are three parties involved instead of two. This is known as a "three-party exchange" or **delayed exchange**. Delayed exchanges are sometimes also called "Starker" transactions after the case that made them famous.

Q: WHAT IS A THREE-PARTY EXCHANGE?

A: A typical three-party exchange goes something like this:

Seller Sam has a small office building he wants to sell. However, he is not anxious to pay the large tax that will be due upon its sale (due both to recapture and to tremendous appreciation in the building). Sam wants to reinvest all the sales proceeds (before tax) in a larger building he has spotted across town. Sam really wants to exchange his smaller building for the bigger building, but the seller of the bigger building has no desire to swap the two buildings. Buyer Ben likes Sam's building and is willing to pay cash for it but does not have anything that Sam wants.

Accordingly, Sam enters into a contract with a third party, Kim, under which Kim agrees to have Sam transfer Sam's building to Kim, with Kim then transferring the building to Buyer Ben for cash. Kim will hold this cash (will not pay it to Sam) and will use it to buy the bigger building from its owner across town. Kim will then transfer this building to Sam. The result is that Sam has swapped his smaller building for a bigger building but is not treated as having received the cash that Kim received and held under the contract. Sam has thus gotten exactly what he wanted.

Q: DOES THIS KIND OF THREE-PARTY EXCHANGE REALLY WORK?

A: Yes. The three-party exchange can be a simultaneous exchange (in which all of the steps outlined above happen at once) or a "delayed exchange." Under a delayed exchange, the steps do not all happen at once. In fact, commonly, the property to be transferred back to the seller in exchange for his property is not even identified at the time the original sale takes place, so there has to be a delay.

The amount of permissible delay is now subject to strict limits, however. Each of two timing requirements must be met. First, the property to be conveyed back to the original seller must be "identified" within 45 days of the original transfer. In the above example, that would mean the building across town that Sam wanted would have to be identified in writing to Kim within 45 days of the time Sam transferred his smaller building to Kim for sale to Ben.

The second timing requirement is that the actual transfer of the substitute property has to be made within 180 days of the original transfer. In the above example, this means the building across town must actually be transferred to Sam within 180 days of the time he transfers his smaller building to Kim. As long as both the 45-day and 180-day time requirements are met, the delayed exchange will qualify as tax-free.

Q: WHAT HAPPENS IF CASH IS ALSO TRANSFERRED IN A LIKE-KIND EXCHANGE?

A: Gain will be recognized on the exchange in the amount of the cash transfer. Obviously, this is a common problem, since frequently the two properties to be exchanged are not of even value. If the transferor receives like-kind property and cash, the cash will result in some tax liability.

Example

Sam exchanges an industrial site he bought on speculation for a corner lot on Main Street that he intends to develop. Sam originally paid $100,000 for the industrial site, and it is now worth $150,000. The lot on Main Street is only worth $125,000. As part of the exchange, Sam receives the equalizing payment of $25,000 in cash. Sam has had a $50,000 gain on the disposition of the industrial site (the $150,000 value he receives in the form of the cash and the corner lot, less the $100,000 basis in the industrial site). However, Sam's gain will be recognized only to the extent of the $25,000 in cash received.

DJI Planning Guide

The necessity of a cash balancing payment of this type is a practical one rather than a legal one. There is no requirement that the properties transferred in the exchange equal the value of the properties received. Different persons may place different values on the properties, and they are free to agree to whatever arrangement they wish (e.g., the exchange of a $30,000 lot for a $40,000 lot involves no tax to either party).

Q: CAN THE TAX ON THE CASH BE AVOIDED BY TRANSFERRING OTHER PROPERTY?

A: It depends. If there is an imbalance between the property transferred and the property for which it is exchanged, some form of compensation will typically be made. If it is not made in cash, it could be made in other property. However, in order for the property to prevent taxation on this equalizing payment, it would have to be "like-kind" property.

Example

Smallco transfers a machine worth $100,000 in which it has a $25,000 basis for a different machine worth $75,000 plus file cabinets worth $25,000. Smallco has transferred $100,000 worth of equipment for $75,000 worth of equipment and $25,000 worth of furnishings. Since these are all like-kind property, Smallco will not be taxed on the exchange.

However, if Smallco transfers its machine for the $75,000 machine plus $25,000 worth of notes, partnership interests, or real estate, then because the notes, partnership interests, or real property are not like-kind property, they will be treated as cash. The same result would apply if the $25,000 of property transferred to Smallco were not property used in a trade or business or for investment (i.e., was to be personal-use property such as kitchen appliances to be used by Smallco's major shareholder).

Q: WHAT HAPPENS WHEN THERE IS A MORTGAGE OR OTHER DEBT ON PROPERTY EXCHANGED?

A: The situation gets more complex here. If a person exchanges mortgaged real estate for other real estate in an exchange that is otherwise like-kind, then the amount of the mortgage on the property he transfers (that he will no longer be liable for) is relieved and is treated like cash. If the exchange is of one mortgaged parcel for another, only the net reduction in the mortgage debt is treated as cash.

Example

Sam owns Building X, which has a basis of $80,000 and is subject to an $80,000 mortgage. He exchanges Building X for Building Y, which has a fair market value of $90,000 and is subject to only a $40,000 mortgage. His entire gain is taxable as shown in the following table.

Fair market value of property received	$90,000
Less mortgage on the property	40,000
	$50,000
Mortgage on the property transferred	80,000
Total consideration received	$90,000
Less basis of property transferred	80,000
Gain realized	$40,000

DJI Planning Guide

With mortgaged property, like-kind exchanges can become very confusing. Unless the mortgage assumed and the mortgage discharged are equal or very close, it is advisable to get professional help before entering into any agreement. The agreement may call for the receipt of property and no cash, yet the mortgage rules may operate to treat the taxpayer as having received substantial cash. In this situation, there may be no cash to pay the tax, and other property may have to be sold to satisfy the tax liability!

INVOLUNTARY CONVERSIONS

Q: WHAT HAPPENS WHEN PROPERTY IS DESTROYED BY FIRE OR OTHER CASUALTY?

A: The destruction of property by fire or other casualty is a disposition of the property. Consequently, if cash is generated, such as from insurance proceeds, then gain or loss could result and depreciation recapture could apply. Because of the inequity in forcing taxpayers to pay tax when they have not chosen to make the disposition, a reinvestment of the proceeds is permitted without tax.

Q: TO WHAT EVENTS DOES THIS TREATMENT APPLY?

A: It applies to any **involuntary conversion**. This includes destruction by fire, flood, earthquake, etc. It also includes a government's seizure of property under its condemnation powers (e.g., condemning a piece of real property in order to build a freeway). So that taxpayers do not have to wait until a lengthy condemnation proceeding is completed, a sale pursuant to a "threat" of condemnation is sufficient for this purpose even though the condemnation action may not yet have been concluded.

Q: HOW DO YOU SECURE THE PROTECTION FROM TAX?

A: The taxpayer must make an election on his or her tax return and make the requisite investment of the condemnation proceeds or insurance proceeds. No gain will be recognized from the involuntary conversion even though insurance proceeds (or money from the condemning authority) may compensate the taxpayer in full for the fair market value of the property.

In order to qualify, the taxpayer must replace the property with property "similar or related in service or use" to the property that was converted. Property is treated as similar or related in service or use to the property converted if it will be used in the same fashion as the property that was destroyed or taken. Thus, if a machine is destroyed, a different model machine or different kind of production equipment can be purchased with the insurance proceeds.

Q: DO THE SAME RULES APPLY TO PERSONAL PROPERTY AND REAL PROPERTY?

A: Yes, but there is a little more latitude in the permissible replacement with real property. If real property used in the taxpayer's trade or business (but not inventory property held for sale) or real property held for investment is destroyed or condemned, then the replacement property has only to be "like-kind" property. Any real property is considered "like-kind" to any other real property. This means that any real property, even if it is not used in the same fashion, can qualify.

Example

Rocketco has one of its raw land rocket testing sites in the desert condemned by a state highway commission. It reinvests the condemnation proceeds in a building it will use for office space. Even though the building has a different use than the rocket testing site, the two properties are both real property (so are of "like-kind"), and the gain on the condemnation will be nontaxable.

Q: WHEN MUST THE PROPERTY BE REPLACED?

A: The taxpayer has two full years after the involuntary conversion or condemnation to acquire replacement property and still avoid tax on the gain. In fact, this replacement period is even extended to three full years in the case of business or investment real property.

Example

Midget Manufacturing Co. has a small warehouse destroyed by fire on which it receives insurance proceeds of $800,000. The fire occurred in 1988, and Midget receives the insurance proceeds in the same year. Midget has three full years (1989, 1990, and 1991) to reinvest the insurance proceeds in a replacement structure in order to avoid recognizing gain on the receipt of the insurance proceeds. Note that if the asset destroyed were something other than real property (such as a machine or the company jet), the period of replacement would be only two full years after the disposition.

CHAPTER 6

COMPENSATING BUSINESS OWNERS AND EMPLOYEES WITH CASH

INTRODUCTION

Compensating with cash is something that every business does and, seemingly, everyone understands. The money is taxable to the recipient and deductible to the payor. But there is considerably more to the topic than this.

For example:

- Is there any limit to the compensation that can be deducted?
- Is there any way to defer the time when the employee will be taxed?
- Can withholding for income tax and Social Security be avoided?
- If withholding cannot be avoided, can its effects be minimized?
- Is it still possible to pay large bonuses at the end of a fiscal year?
- If income is deferred under a deferred compensation agreement, is it possible to secure the ultimate payment?

And there are many other issues that are important for virtually every business, regardless of the form in which the business is conducted. These issues can also be critical to employees, consultants, and independent contractors, since few things are more basic than the amount and timing of income.

Q: ARE THERE ANY LIMITS TO THE AMOUNT OF COMPENSATION THAT CAN BE PAID TO EMPLOYEES AND DEDUCTED BY THE EMPLOYER?

A: Yes, there are limits from a tax standpoint. Although obviously any amount of compensation can be paid to employees or business owners, the question is how much the employer can deduct as compensation. The answer is that only compensation that is "reasonable" can be deducted.

Q: WHAT IS REASONABLE COMPENSATION?

A: What constitutes **reasonable compensation** depends on the services rendered, the industry, the locality, and other factors. Generally speaking, the IRS challenges the reasonableness of compensation only in the context of closely held businesses. Abuses are greatest in this context since there is an incentive for shareholders of a corporation to have large amounts paid out to themselves as compensation (for which the company will get a deduction) rather than paid to them in the form of dividends (for which the company will get no deduction).

Occasionally, the IRS has argued that compensation paid to an employee or consultant outside the context of a closely held business is unreasonable, but generally speaking the point is confined to closely held businesses.

Q: WHAT HAPPENS IF COMPENSATION IS DEEMED UNREASONABLE?

A: The compensation cannot be deducted if it is unreasonable. This means that the company will pay tax on money it has already paid out to an executive or employee. The company will get no deduction, and normally the employee (if he is a shareholder) will get dividend income.

Example

Norman is a major shareholder and Chief Executive Officer of Merchandise, Ltd., a retail chain store. The company paid him $800,000 in compensation in 1988. If $400,000 is treated as unreasonable, then the company gets no deduction for it even though it did in fact pay it to Norman. This treatment increases the company's income tax. $400,000 of income at the company's 34 percent federal tax rate would add another $136,000 of tax! The $400,000 might also constitute dividend income (as opposed to compensation income) to Norman. This latter point is unimportant now that dividends and compensation are taxed at the same individual tax rates.

Q: HOW CAN THE PROBLEM OF UNREASONABLE COMPENSATION BE AVOIDED?

A: The best way to avoid this problem is to properly document the services performed and, where available, to back up your documentation with information about other businesses. Commercially prepared services are available that document industry compensation standards on an annual basis. If the company can show that the amount it pays its executives and shareholder/employees is in line with similar businesses, then it should go a long way toward alleviating the problem of unreasonable compensation. It is also appropriate to insure that services are in fact being rendered by the persons being paid.

DJI Planning Guide

In the case of consultants or retired executives who are being paid a large amount and perhaps doing little work, it may be a good idea to have the employer and employee enter into a consulting agreement. The agreement could require the consultant to remain available to do work within certain specified hours and to be available by telephone during all business hours. Even if the employee in fact does very little work, his scheduled availability itself constitutes the performance of services. If the employer and consultant can document that some services were actually provided and that the employer required the consultant to remain available, then a claim of unreasonable compensation may be rebutted. A covenant not to compete also constitutes the rendering of services for which compensation may be paid.

Q: DOES THE TIMING OF THE PAYMENT HAVE ANYTHING TO DO WITH REASONABLENESS?

A: Yes. Although the ultimate question is whether the compensation is "reasonable" for the services rendered, historically the IRS and the courts have looked at large year-end bonuses with great scrutiny. When a company pays most of its compensation to an employee as a bonus—especially if the employee is a shareholder of the company—it may look as though the company is siphoning off earnings at the end of the year in lieu of paying a dividend.

DJI Planning Guide _____

When it is desirable to pay large year-end bonuses, it is a good idea to document in corporate minutes and resolutions—or even in correspondence—that the services performed were really extraordinary and that a bonus was determined to be appropriate based on performance. After all, it is frequently difficult to effectively evaluate performance until the year-end results of operations are available.

Q: ARE FISCAL-YEAR OPERATIONS STILL PERMISSIBLE?

A: Yes, in some cases. Corporations other than personal service corporations may still maintain fiscal years. However, personal service corporations, S corporations, and partnerships are largely confined to a calendar year. This makes a regular "C" corporation more attractive. (Regarding the difference between a C and an S corporation, see Chapters 1 and 2.) Personal service corporations, S corporations, and partnerships can use a fiscal year but have to pay a tax deposit on behalf of the persons who are entitled to the deferred income. The tax deposit is designed to offset the tax benefits of the fiscal year.

Personal service corporations are subject to more strict rules. They are limited in the amount they can deduct for these tax deposits unless they make certain minimum distributions before the end of the calendar year.

Q: WHAT ARE THE TAX EFFECTS OF A FISCAL YEAR?

A: In the context of a discussion about compensation, the main effect concerns bonuses. A fiscal year enables the employer to pay compensation payments (such as bonuses) toward the end of its fiscal year and yet achieve deferral for employees. It works like this:

Example

Largeco's fiscal year (its tax year) is from February 1 through March 31. Every year in January, it pays bonuses to all of its employees, with very large bonuses going to the top management. It can deduct these payments in its tax year ending January 31 (assuming the payments are reasonable compensation and assuming the corporation is not a personal service corporation). However, since the employees operate on a calendar year because they are individuals, they receive their bonus checks in January and do not have to report the income and pay tax on it until *the following* April 15, on year and three months later!

Q: WHY DO SOME INDIVIDUALS PREFER INDEPENDENT CONTRACTOR STATUS TO EMPLOYEE STATUS?

A: The basic incentive lies in the rules concerning withholding and employment taxes. If someone is an **independent contractor** rather than an employee, then the employer (whether a partnership, corporation, or proprietorship) is not required to withhold on wages. The independent contractor can be paid a lump sum without deductions.

Furthermore, amounts paid to an independent contractor are not subject to Social Security taxes (sometimes called FICA taxes). In contrast, wages paid to employees are subject to Social Security taxes, and the employer and the employee must each pay half of the Social Security tax. In the case of an independent contractor, the employer does not have to pay the Social Security tax. The independent contractor also receives full compensation without reduction for his or her portion of the Social Security tax (although the independent contractor would be subject to the self-employment tax).

Q: HOW DOES ONE BECOME AN INDEPENDENT CONTRACTOR?

A: The basic question in determining whether someone providing services is doing so as an employee or as an independent contractor is whether the employer paying for the services has a "right to control" the person providing them. This distinction really depends on whether the person paying for the services is paying for a finished product or has the right to direct *how* the task is performed along the way (e.g., purchasing a finished kitchen of a certain quality versus directing the construction crew at each step of the way).

However, there are also other factors. For example, whether the employer provides a workplace and tools to the person, fringe benefits, and the like is relevant. (These factors indicate employee status.) If the employer requires particular hours of work, then employee status may also be indicated, whereas an ability to set one's own hours indicates independent contractor status. It may even be relevant whether other persons retained by the employer are treated similarly.

Q: IS THE EMPLOYER AT RISK IF THE IRS LATER TRIES TO CLASSIFY AN INDEPENDENT CONTRACTOR AS AN EMPLOYEE?

A: Yes. If the employer treats someone as an independent contractor who is later determined to be an employee, then the employer is technically liable for all of the employment taxes that should have been withheld.

DJI Planning Guide

There are ways to avoid this risk. If the employer treats a person as an independent contractor, then it is a good idea for the employer to get a written agreement from the individual indicating that he is aware of his independent contractor status. Furthermore, the agreement should indicate that if the IRS later claims otherwise, any applicable withholdings and taxes will be promptly paid by the independent contractor. Of course, if the independent contractor has no money to pay the tax, then the employer may still be saddled with the tax liability.

Q: WHAT ABOUT WITHHOLDING? WHAT ARE THE REQUIREMENTS?

A: Withholding is required on all wage payments made to employees. There are several types of withholding: federal income tax withholding, Social Security tax withholding (FICA), and, depending upon the state in which the compensation is paid, state income tax and disability income insurance withholding.

Q: WHAT ABOUT INCOME TAX WITHHOLDING ON WAGES? HOW DOES THAT WORK?

A: Withholding is required on "wages," which includes all remuneration for services, whether paid in cash or not. Salaries, fees, bonuses, commissions, and even taxable fringe benefits are treated as compensation subject to withholding. There are two major methods of withholding on this compensation: the "percentage method" and the "wage bracket method."

Q: WHAT IS THE PERCENTAGE METHOD OF WITHHOLDING?

A: Under this method, the employer must multiply the amount of the withholding exemption for the payroll period by the number of exemptions claimed by the employee. The employer then subtracts that amount from the employee's wages and determines the amount to be withheld by using the percentage rate table available from the IRS.

Q: WHAT IS THE WAGE BRACKET METHOD?

A: The wage bracket method employs tables provided by the IRS; separate tables are provided for single persons and married persons. These tables provide separate columns to be used according to the number of exemptions an employee claims. The final result is basically the same as the percentage method.

Q: CAN EMPLOYEES CLAIM THEY ARE EXEMPT FROM WITHHOLDING?

A: Yes, they can fill out a Form W-4 claiming to be exempt from withholding. If they claim exemption, then the employer is required to submit a copy of the employee's Form W-4 to the IRS. This procedure is to insure that only employees who really expect not to owe tax at all for the year will be exempt from withholding.

If the IRS determines that the employee's "exempt" claim is erroneous, then the employer will be instructed to withhold despite the employee's claims of exemption. This same basic treatment applies when employees claim large numbers of withholding allowances (i.e., in excess of 13 allowances).

Q: WHAT KINDS OF PAYMENTS ARE NOT SUBJECT TO INCOME TAX WITHHOLDING?

A: For one, payments to independent contractors (see discussion above). In addition, strike benefits paid by a union to members are not subject to withholding. The following kinds of payments are also exempt: reimbursements to employees for traveling, meals and other business expenses; death benefits paid to beneficiaries or to the estates of deceased employees; and workers' compensation benefits.

Q: WHAT ABOUT WITHHOLDING OF SOCIAL SECURITY TAX?

A: Social Security withholding, or FICA (this stands for Federal Insurance Contributions Act), is required on all "wages" up to a certain level. This level was $43,800 for 1987 and is adjusted upward for inflation each year. For 1988 it is $45,000.

The employer and the employee each pay half of the FICA tax. (Each pays 7.15 percent of wages up to this level for each year.) When an employee works for more than one employer, however, the employee is entitled to credit for the amounts withheld by one of the employers. Thus, the employee pays a maximum of 7.15 percent times the wage base ($43,800 for 1987 and $45,000 for 1988).

Q: WHEN IS THE SOCIAL SECURITY TAX WITHHELD BY THE EMPLOYER?

A: As with income tax withholding, Social Security taxes are withheld on an ongoing basis from each payment. The employer files a quarterly return that combines reporting of income and of Social Security taxes withheld from wages. The quarterly return (on IRS Form 941) is filed by the employer and accompanied by the withheld taxes. However, the payment schedule is really determined by the extent of an employer's withholding.

Q: ARE ALL WITHHELD TAXES PAID QUARTERLY?

A: No. If the employer has a liability of $500 or more but less than $3,000 for any one month, then the employer must deposit it by the 15th of the following month. This liability would be the combination of the withheld taxes plus the employer's share of the Social Security taxes. Deposits are made with the Federal Reserve Bank or an authorized commercial bank depositary. If the employer has a liability of $3,000 or more at the end of any month, it must be deposited within three banking days after the close of that period.

Q: WHAT HAPPENS IF THE EMPLOYER FAILS TO WITHHOLD OR PAY OVER THE TAX?

A: The IRS hates employers who fail to withhold. Even worse are employers who withhold but use the funds for something else. This is one of the reasons the deposit requirements are so strict (see above answer). If the employer fails to withhold or fails to pay over the withheld tax, then the employer is liable for it.

DJI Planning Guide _____

The IRS vigorously pursues businesses that fail to collect and pay over withholding taxes. The issue comes up most commonly when a business fails and the IRS begins looking for a "responsible party," which can be any officer of the company or partner in the case of a partnership. The IRS' position is that *every* officer or partner is personally liable for the withholding taxes, even if they had no knowledge of or responsibility for the collection or payment. Consequently, every officer or partner should be on the lookout for any sign that the payroll taxes are not being properly withheld and paid.

Q: ARE YEAR-END BONUSES SUBJECT
TO WITHHOLDING?

A: Yes, but at a reduced rate. Generally speaking, an employer can withhold a flat 20 percent on unusual items such as bonuses. In addition to the use of fiscal years discussed previously, bonuses are attractive to employees because of this reduced withholding rate. Because of the 20 percent flat withholding rate, an employee may receive more when an amount is paid as a bonus rather than as a regular paycheck.

DEFERRING COMPENSATION

Q: IS IT POSSIBLE TO DEFER
THE RECEIPT OF INCOME?

A: Yes, but it must be done carefully. It is obviously desirable for an employee who does not need cash immediately to defer the receipt of the income for a period of time. For example, if an employee were otherwise entitled to a big bonus in December, the employee might prefer to wait a few days until January so the tax on the income will not come due until the next year.

Q: IS THIS SORT OF DEFERRAL
PERMITTED?

A: Yes, but not if the employee is entitled to receive the funds. If the employer indicates willingness to make the payment and the employee protests, then the employee will be taxable on the amount even if it is not paid until January. This concept is usually referred to as **constructive receipt**. Even though the employee may not have actually received the money, he clearly *could* have gotten it and therefore will be taxable on it.

**Q: IF AN EMPLOYEE CAN HAVE
"CONSTRUCTIVE RECEIPT," HOW
CAN INCOME BE DEFERRED?**

A: For the deferral to work, there must be an agreement between the employer and employee prior to the time the services are rendered that will give rise to the compensation. Under the agreement, if must not be possible for the employee to get the money prior to the time when it is stated to be payable.

> **Example**
>
> Julia and her employer agree in writing in November that the salary that would otherwise be payable to her in December will be paid in January. Julia will not have constructive receipt of the December compensation because she has not yet performed her December services. Julia will be taxable on the December check when she actually receives it in January. Note that the fact that Julia's employer would be quite willing to pay Julia in December is irrelevant as long as the written deferral agreement is entered into before the services are performed. This procedure only works, however, if the compensation that would otherwise be payable in December is calculated solely on December performance.

**Q: WHAT ABOUT AN ANNUAL BONUS?
MUST THE AGREEMENT TO DEFER
COMPENSATION BE ENTERED INTO
PRIOR TO THE TIME *ANY* SERVICES
ARE PERFORMED?**

A: Yes. And the same rule applies for other compensation as well. The employer and employee may agree in September that the employee's monthly paychecks for October, November, and December will be paid in January. As long as the agreement is in writing and the employee has no ability to accelerate the payments, the deferral should be effective.

Q: IS IT EVER POSSIBLE TO DEFER THE INCOME *AFTER* THE SERVICES ARE RENDERED?

A: Yes, in some cases. Deferring income after the services are rendered is permissible as long as the *likelihood* or *amount* of the payment can still not be determined on the date of the deferral.

Example

Sam and his employer are under a contract that calls for Sam to be paid a salary plus a bonus. The bonus is to be paid in 1988 based upon the employer's 1987 profits. The 1987 profits are to be calculated in 1988, and the amount will be paid then. In November of 1987, Sam and his employer agree to defer the bonus until 1989. There should be no constructive receipt in this case. That means that Sam will not be taxable upon the bonus until he actually gets it in 1989.

Q: WHAT IF THE EMPLOYEE WHO DEFERS THE INCOME NEEDS TO GET IT BEFORE IT COMES DUE UNDER THE DEFERRAL AGREEMENT?

A: This is a common problem. The employee cannot have it both ways. If the employee even has the *ability* to accelerate the payment—although that ability might not be exercised— the payment will be considered constructive receipt.

Example

John and his employer enter into a deferral agreement in October relating to John's November and December 1988 paychecks. Under the agreement, the deferred salary will be payable on January 1, 1990. The agreement provides, however, that John can get the deferred money prior to January 1, 1990 (at any time during 1989), in the event of an emergency. Based upon these facts, John has constructive receipt of the money in 1989 *even if* he does not have an emergency and does not exercise his right to get the money.

Q: IS IT POSSIBLE TO KEEP ROLLING OVER A DEFERRAL?

A: Yes. If the employer and employee enter into an agreement calling for a deferral of compensation, and if before the due date for the payment arrives, the employer and employee modify the agreement to provide for payment at a still later date, then this deferral will be respected.

Example

Frank and his employer enter into a written agreement in July that Frank's August through December compensation for 1988 will be payable on January 10, 1989. In November, Frank goes to his employer and indicates that he would like to amend the agreement to provide that this compensation will not be payable on January 10, 1989, but instead will be payable on January 10, 1990. The employer agrees that they should amend the contract. Frank should not be taxable until he actually receives the funds in 1990.

Q: WHAT ABOUT GETTING SECURITY FOR THE DEFERRED PAYMENT FROM THE EMPLOYER?

A: The IRS views any security for performance in this context as a no-no. If the employee gets security for the paychecks that will be paid in January, then the IRS position is that the employee has already received an "economic benefit" that will trigger current taxation.

In the IRS view, even setting aside the deferred money in a separate account (such as a trust account or an escrow) is generally close enough to a current economic benefit (and perhaps to a real secured obligation) to require that the funds set aside must be currently taxed.

Q: IS THERE ANY WAY TO OBTAIN SECURITY FOR A DEFERRED COMPENSATION OBLIGATION WITHOUT INCURRING TAX?

A: Yes, if it is done carefully. It is now possible to set up a **Rabbi Trust** under which money is set aside for the account of the employee but is still not taxed to the employee until payment is actually made.

Q: WHAT IS A RABBI TRUST?

A: A Rabbi Trust, which got its name because a rabbi was the first one to set one up, involves a trust agreement between the employer and employee under which the money can accumulate in the trust tax-free for later payment to the employee. The trust has to be subject to the employer's general creditors so that the trust is not secure from attacks by creditors.

However, the money is at least set aside in the separate account, giving the employee some sense of security that the funds will in fact be paid. An independent trustee must make the payment of amounts to the executive under the terms of the trust upon specified events (such as retirement). The payment may be all in a lump sum or in installments over time.

DJI Planning Guide _____

Rabbi Trusts have become very popular in recent years because they do involve a setting aside of amounts for the account of the employee (which normally would result in current taxation to the employee) without tax consequences. The only real disadvantage of a Rabbi Trust is that the trust must be subject to the creditors' claims of the employer. Obviously this makes a Rabbi Trust fairly attractive when the employer is very secure financially (such as a public company or a very solvent entity with few claimants). Conversely, Rabbi Trusts may not be very attractive to employees where there is a real possibility that creditors may attack the trust that is set up for the employee's benefit.

Q: ARE THERE ANY OTHER METHODS OF SECURING AN EMPLOYEE'S INTEREST IN DEFERRED COMPENSATION BENEFITS?

A: Yes, but their tax outcome is uncertain. For example, employers and employees, with varying degrees of success, have used surety bonds, escrow accounts, and even letters of credit to attempt to secure an obligation to pay the employee funds.

Although these techniques can be used, ultimately the problem is this: the IRS does not like to see employees having the security of knowing their money will be paid to them in all events, and yet not being taxable on it. With qualified retirement and pension plans, this result is permissible and even encouraged (on this topic see Chapter 8), but it is generally not permissible with nonqualified deferred compensation arrangements.

CHAPTER 7

COMPENSATING OWNERS AND EMPLOYEES WITH STOCK

INTRODUCTION

Sooner or later, virtually every incorporated business looks at the possibility of compensating with stock. The goal may be to give a broad class of employees a stake in the company in order to improve their performance, to give them an additional incentive to remain with the company, or to provide further compensation to them over and above the cash compensation the company is able to pay. Stock compensation plans may also be attractive as a means of rewarding specific employees who are key to the operation of the business.

Apart from the desirability of such plans, there are a myriad of available choices, including several different types of stock options, different types of share purchase and stock bonus plans, and even plans that seek to have the best of both worlds. The latter are commonly called "stock appreciation rights" or "phantom stock" plans. Under this type of arrangement, participants receive the economic equivalent of stock ownership (appreciation in the value of the shares) but do not receive any voting power along with their share appreciation rights or phantom shares.

Perhaps the most common mistake in dealing with any stock compensation arrangement is the failure to consider exactly what the goals are from both a tax and business standpoint.

Q: WHAT TYPES OF STOCK OPTIONS ARE AVAILABLE?

A: Stock options fall into two categories: **nonqualified options** and **incentive stock options**. A third category, known as the **qualified stock option**, can no longer be issued.

A nonqualified stock option gives the holder the right to buy stock at a specific price for a definite period of time. Although the option price can be set at any level, it usually is set at the fair market value of the stock at the time the option is granted. Some employers institute plans over a period of 10 or more years with gradual vesting of rights to exercise the options over several years.

In contrast, an incentive stock option is subject to a number of detailed rules. The option price must at least equal the fair market value of the stock on the date of the grant. This requirement makes it impossible with incentive stock options to allow purchases of stock based on an option price less than the value of the stock on the date the option is granted. There is also an overall limit of $100,000 on the incentive stock options that can be awarded per recipient each year.

Q: HOW ARE RECIPIENTS OF NONQUALIFIED OPTIONS TAXED?

A: With nonqualified options, there is no tax when the option is granted. Any appreciation from the grant date to the exercise date is taxed as ordinary income at the time of exercise of the option.

Example

Fred receives options to purchase 50 shares in his employer at a time when the market value of the shares is $20. The option price is set at $22. Six months later, the stock is selling for $25 and Fred exercises his option. He has $3 of income ($25 minus $22) at the time of exercise.

Q: HOW ARE RECIPIENTS OF INCENTIVE STOCK OPTIONS TAXED?

A: With incentive stock options, there is no tax to the participant when the option is granted or when it is exercised. The employee pays tax only when the shares are actually sold. Any appreciation from the date of grant to the date the shares are sold is taxed at the capital gains rate provided that certain rules are met. With incentive stock options, one of the primary benefits has traditionally been the fact that the appreciation in the shares is taxed as a capital gain instead of ordinary income.

Q: WHICH IS BETTER FOR THE RECIPIENT, NONQUALIFIED STOCK OPTIONS OR INCENTIVE STOCK OPTIONS?

A: Since ordinary income and capital gains rates are now the same, the only benefit that incentive stock options have over nonqualified options is that incentive stock options give the optionholder the ability to defer paying taxes from the date of the exercise of the options (the event of taxation in the case of nonqualified options) to the date of sale (the date of taxation in the case of incentive stock options).

However, the disadvantages of incentive stock options make nonqualified options comparatively more attractive.

DJI Planning Guide

From the company's perspective, with a nonqualified option, it will receive a deduction equal to the taxable income of the recipient at the exercise of the option. In contrast, with an incentive stock option, the company will *never* receive a deduction. (No deduction is available at the time of grant, exercise, or sale.) From an employer's viewpoint, therefore, incentive stock options are not attractive at all insofar as tax planning is concerned.

Q: WHICH IS MORE POPULAR, INCENTIVE STOCK OPTIONS OR NONQUALIFIED OPTIONS?

A: As noted above, incentive stock options produce capital gains, while nonqualified options produce ordinary income. This difference has made incentive stock options very popular in recent years. However, the tax rates on ordinary income and capital gain are now the same. With a nonqualified option, the holder of the option is taxed at the time of exercise, while with incentive stock options, the tax is not incurred until the shares (acquired pursuant to the option) are ultimately sold. This feature makes the incentive stock option marginally more attractive to the employee.

However, for a variety of reasons, the nonqualified option plan is more attractive to the employer now. The primary reason is that the employer gets no deduction at all for incentive stock options, while the employer does get a deduction for nonqualified options. Incentive stock options are also subject to the individual alternative minimum tax. This means that when the employee exercises his incentive stock options, the excess of the fair market value of the options over the exercise price is an item of tax preference. At the present time, nonqualified stock options are therefore more widely used.

Q: WHAT OTHER STOCK COMPENSATION METHODS ARE THERE BESIDES STOCK OPTIONS?

A: Instead of awarding options to employees, an employer may give stock bonuses or may sell shares to employees under a stock purchase plan. In the case of a stock bonus program, the shares are typically awarded without cost to participants but generally with restrictions affecting their resale. The shares typically become available to participants as restrictions lapse over time, generally after a specified period of continuous employment.

Q: WHAT ARE THE ADVANTAGES OF A RESTRICTED STOCK PLAN?

A: The advantages of a **restricted stock** bonus program of this sort is that it is extremely flexible, and restrictions can be established that lapse over time or that are based on performance criteria. Participants can be allowed to vote shares and earn dividends on the shares during the time they are restricted, but there is little danger of the shares being sold to outsiders because of the restrictions on resale.

When the restrictions ultimately lapse, the participant in this sort of plan is taxed on the value of the stock at ordinary income rates. This means that, assuming the shares bear restrictions, there will be no tax to the employee at the time he receives the shares, and he will be taxed at ordinary income rates only when the restrictions lapse.

If the employee wishes, he can elect to be currently taxed on the shares, notwithstanding the restrictions. This election was once desirable as a means of insuring that future appreciation on the shares would be taxed as a capital gain. However, with the elimination of favorable capital gains rates, this election is now generally undesirable.

DJI Planning Guide

One obvious advantage of a restricted stock plan is that it is an effective means of holding onto valuable employees. The schedule over which the restrictions on the stock will lapse can serve as a carrot to keep the employees in place at least until the restrictions lapse. Several blocks of stock can be subject to successive restrictions to prolong this "forced employee loyalty" effect.

Q: WHAT IF THE EMPLOYEE PAYS SOMETHING FOR THE SHARES?

A: If the employee pays something for the shares, they can still be subject to a variety of restrictions. From a tax perspective, if the employee pays full market value for the stock, then there is no compensation element, and it is treated as if the employee had purchased the stock in any other company. However, most commonly, under stock purchase plans the employee makes a purchase for a bargain price. In this event, any difference between the bargain price and the market price is treated the same as a bonus share would be treated.

Example

Sam purchases 500 shares of Smallco stock from his employer for $30 a share at a time when the stock is selling for $40 a share. The stock is subject to restrictions under which he must resell the shares to the company for a specified formula price if he leaves the company within five years. Sam has no current income now based on this stock purchase. However, when the five-year period lapses and the restrictions disappear, the stock is worth $50 a share. Sam will have $20 of income per share at that time.

Q: HOW DO RESTRICTED STOCK PURCHASE AND RESTRICTED STOCK BONUS PLANS COMPARE TO INCENTIVE STOCK OPTION AND NONQUALIFIED OPTION PLANS?

A: Restricted stock purchase and **restricted stock** bonus plans are probably more effective than stock options in retaining key personnel. Restricted stock plans are also extremely flexible, and the costs are typically low. From the company's perspective, the restricted stock purchase and stock bonus plans suffer from disadvantageous accounting treatment.

Q: WHAT IS A PHANTOM STOCK PLAN?

A: A **phantom stock** plan is a plan involved in the creation of units that are analogous to shares of the company's stock. Employees are granted rights in appreciation in the value of these shares. A variation of a phantom stock plan is a "stock appreciation rights" plan. Basically, both phantom stock plans and stock appreciation rights plans create fictional shares that are awarded to employees and that may increase in value over time.

These plans seek to give employees essentially what they would have gotten by holding shares, but the employees do not have to purchase the shares and do not have voting rights.

DJI Planning Guide

This means that the employer (and the control group) do not have to worry how the shares will be voted, and the employer does not have to worry about enforcing the resale restrictions on real shares to ensure that real stock is not acquired by a corporate raider or a competitor. Thus, phantom stock and stock appreciation rights have real practical advantages.

Q: HOW IS A PARTICIPANT IN A PHANTOM STOCK PLAN OR STOCK APPRECIATION RIGHTS PLAN TAXED?

A: There is no tax when the phantom shares are granted. Any appreciation from the date of grant to the date of payment is taxed as ordinary income at the time of payment. The company will receive a deduction for the payment at the time it is made.

Q: WHEN SHOULD THESE PLANS BE USED?

A: Phantom stock plans are most useful where control is a major issue, such as in any closely held corporation. Since the plans are wholly artificial, some method must be developed for evaluating the shares at the commencement of the plan and upon various new valuation dates needed for payments to participants. The valuation problems can be severe.

Another disadvantage is the accounting treatment of such plans, since for accounting purposes the value of the phantom shares is a compensation expense that must be accrued annually and charged against the company's earnings.

Case Studies

The best way to see the rules governing stock compensation is to see several real-life situations.[1] This is particularly true with stock compensation arrangements because the tax considerations are so intimately connected to the business goals.

Imagine that you are on the compensation committee of a Board of Directors, or if there is no compensation committee, on the Board itself. In either case, you are forced to analyze compensation problems and to attempt to determine which compensation plan best suits the situation. Although it is customary to rely upon professional advisers to some extent in this process, it is important to understand some of these considerations that bear on the appropriate plan. These issues arise with companies of all sizes.

Here are three hypothetical situations to illustrate the factors that come into play.

CASE 1

Martin Mover-Shaker, age 36, is a manager of Pirouette Ballet Supplies, Ltd., a company that is experiencing tremendous growth due to the revival of classical ballet in the U.S. 75 percent of Pirouette's stock is held by various members of the Petrouchka family, with 3 percent still held by Pavlov, Papa's son and the current CEO of the company. The remaining 25 percent is held by Aussie N. Harriet (the noted Australian corporate raider), who obtained his shares when the company was in financial difficulty several years ago.

Martin Mover-Shaker has pushed hard for ownership in the company, which he has correctly perceived to be on a marked upswing. He claims he will leave the company if he is not offered "a piece of the action" (his words) and insists there are a number of other managers and executives who feel the same way.

---

[1]These purely fictional (but realistic) case studies are adapted from Robert Wood, "Three Cases of Compensating with Stock and Stock Substitutes," 12 *Directors & Boards*, 37 (1987), copyright 1987 The Hay Group.

Papa and Pavlov Petrouchka would hate to lose Martin, who has been with them for six years, but they are concerned about maintaining control of the company, particularly because of the other key employees who should logically be rewarded if Martin is. In this connection, they note that a number of shares in the company are held by various cousins and siblings, several of whom are currently involved in marital difficulties.

Q: WHAT TYPE OF COMPENSATION FOR MARTIN WOULD BE APPROPRIATE?

A: This is a fairly clear case for a form of stock appreciation rights (SAR) plan or phantom stock plan. It is apparent that control is an issue. There is a corporate raider with significant stock ownership, stock might possibly go to spouses in divorce proceedings, and there is a relatively small percentage now owned by Papa and Pavlov. Indeed, Papa and Pavlov are expressly (and probably appropriately!) concerned about maintaining control.

A number of employees will evidently be included in the plan in addition to Martin, in which case granting a single bonus of shares only to Martin is out of the question. Note that Martin's age and tenure with the company may also cut against actual stock ownership.

It should be possible to give "a piece of the action" through an SAR or phantom stock plan that gives additional compensation for growth in the company. It gives employees a stake. From what we know, Martin is more concerned with capital appreciation than with having a voice as a shareholder.

Q: WHAT IF MARTIN REALLY WANTS "REAL" STOCK?

A: An SAR or phantom stock plan can have a real stock component. Appreciation shares can be payable at some future date in real stock. (Typically, participants have the option to receive benefits in cash or in stock rather than being forced to receive stock.)

Although awarding stock may not be called for here, paying off appreciation shares in real stock can be a way of delaying the ultimate issuance of shares when owning stock is one real objective of the participants. If Martin and the other employees who are expected to be participants are really seeking appreciation but also eventually want stock ownership, then having optional share awards in the SAR plan may be appropriate.

CASE 2

Emerging Electronics is a medium-sized Silicon Valley company specializing in the recycling of silicon chips. Its CEO is Charlie Chairman, who has just navigated the company through the 1983–87 economic slump. Emerging's stock is traded on the over-the-counter market, although 30 percent of the stock (constituting effective control) is still owned by Chip Wafer, the founder.

Emerging's management and board are convinced that a broad program of employee ownership is appropriate at this time. As the primary goal of the program would be to enhance employee incentives, they want to ensure that employees remain with the company for at least several years.

Cash compensation by Emerging is a bit on the low side. The company's accountants and investment bankers have indicated that equity compensation would be desirable because the company does not have very high book earnings; they are concerned that higher direct compensation (as opposed to compensation in the form of equity) would result in an even smaller figure for the company's earnings.

Q: WHAT KIND OF PLAN IS APPROPRIATE HERE?

A: Emerging's Board might consider the following alternatives.

• *Stock Bonus Program (Restricted Stock).* Certain employees would be granted shares at the end of the fiscal year based on perceived merit. The shares would be subject to restrictions under which the employees would be required to resell the shares to the company at the book value then prevailing if they should leave the company within three years.

• *Stock Option Plan (Nonqualified)*. Certain employees would be granted options to purchase shares in the company exercisable in installments over a four-year period after the date of grant. The option price would be fixed about 5 percent below the over-the-counter trading price for the company's stock at the time the options were granted. This low option price would give some compensation to grantees even if the stock price does not go up significantly.

• *Stock Option Plan (ISOs)*. This plan is basically the same as the plan described above, but the exercise price would be at least 100 percent of the market value of the shares on the date of grant (or 110 percent for 10 percent owners). Thus, the possibility for employee gains would lie in the ultimate appreciation in the shares rather than in the immediate difference between the option price and the price of the shares.

• *Phantom Stock Plan*. Under this alternative, employees would be awarded "performance shares" keyed to the market value of the company's stock, with future increases in the stock's value giving rise to cash or stock benefits. Under the plan, benefits would not be payable until three years from the date of grant, and participants could elect whether to receive cash or stock.

Q: IS ONE PLAN BETTER FOR EMPLOYEES THAN OTHERS FROM A TAX STANDPOINT?

A: Yes, but not dramatically. After the 1986 Tax Reform Act, any of these stock plans will suffer from the lack of opportunity for capital gains in the tax law. Each plan is discussed more fully below.

Q: WHAT IS GOOD ABOUT THE STOCK BONUS PROGRAM?

A: The Stock Bonus Program (Restricted Stock) can be quite flexible, since there are no legal constraints on duration, vesting, and other such features. The restrictions can require employees to remain with the company for a considerable time in order to receive their benefits.

Participants will be taxed (as ordinary income) when the restrictions on their shares lapse. The participants can make an election to include the value of their shares in income currently, even though the restrictions have not lapsed. This tended to be a desirable election when capital-gains rates were in effect, but it is typically not desirable now.

Q: WHAT ABOUT THE COMPANY'S TAX PLANNING?

A: The company will not receive a tax deduction for any of this restricted stock compensation until the employees have to include it in income. Thus, the employer receives no current tax break. From an accounting standpoint, the projected expense of the stock is generally accrued over the life of the restriction period based upon the fair market value of the shares on the date of the grant. This means that for purposes of the company's balance sheet and annual report, it is treated as spending money (compensation) over the restriction period.

Q: WOULD THE RESTRICTED STOCK OR STOCK OPTION PLAN BE MORE FAVORABLE?

A: Probably the greatest advantage of the restricted stock plan is its effect in retaining key employees. Its flexibility and low cost to participants is also attractive. However, the accounting treatment of the plan and awards makes it less desirable to the company than stock option programs.

The Stock Option Plan (Nonqualified) allows employees to get instant appreciation—the option price could be fixed at below the current market value. The duration of option periods and exercise periods and participation are all flexible. The participant is not taxed when he gets the option and is only taxed on the appreciation at the time he exercises the option.

Likewise, the company gets a deduction for compensation

expense at the time of the exercise. Although currently the company is not required to charge earnings for options on the date of the grant or the date of exercise (or even the eventual sale of the shares!), the Financial Accounting Standards Board (which regulates accounting practices) may change this rule.

Q: IS AN INCENTIVE STOCK OPTION PLAN MORE RESTRICTED?

A: Yes. The Incentive Stock Option Plan has more constraints than the nonqualified option plan. For example, the option price must at least be 100 percent of the fair market value at the date of grant (and 100 percent of fair market value for owners of 10 percent or more of the company's stock). This factor is limiting, but after the 1986 Act, options need no longer be exercised in the order received. The life of the plan and the exercise period for the options may not exceed 10 years. And the maximum award per individual may only be $100,000 per year.

There is no tax when the option is granted or exercised. Any appreciation from the date of grant to the date the shares are sold is taxed currently (as capital gains) if the sale occurs no sooner than one year from the date of exercise and two years from the date of grant. Note that with repeal of capital-gains rates, the only advantage of ISOs over nonqualified options is the ability to defer the payment of the tax from the date the option is exercised to the date of sale.

Q: WHAT ARE THE OTHER DISADVANTAGES OF INCENTIVE STOCK OPTIONS?

A: The company receives no deduction for compensation expense when ISOs are granted, exercised, or sold. This is a big disadvantage compared to nonqualified options. For accounting purposes, no charge to earnings is made under the current rule, but as with nonqualified options, the Financial Accounting Standards Board may change this practice.

For closely held companies, the ISO accounting is the same as for nonqualified options. In general, the lack of a tax deduction at any time to the company makes ISOs less attractive than nonqualified options.

Incentive stock options are also subject to the individual alternative minimum tax. When an employee exercises his options, the excess of their fair market value over their exercise price is preference income subject to the alternative minimum tax.

Example

Orville receives incentive stock options to buy 1,000 shares of his employer's stock at $10 per share. Four years later, Orville exercises his options when the market price for the stock is $25 per share. Orville has $15,000 of preference income.

Note

Whether preference income will be taxable depends on a variety of factors, including the taxpayer's other income. However, there is a threshold alternative minimum tax exemption of $40,000 on a joint return and of $30,000 on a single return. So Orville should not owe the tax just by reason of this exercise. But in some cases, the alternative minimum tax can be a big problem.

Q: WOULD A PHANTOM STOCK PLAN BE DESIRABLE?

A: The Phantom Stock Plan is flexible and can afford participants the option of receiving cash or stock. There is no tax to the employee when the phantom shares are granted, and any appreciation from the date of grant to date of payment is taxed as ordinary income at the time of payment. The company receives a deduction for compensation expense when the participant is taxable on it.

For accounting purposes, any appreciation in the value of the phantom shares is a compensation expense that must be accrued annually and charged against earnings.

Example

Suppose that the company's stock, and consequently the phantom shares, goes up in value $10 per share and that there are 5,000 phantom shares outstanding to plan participants. The company will be treated for accounting purposes (in its balance sheet and annual report) as having *spent* $50,000!

This accounting treatment can create a very large liability against the company's earnings and may cause serious problems. Note that the same rule applies to stock appreciation right plans, where instead of being credited with phantom shares, employees are awarded rights to cash in on the appreciation in the company's stock.

Currently, a great disadvantage of phantom stock and SAR plans is the unfavorable accounting treatment they receive as compared to stock options, but this imbalance may change if (as is currently proposed) the Financial Accounting Standards Board does change the accounting treatment of stock options.

CASE 3

Charlene Chairperson heads Pet Products, Ltd., a successful privately held company. Under arrangements with Pet Products' investment bankers, the company will go public within the next year. Charlene's own small holdings in the company stand to increase in value by 15 or 20 times. The board has determined that it is appropriate to make awards for exemplary service in the past year, leading, at least in part, to the likelihood of a public offering in the near future.

The Board has discussed the following kinds of awards.

• *Cash Bonuses.* Selected employees would receive discretionary cash bonuses.

• *Stock Bonuses.* Selected employees would receive share awards. The shares would be subject to restrictions requiring their resale to the company at a formula price if the employee should leave the company within three years.

• *Stock Options.* Either nonqualified options or incentive stock options would be distributed to selected employees.

**Q: CHARLENE OPENS THE BOARD
MEETING BY ASKING: WHAT
CONSIDERATIONS SHOULD PLAY
A PART IN CHOOSING AMONG
THESE ALTERNATIVES?**

A: At the heart of determining which type of program Pet
Products should pursue is the extent of the benefit it wishes
to confer upon its employees. It may be undesirable to grant
significant stock bonuses—even if the shares were subject to
substantial restrictions—since the company's stock may go public and increase dramatically in value within a relatively short
period.

Both incentive stock options and nonqualified stock options
here would suffer from this same fundamental problem.
Although there is less employer cost involved in awarding
shares or stock options than in awarding cash, the stock bonuses
and stock options may be inadvisable for this reason.

**Q: WHAT ELSE MAKES THE STOCK PLANS
ATTRACTIVE HERE?**

A: Either stock bonuses or stock options may be very attractive, particularly if executives are also to be included within
the program, precisely because of the possibility of a marked
upturn in the stock's value. The board will have to balance this
fact with the potential detriment of the large awards to other
program participants. Furthermore, the company's investment
bankers may well have input on the appropriateness (and the
extent) of employee stock bonuses or stock options.

**Q: WHAT TAX CONSIDERATIONS ARE
THERE IN THE DECISION?**

A: If the company makes cash awards, they will be deductible when paid. Stock bonuses will be deductible when the
restrictions on the shares lapse (unless recipients elect cur-

rent taxability). By the same token, the inclusion in income to employees when the restrictions lapse would be based on the then-current market value of the shares, which could be huge if the company does go public.

With incentive stock options, there will be no deduction for the company at any time. However, with nonqualified options, the company would at least receive a deduction when the recipient exercises the options.

Also note that, from the employee's perspective, any stock compensation that has as one of its goals converting ordinary income to capital gains has less appeal since ordinary income and capital gains are now taxed at the same rates.

CHAPTER 8

DEFERRED COMPENSATION PLANS

INTRODUCTION

Our tax laws have long given special tax breaks to businesses that establish and fund retirement benefits. The employees who receive the benefits are also given favorable tax treatment. The basic tax benefit of qualified retirement plans is that the employer can currently deduct contributions made for the employee's benefit, yet the employee will not have to include the contributions in income.

Nor will the employee have to include the earnings from the qualified retirement plan account in his income. This means that the earnings accumulate on a "tax-deferred" basis, so the income in the qualified retirement account is able to grow at a much faster rate than if it were currently subject to tax.

The employee must pay tax on the amounts distributed to him from the plan. Generally this payment occurs upon retirement. As an incentive to accumulate the funds until retirement, the law provides favorable tax treatment for the recipient on retirement. On the other hand, to discourage withdrawals before retirement, penalties are imposed on premature distributions of retirement funds.

Retirement plans provide wonderful employee incentives to remain with the company. In addition to assisting employees in planning for their retirement, they may make a business' overall compensation package attractive. The various types of qualified retirement plans are widely used in this country and account for billions of dollars. Every business, whether it maintains qualified plans or not, needs a basic understanding of the rules governing these plans.

Q: WHAT IS A QUALIFIED RETIREMENT PLAN?

A: A qualified retirement plan is a program of benefits maintained by either an employer or union that is entitled to the following tax advantages:

- The employer can take a current tax deduction for contributions it makes.
- The earnings on the amounts in the qualified plan are not currently taxed, so they accumulate tax-free.
- The employees are not taxed until benefits are distributed to them.
- When the benefits are paid to retired employees, favorable tax treatment may apply.

Q: WHAT TYPES OF QUALIFIED RETIREMENT PLANS ARE THERE?

A: The two basic types of qualified retirement plans are **defined benefit plans** and **defined contribution plans**. A defined benefit plan involves the employer's promise to pay an employee a particular benefit upon retirement, such as a fraction of salary or some other specified benefit. A defined contribution plan involves a stated contribution each year rather than a stated benefit provided upon retirement. Depending upon earnings and market conditions, and even the group of employees the plan will cover, either type of plan may prove to be more beneficial than the other in a given situation.

Q: HOW CAN THE EMPLOYER PROMISE TO PROVIDE A PARTICULAR BENEFIT ON RETIREMENT?

A: With a defined benefit plan, the employer promises to pay a particular benefit on retirement. In order to determine what contributions to make every year to create a large enough fund to provide that benefit for employees, the employer must hire an actuary or plan consultant who makes actuarial and other calculations to determine the amount of necessary annual contributions. It is not enough just to make sure there is sufficient money in the plan, as it is also generally undesirable to contribute too much (to "overfund") the plan. A defined benefit plan therefore requires a greater degree of diligence (and typically expense) to operate.

Q: WHY WOULD ANYONE USE A DEFINED BENEFIT PLAN?

A: For one thing, to take advantage of the relatively low cost of benefits. For large groups of employees, defined benefit plans can be more cost efficient (in terms of employer contributions), even though they are more expensive to administer. Furthermore, as is discussed more fully below, defined benefit plans may be used to obtain large contributions for older persons (approximately over age 50). The larger contributions are attractive if these persons are the owners or key executives of the business, but such contributions may be very unattractive if they are not.

DJI Planning Guide _____

In considering the implementation or operation of any qualified plan, two distinct perspectives must be kept in mind. One is the employee's, and the other is the employer's. The employer generally has an incentive to keep costs low, to exclude as many high-turnover employees as possible, and to stretch out the rates at which benefits vest. Yet the employer often also wants high contributions for key employees.

The employee typically wants as much as possible as soon as possible in the way of plan benefits. Some employees may want the option of taking cash currently in lieu of plan benefits.

Q: WHAT REQUIREMENTS APPLY TO QUALIFIED PLANS?

A: Whether a plan is a defined benefit or defined contribution plan, certain requirements must be met in order for the plan to qualify for favorable tax treatment. To begin with, several technical rules apply to ensure that the plan will benefit a large percentage of employees, including lower-paid or "rank and file" employees. A plan that benefits only a small percentage of employees or only the highly compensated persons will not qualify.

There are also standards governing the rate at which a plan participant becomes entitled to benefits. Known as the "vesting" requirements these rules seek to prevent a plan from requiring an employee to remain with the company for too long before the benefits "vest" (that is, before they become nonforfeitable, even though the employee may not be able to get them until retirement age).

Q: HOW FAST MUST A PLAN PARTICIPANT'S BENEFITS VEST?

A: Generally speaking, a plan has to provide vesting (a so-called "vesting schedule") that is at least as favorable as the schedules indicated in the following table.

The plan can provide a more generous vesting schedule so that participants vest more quickly, but these are minimum

Number of Years with Employer	Percentage of Benefits Vested
3	20%
4	40
5	60
6	80
7 or more	100

standards. The "vesting schedule" in the plan will determine the rate at which an employee's benefits vest.

Example

Hank is a computer technician for Silicon Valley, Inc. Under the company's pension plan, Hank's benefits vest in accordance with the minimum vesting schedule set forth in the preceding table (20 percent per year between years 3 and 7). After five years of employment, Hank quits and goes to work for a competitor. He is 40 percent vested in the Silicon Valley plan, so he will be entitled to 40 percent of the benefits when he does retire. Most plans provide Hank with the option of taking his distribution now (when he leaves Silicon Valley), although the distribution would be subject to a penalty tax. Alternatively, Hank could put the distributed money into an Individual Retirement Account (a so-called "IRA rollover").

Q: AREN'T THERE DIFFERENT TYPES OF RETIREMENT PLANS?

A: Yes. There are two basic types mentioned above, defined contribution plans and defined benefit plans. Moreover, there are different types of plans within these broad categories. A defined contribution plan may be any one of the following.

• *Money Purchase Plan.* Sometimes considered the classic pension plan, a "money purchase" plan mandates annual contributions by the employer, typically based on a percentage of the employee's compensation. Annual contributions are limited to $30,000 or 25 percent of the participant's compensation, whichever is less.

• *Profit Sharing Plan.* This type of plan gives the employer more flexibility, since contributions are not mandatory but are generally based upon employer discretion.

• *Stock Bonus Plan.* As the name suggests, a stock bonus plan involves payment in stock. Normally, the participant will have a right to demand that the benefits be paid in stock instead of in cash.

Two more types of defined contribution plans are **Employee Stock Ownership Plans** (ESOPs) and **401(k)** or, "Cash or Deferred" Plans.

Q: WHAT IS AN ESOP?

A: ESOP stands for **Employee Stock Ownership Plan**. Contributions are made by the employer in cash, as in the case of a money purchase plan or a profit sharing plan. With an ESOP, the big difference is that these contributions in cash are then used to buy stock in the employer.

DJI Planning Guide ——————————————————————

ESOPs have become tremendously popular in the last few years because they may assist management in avoiding takeover attempts and other types of acquisitions. The ESOP serves as an alternate buyer for the stock. Once the stock is sold to the ESOP, it can generally still be voted by the employer.

Furthermore, as is discussed in more detail in Chapter 9, the shareholders who sell stock to an ESOP are taxed very favorably. Finally, ESOPs themselves are entitled to favorable tax provisions. These rules encourage a company or shareholders to sell all of the company's stock to an ESOP so that the employees will ultimately own the company. Many widely publicized "employee take-overs," are based on these rules.

Q: WHAT IS A 401(k) PLAN?

A: A 401(k) plan (named after the Internal Revenue Code Section) is also sometimes called a "Cash or Deferred" plan or a "Cafeteria Plan" (because it involves employee choice). It is sponsored by the employer and allows participants to make retirement plan contributions *if they so elect*. The contributions come from the employees, not the employer. Assuming that the employees elect to participate, however, the contributions come off their pre-tax earnings rather than their after-tax earnings.

Essentially, under such a plan, the employees tell the employer that they would rather have a portion of their compensation contributed to the 401(k) plan rather than to receive it in cash. The employer pays the amount into the plan and takes a deduction for it. Under the current annual limits on a 401(k) plan, the employee cannot elect to have more than $7,000 per year contributed to the 401(k) plan.

Q: CAN MORE THAN $7,000 A YEAR BE PUT INTO A 401(k) PLAN?

A: It depends. The $7,000 limit applies to "voluntary contributions," meaning that when the employee requests the employer to reduce his salary and make corresponding contributions to the 401(k) plan, he can do so with no more than $7,000. The $7,000 limit does not apply to nonvoluntary contributions, with which the employer (rather than the employee) decides to make a 401(k) contribution. Granted, it seems unlikely that an employer would *require* plan contributions at the expense of current salary payments to the employee, but this is the distinction drawn in the law.

Example

Tom's salary from Largeco is $90,000 a year. If he elects to have a portion of his salary contributed to the company's 401(k) plan on his behalf, then he will be subject to the $7,000 limit. (He will not currently be taxable on up to $7,000 contributed to the plan, but the balance of his salary will be currently taxable to him.) However, if the *company requires* the contribution, then the limit does not apply. Suppose the company tells Tom his compensation package for the year will consist of $70,000 in cash and a $20,000 401(k) contribution. This employer-mandated contribution would not be subject to the $7,000 limit.

DJI Planning Guide

The preceding distinction certainly seems artificial, since it is hard to imagine an employer *forcing* an employee to reduce his salary to make plan contributions. However, the distinction can be used to advantage when larger contributions are desirable. Whether the employee requests the reduction in salary and the 401(k) contribution or the employer requires it is a factual question. An employer may appear to be the instigator of the arrangement even though it may really amount to an accommodation to a valued employee.

Q: WITH ALL THESE TYPES OF DEFINED CONTRIBUTION PLANS, WHEN ARE DEFINED BENEFIT PLANS USED?

A: Since a defined benefit plan promises a specific benefit on retirement, it can be particularly advantageous to an employer when retirement for most employees is a long way off. Contributions can be very small if there are many years left before an employee's retirement. Conversely, if it is just a few years until retirement for some employees, the cost of the plan to the employer may be enormous. This fact can be used to advantage in a closely held business.

The maximum amount that can be contributed annually for a participant in defined benefit plan is much larger than the amounts that can be put into a defined contribution plan. The maximum defined benefit contribution that can be paid to a participant in a defined benefit plan is the smaller of $90,000 per year or 100 percent of the participant's average compensation over the three highest years of his compensation. The maximum amount of compensation that can be considered is $200,000. In addition, the $90,000 figure is reduced if the person retires before age 65.

DJI Planning Guide

A defined benefit plan can be used to advantage in a closely held business with older owners. The amount of the contribution is determined by taking into account the age of the participant and the number of years until his or her retirement. If the person has only a few years left until retirement, then large contributions will have to be made in order to pay the desired benefit.

Depending upon the age of the participants, the owners of a closely held business may be able to contribute large amounts of income into the retirement plans on a deductible basis, while at the same time making relatively modest contributions for most employees.

Q: ISN'T MAKING LARGE CONTRIBUTIONS FOR THE OWNERS AND SMALL CONTRIBUTIONS FOR MOST EMPLOYEES DISCRIMINATION?

A: In a way, but it is not considered discrimination to provide benefits based on a percentage of salary and to fund those benefits with large contributions for the older employees.

Example

Bubbleco, Inc.'s plan promises all employees a benefit on retirement of 50 percent of their average salary for the last five years of their employment. Highly paid employees obviously will get a larger retirement benefit than others, but this percentage of compensation formula is not considered discriminatory. The kind of discrimination that is *not* allowed is to promise dramatically disparate benefits on retirement in the case of a defined benefit plan.

In the case of a defined contribution plan, making contributions of a low percentage of compensation for lower-paid persons and a high percentage of compensation for highly paid employees would be discrimination. Certain other practices are also considered discriminatory under detailed antidiscrimination rules.

Q: WHAT ARE THE LIMITS ON CONTRIBUTIONS TO DEFINED CONTRIBUTION PLANS?

A: There are two basic limits applicable to contributions to defined contribution plans. For the employer's tax deduction, a contribution equal to as much as 15 percent of the total compensation paid to all participants during the year can be deducted. The second limit applies to amounts allocated annually to each participant's account. This amount cannot exceed $30,000 or 25 percent of the participant's compensation, whichever is less.

Note that most defined contribution plans can be "integrated" to some extent with Social Security. This means that the payments the employer makes for Social Security tax for each employee can be treated as contributions made by the employer and will count toward the employer's obligation to make contributions. This integration is no longer unlimited as it once was, but it can still be a cost-saving device for an employer.

Q: WHAT IS THE EFFECT OF A PLAN'S INTEGRATION WITH SOCIAL SECURITY?

A: The effect is that the employer is able to divert more contributions to highly paid persons such as executives and principals of the business.

Example

Manufacto, Inc. pays a flat 10 percent of compensation in excess of the Social Security wage base to its defined contribution plan for all employees. By integrating with Social Security contributions, Manufacto can make only a 5 percent contribution on compensation up to the Social Security wage base. Since most employees are paid less than the Social Security wage base of $43,800, in effect, most of the contribution for these employees is funded by the employer's payment of the Social Security tax, something the employer would be required to pay in any case. This practice effectively allows the company to make contributions to highly paid persons such as executives with no corresponding contribution to the lower-paid employees.

Q: CAN LOANS STILL BE MADE FROM QUALIFIED RETIREMENT PLANS?

A: Yes, subject to limits and restrictions. One of the greatest "games" in tax planning has been the ability to make contributions to qualified retirement plans for employees, so that the employer receives a deduction for the payment and the employee still does not have to include it in income. Then the employee borrows the money out of the plan to use it for the employee's purposes. Since there is an obligation to repay it, the amount is still not taxable to the employee. Consequently, the employee gets the use of the cash without having to pay tax on it.

The rules have tightened up substantially on retirement plan loans in recent years. A plan can still permit a participant to borrow, normally at a more favorable interest rate than a participant might obtain elsewhere. The plan loan cannot exceed $50,000.

Q: WHEN DOES A PLAN LOAN HAVE TO BE REPAID?

A: Both principal and interest on the loan have to be repaid in quarterly installments over five years. In order to prevent plan participants from paying off a loan and taking out a new loan every five years (effectively allowing the loan to go on forever), there are restrictions on the amount of new loans if the participant has had a plan loan outstanding during the preceding 12 months.

Plan loans can exceed the five-year general rule if they are taken out to allow the participant to purchase a principal residence.

DJI Planning Guide

Even with the new restrictions on plan loans, they can be of tremendous benefit. Plans that are maintained by unincorporated entities such as partnerships or proprietors (called **Keogh plans**) are not allowed to loan money to owners of the business at all. Consequently, borrowing represents a large advantage that corporate plans still enjoy over plans operated by unincorporated entities.

Q: HOW ARE BENEFITS TAXED FROM A QUALIFIED RETIREMENT PLAN?

A: Benefits can be provided from a qualified retirement plan in one of several ways. If the money is paid out all at once, then it is known as a **lump-sum distribution**. A person who receives this of lump-sum payment generally must include the total amount in current income.

Example

Roger Retiree just retired from Megafirm, Inc. Over the years, his retirement account in Megafirm's qualified plan grew to $900,000. If he receives the whole amount when he is 65, it will all be taxable.

Q: CAN THE LARGE TAX ON THE LUMP-SUM DISTRIBUTION BE REDUCED?

A: Yes, in one of two ways. Taxes can be postponed on all or a portion of the distribution if the participant who receives the distribution transfers it to an **Individual Retirement Account** (IRA) or another qualified retirement plan within 60 days after the distribution. This transfer of a retirement plan distribution to an IRA is usually referred to as a "rollover." (More on IRAs follows.)

Secondly, if the IRA rollover mechanism is not desirable, the person can elect to have the distribution taxed under a special five-year averaging method. The tax is calculated as if the plan distribution were paid in installments over five years rather than in one year, so the tax is reduced. Actually, the money is still all distributed in one year.

Q: HOW DO YOU QUALIFY FOR FIVE-YEAR AVERAGING ON A PLAN DISTRIBUTION?

A: To qualify for this five-year averaging, these three requirements must be met:

- The person must have been a participant in the plan for at least five years prior to the distribution.
- The person must have been at least 59 1/2 years old when the distribution was made.
- No part of the distribution can be rolled over to an IRA or to another qualified plan.

Note

This 5-year averaging rule replaces an even more favorable 10-year averaging rule. The 10-year averaging rule can still apply to a participant who reached age 50 before January 1, 1986.

Q: DOES IT MAKE SENSE TO USE FIVE-YEAR AVERAGING WHEN THESE REQUIREMENTS ARE MET?

A: For a plan participant who receives a lump-sum distribution, either a rollover to an IRA or the five-year averaging can be beneficial depending on his situation. Generally speaking, persons who receive small plan benefits and who may need the funds to live on are better off to elect five-year averaging. Five-year averaging reduces the tax burden on the distribution but ensures that the money is available to the participant.

In contrast, recipients of large benefits who do not currently need the money are frequently better advised to roll the lump-sum distribution in to an IRA or another qualified plan.

Note

An IRA **rollover** removes the tax burden imposed on the distribution altogether. It also insures that the money can keep compounding on a tax-deferred basis.

Q: CAN BENEFITS BE PAYABLE IN OTHER FORMS?

A: Yes. Other than cash, the most common method of payment is the annuity, under which payments are made over a period of years, typically for life. An annuity is generally taxed as payments are received. Obviously, this means that the tax liability associated with the payments is also spread out over a number of years. Many participants like an annuity because of the consistent cash flow it produces. Unlike a lump-sum distribution, an annuity provides a guaranteed source of income.

Q: CAN A PARTICIPANT IN A PENSION PLAN ALSO HAVE AN IRA?

A: Yes, depending on the income of the participant. If you are *not* an active participant in a qualified plan, then you can make deductible IRA contributions no matter what your income.

If you *are* an active participant in a plan, you can still make deductible IRA contributions as long as your adjusted gross income is under $25,000 individually or $40,000 on a joint return. If you are an active participant in a plan and your adjusted gross income is under $35,000 (but over $25,000) individually or under $50,000 (but over $40,000) on a joint return, then IRA contributions are partially deductible. If your adjusted gross income is over $35,000 individually or over $50,000 on a joint return, IRA contributions are totally nondeductible.

See Table 8–1 for a summary of the rules pertaining to allowable IRA contributions for pension plan participants.

Q: IF I CANNOT MAKE IRA CONTRIBUTIONS ON A DEDUCTIBLE BASIS, CAN I MAKE NONDEDUCTIBLE IRA CONTRIBUTIONS?

A: Yes. Contributions to an IRA can still be made on a nondeductible basis. Because of the power of tax-deferred compounding, even IRAs funded with nondeductible contributions can perform dramatically.

Example

Fred participates in his company's pension plan, so he cannot make deductible IRA contributions. However, he can make nondeductible contributions. If Fred contributes $2,000 every year for 30 years, and his money earns 10 percent interest yearly, then he will have over $277,000 in his IRA. If he were to invest the same $2,000 per year for 30 years in taxable investments earning 10 percent (paying 28 percent tax on the interest every year), then he would have only about $210,000. In this case, tax-deferred compounding produces a savings of over $67,000.

TABLE 8–1
Deductibility of IRA Contributions

Adjusted Gross Income		Are Either You or Spouse Covered by a Pension Plan?	Type of $2,000 Contribution
Joint Return	Individual Return		
Under $40,000	Under $25,000	Yes	Fully deductible
Under $40,000	Under $25,000	No	Fully deductible
$40,000–50,000	$25,000–35,000	Yes	Partially deductible
$40,000–50,000	$25,000–35,000	No	Fully deductible
Above $50,000	Above $35,000	Yes	Nondeductible
Above $50,000	Above $35,000	No	Fully deductible

DJI Planning Guide —————————————————

Nondeductible IRA contributions may seem unattractive at first glance. However, as the above example illustrates, they still perform very well as compared with a taxable investment.

—————————————————————————————

Q: ARE THERE DIFFERENCES BETWEEN QUALIFIED PLANS COVERING CORPORATIONS AND THOSE COVERING PARTNERSHIPS AND PROPRIETORSHIPS?

A: There used to be tremendous differences. Currently, there are very few distinctions. It used to be that much larger contributions could be deducted for contributions to corporate plans, but this disparity has been eliminated. One of the few remaining distinctions is that borrowing is permitted from corporate plans but not from plans maintained for partners for proprietors. (See earlier questions concerning plan loans.)

Q: WHAT KINDS OF FRINGE BENEFIT PLANS CAN BE PROVIDED FOR EMPLOYEES?

A: Virtually any type of fringe benefit program can be provided for employees. The question is whether the employees will be taxable on these benefits or not. Certain types of fringe benefit programs are explicitly excluded from taxation. They include the following.

- No-additional-cost services (for example, free standby airline flights provided by airlines to employees).
- Qualified employee discounts (for example, a discount sale price on products sold by the employer).
- Working condition fringe benefits (for example, company cars used for business purposes).

- Small and insignificant fringe benefits (so-called *de minimus* fringe benefits, such as employer-provided coffee and personal use of the employer's copy machines and other office equipment).
- Use of on-premises athletic facilities provided and operated by the employer.

Q: DO ANY SPECIAL REQUIREMENTS APPLY TO THESE TYPES OF BENEFITS?

A: Yes. Probably the most important requirement is compliance with the strict nondiscrimination rules that apply to most fringe benefits. Although certain exemptions from the nondiscrimination requirements apply, in general these rules insure that the exclusion from income for these types of fringe benefits will be available only if the benefits are provided to a broad cross section of employees.

Q: WHAT ABOUT OTHER TYPES OF FRINGE BENEFITS PROVIDED BY THE EMPLOYER?

A: Employers may provide child or dependent care services, prepaid legal services, educational expenses, and food and lodging, all of which may be excludable from the employee's income provided that certain requirements are met. Specific statutory provisions govern prepaid legal service plans, under which the employer makes contributions on a deductible basis to the plan and the plan provides nontaxable benefits in the form of legal services for employees and their dependents.

Employers may maintain an educational expense plan under which up to $5,250 per year received by an employee for tuition, fees, books, and supplies may be excluded from the employee's income but will nevertheless be deductible to the employer. Once again, the plan must be written, and strict nondiscrimination rules and limits apply.

Q: CAN CHILD CARE BENEFITS
BE PROVIDED TAX-FREE?

A: Employers may provide child or dependent care services under a nondiscriminatory written plan that will not be includable in the employee's income. The cost, however, will be deductible by the employer. Only $5,000 per year may be excluded to the employees under this plan, and certain other limits apply.

Q: ISN'T FOOD AND LODGING
PROVIDED BY THE EMPLOYER
ALWAYS EXCLUDED?

A: No. The value of meals and lodging furnished by an employer to an employee (and the employee's spouse and dependents) is not includable in the employee's gross income if such provisions are furnished for the employer's convenience. Basically, this means that the meals or lodging must be provided to suit the employer, as when the operator of a hotel requires the employee to take meals in the hotel dining room.

Furthermore, meals must be furnished on the employer's business premises. In the case of lodging, the employee must be required to accept the lodging as a condition of employment. Cash reimbursements of meals would be included in gross income, however.

Example One

Ralph works as a manager on an oil rig in the North Sea. He is required to take his meals and to sleep on the rig. The value of meals and lodging are not taxable to Ralph.

Example Two

Betty is vice president of a large manufacturing company and is in charge of its largest plant located 10 miles outside of Detroit. She is not required to take her meals on the premises, but any she does take in the company cafeteria are free. The cost of these meals should not be taxable to Betty even though she is not *required* to take them, as long as they are furnished for her employer's convenience (e.g., to encourage shorter lunch breaks by keeping people on the premises).

However, if the company were also to offer lodging on a similar basis, the value of any lodging Betty accepted would be includable in her income. In order not to be taxable, the lodging would have to be something she was required to accept as a condition to employment (as in the case of a hotel manager who must sleep on the premises).

Q: WHAT RULES GOVERN HEALTH AND WELFARE BENEFITS PROVIDED TO EMPLOYEES?

A: Many employers finance accident and health insurance plans. The amounts received by employees under such plans are not taxable, yet the employer can deduct the cost of the plan as a business expense. The employer can fund such a plan directly (as by reimbursing employees for the medical and/or accident expenses they incur for themselves and their families). More commonly, however, the employer funds the arrangement through medical and/or accident insurance.

As in the case of other employee benefits, the main rule governing accident and health plans is one of nondiscrimination. The plan must benefit a broad cross section of employees rather than merely the highly paid or control persons.

CHAPTER 9

COMBINING BUSINESSES: MERGERS AND ACQUISITIONS

INTRODUCTION

One needs only to open a newspaper to become well acquainted with the "merger mania" currently prevailing in the business community. The trend has truly blossomed in recent years.

To a far greater extent than ever before, mergers and takeovers have been the constant talk in the business world. And even outside the business world, the players have become popular cult figures. The latest transactions have become cocktail party conversation.

Obviously, the biggest splashes in this arena have been with large companies and colorful takeover entrepreneurs. However, it is deceptive to think the trend is limited to these big players. In fact, many mergers and acquisitions occurring today involve companies of relatively modest size.

Regardless of the size of a business, it is more essential than ever before for the owners, officers, and executives to understand the rudiments of mergers and acquisitions.

- What makes them viable?
- How do they work?
- Who gets what?

No factor is more decisive in these transactions than income taxes. Our tax system sometimes drives the transactions to begin with. And even where tax dollars do not drive the transaction, they certainly play a critical role in structuring the transaction and carrying it out.

By their very nature, most of these transactions involve corporations. Either a corporation is being bought or it is being sold. In many cases, the other party to the transaction (the buyer or seller) is also a corporation.

However, this does not mean that businesses conducted as proprietorships or partnerships cannot be bought or sold. They certainly can. Some of the discussion below concerns purchases and sales of partnerships and proprietorships. Yet the focus in this chapter is on the corporate form. That is where all of the flexibility lies.

It is also where the action is!

PROPRIETORSHIPS

Q: WHAT HAPPENS WHEN A PROPRIETORSHIP IS SOLD?

A: When a proprietorship is sold, the proprietor will have taxable income or loss. Since there is no separate entity with a proprietorship (in that the business assets are actually held by the proprietor himself), there is no separate tax imposed. The proprietor simply has a larger gain (or smaller loss) for the year.

Traditionally, the tax on the sale of a business held as a proprietorship was at the capital gains rate except for certain special items. Beginning in 1988, however, there is no distinction between the tax rates imposed on ordinary income and those on capital gains. But this seems likely to change in the near future.

Note

Congressional leaders and even the President have made repeated statements about the need to bring back a more favorable capital gains rate. Several bills have even been introduced to do just that. Sometime within the relatively near future, capital gains rates seem likely to come back.

Q: HOW IS THE TAX MEASURED ON
THE SALE OF A PROPRIETORSHIP?

A: The proprietor pays tax on the difference between the money and the value of any property received in exchange for the business assets and his basis in the assets.

Example

Floyd conducts a proprietorship that sells golfing equipment and supplies. Over the years, he has invested $300,000 in the business, but as a result of depreciation deductions taken on certain assets, his "adjusted basis" in the business assets is $225,000. When he sells the business to a competitor for $700,000, he has $475,000 of gain ($700,000 minus $225,000). This $475,000 is reported on his individual tax return.

Q: IS IT POSSIBLE TO COMBINE
TWO PROPRIETORSHIPS?

A: In a way. One proprietor can sell the assets he uses in a proprietorship to another proprietor. The buying proprietorship would get bigger and would continue, and the selling proprietorship would cease.

The other possibility is that the two proprietors would form a partnership, each contributing their respective assets. Both proprietorships would cease. So while proprietorships can be combined, there is no analog, for example, to a corporate merger.

PARTNERSHIPS

Q: WHAT HAPPENS WHEN A PARTNERSHIP
IS SOLD?

A: Here, the answer is more complex. There are at least two possibilities for accomplishing a cash sale. In one case, the partnership sells the business assets and each partner receives a share of the proceeds in accordance with his percentage partnership interest.

Example

Video Co., a partnership that produces videotapes, is sold to a conglomerate for $5 million. The partnership itself sells its assets and distributes the sales proceeds to the partners of the partnership in accordance with the percentage shares of the partners. Each individual partner then has gain or loss depending on how much that partner paid for his partnership interest. For example, if a partner paid $50,000 for his partnership interest and received sales proceeds of $250,000, then he has $200,000 of gain on the sale of the partnership assets.

Q: HOW ELSE COULD A PARTNERSHIP SALE BE STRUCTURED?

A: The other possibility is that the individual partners could sell their partnership interests to the buyer. The tax result to the individual partners would normally be the same as it would in a case where the partnership itself sells its assets. (See previous example.) Sometimes this type of transaction is favored by a buyer who wants to keep the partnership in existence.

However, this kind of partnership sale will usually not be motivated by tax considerations on the part of the buyer. Whenever 50 percent or more of the total partnership interests change hands during any 12-month period, the partnership is treated as "terminating" for tax purposes with a new partnership being formed thereafter.

Q: WHAT HAPPENS WHEN A PARTNERSHIP TERMINATES?

A: It is almost always a bad thing from a tax viewpoint. If there is any depreciation or investment tax credit recapture inherent in the assets, it will generally be taxed upon the termination. Depreciation methods terminate, the fiscal year is lost, and applicable tax elections are terminated.

When a partnership is being sold, termination may not be such a terrible result. But when some interests are simply being transferred, a termination is almost always something to be avoided. A termination occurs when 50 percent or more of the total partnership interests are transferred during any 12-month period.

Example

Albert, Barry, Claude, and Denise are equal partners (each owns 25 percent) in a partnership that operates a restaurant. Barry transfers his interest to an investor. Eleven months later, Denise transfers her interest to her daughter.

The partnership is considered to "terminate" upon this transfer by Denise, because 50 percent or more of the partnership interests have changed hands within a 12-month period. Note that it does not make any difference whether the transfer by Barry and Denise occurred in separate tax years (e.g., one in 1988 and one in 1989).

DJI Planning Guide

Because of the problems associated with the termination of a partnership, it is a good idea for businesses being conducted in the partnership form to maintain a current log of *any* transfers of partnership interests. In this way, the 50 percent threshold on transfers can be monitored. Although it may seem silly in the context of a simple example like the one above, transfers of partnership interests can be very confusing in the case of a large partnership with many partners (many of whom may be limited partners). The termination of a partnership rule draws no distinction between general partnership interests and limited partnership interests on this point.

Q: CAN PARTNERSHIPS BE COMBINED?

A: Yes. Normally, one partnership will terminate and become part of the other partnership.

Example

Partnership A has five partners conducting a consulting business. A competitor, Partnership B, has three partners. The two groups of partners agree to a "merger," with a new partnership name. From a tax standpoint, they can structure the transaction as the transfer of the Partnership A interests, a transfer of the Partnership B interests, or a transfer of both.

DJI Planning Guide

Because of the often adverse tax effects of a partnership termination, it is generally attractive to treat one of the partnerships as remaining in existence. In the above example, that means that one of the two partnerships would be acquired by the other. One would be treated as remaining in existence, and one would be treated as terminating.

CORPORATE MERGERS AND ACQUISITIONS

Q: WHAT HAPPENS IN A CORPORATE MERGER?

A: The term *merger* is often used loosely. Technically, it means that two or more corporate businesses are combined. The shareholders of both companies hold stock in only one company after the smoke clears.

There are several different ways in which these transactions are structured. A common scenario looks like this:

Example

Mom & Pop, Inc., operating a retail pharmacy, is approached by Chain Drug, Inc. The shareholders of Mom & Pop have a very low basis in their stock because they started the company 20 years ago with $5,000). Chain Drug has estimated the value of Mom & Pop at about $1 million. The shareholders of Mom & Pop do not really need the money currently and would prefer to receive marketable securities. Chain Drug therefore proposes to merge with Mom & Pop, with Mom & Pop disappearing in the merger. Each outstanding share of Mom & Pop, Inc. will be exchanged for a share in Chain Drug, Inc. in the merger.

The result is that the two companies are combined, and the shareholders of Mom & Pop end up owning shares in Chain Drug,

Inc. Note that the conversion of the shares is not necessarily done on a share-for-share basis. Depending on the relative values of the shares, each share of Mom & Pop might be worth 50 or 100 shares of Chain Drug, Inc. or vice versa. The result of the whole transaction is that there is no tax.

In diagram form, a simple merger looks like the sequence portrayed in Figure 9–1.

Q: DOES THIS KIND OF TAX-FREE MERGER REALLY WORK?

A: Yes, and these basic rules have not changed too much in many years. Of course, keep in mind that in the preceding example, the shareholders of Mom & Pop will still have to pay a tax someday. If they had only a $5,000 basis in their shares in Mom & Pop, Inc., they will also have only a $5,000 basis

FIGURE 9–1

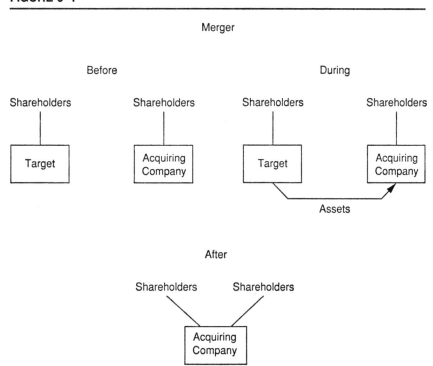

Merger

in their shares in Chain Drug, Inc. However, they can choose *when* to dispose of the shares in Chain Drug, for what price, and over what period of time.

Q: ARE THERE ANY LIMITATIONS ON THE USE OF THIS KIND OF TAX-FREE ACQUISITION?

A: Yes, most definitely. In fact, there are many restrictions that make the area of so-called "corporate reorganizations" one of the most complex areas in the tax law. For example, the parties to the reorganization must have a continuing interest in the surviving entity. This is usually called the "continuity of interest" requirement. If the shareholders of Mom & Pop in the above example were to dispose of all of their stock in Chain Drug, Inc. shortly after the transaction, there would be no continuity of interest, and the transaction probably would not qualify as a tax-free reorganization.

Note

If Mom & Pop's shareholders disposed of half of their stock in Chain Drug, there would still likely be continuity of interest, but the sale of the shares would, of course, produce taxable gain.

There is also a requirement that in a tax-free reorganization, the acquiring corporation must acquire a controlling stock interest in (or substantially all of the assets of) the acquired corporation. In a merger, this acquisition really happens automatically, but in other types of reorganizations this requirement must be met.

These and various other technical requirements must be observed for a reorganization to be tax-free.

Q: HOW IS A STOCK SALE OF A COMPANY TAXED?

A: One alternative to a tax-free reorganization is simply a taxable sale of the stock. To follow along with our example of Mom & Pop, a taxable stock sale would look like this:

Example

The shareholders of Mom & Pop, Inc. have a basis in their Mom & Pop stock of $5,000. They are offered $1 million for their stock by Chain Drug, Inc., a major retailer. If they sell their stock, they will have a capital gain of $995,000. Note that under the current tax rate structure, this gain is taxed at up to 28 percent, so there is no longer any tax rate benefit for capital gain treatment.

Q: WHAT HAPPENS IF THE COMPANY SELLS ITS OWN STOCK INSTEAD OF THE SHAREHOLDERS SELLING THEIRS?

A: If the company sells its stock to the acquiring company, it is possible that the acquiring company will gain control over the acquired entity. In order to "cash-out" the existing shareholders, however, it is necessary to have the stock of the existing shareholder repurchased by the company. This process is known as a "redemption." The transaction goes something like this:

Example

Mom & Pop, Inc. issues new stock to Chain Drug, Inc. for $1 million. Afterward, Mom & Pop, Inc. "redeems" (buys back) the stock in Mom & Pop, Inc. held by Mom & Pop's old shareholders for $1 million. The tax result to the shareholders of Mom & Pop is exactly the same as in the preceding example. The shareholders of Mom & Pop had a basis in their Mom & Pop stock of $5,000 and received $1 million for it. So their taxable gain is $995,000.

Q: IF THE ACQUIRING CORPORATION DOES PURCHASE STOCK, HOW IS THE PURCHASE TREATED TO THE BUYER?

A: Since the buyer is buying stock for cash, the buyer will have a basis in the stock of whatever the purchase price is. The assets of the acquired company, in turn, will have the same basis as they did prior to the acquisition. The only exception to this tax treatment occurs when the buyer elects to have its purchase of stock treated as a purchase of assets for tax purposes.

Q: HOW IS THIS ELECTION MADE?

A: If a corporate purchaser buys a controlling stock interest in another company, it may then elect (by filing an election with the IRS) to have the stock purchase treated for tax purposes as an asset purchase. This election is normally made when the buyer wishes to have its higher purchase price of the stock apply to the assets so that the assets can be depreciated. There is a variety of very complex requirements and qualifications applying to such elections. While this election was sometimes very desirable in the past, it is not very attractive since the 1986 Tax Reform Act.

Q: WHY IS THIS ELECTION NO LONGER ATTRACTIVE?

A: Because when a corporation makes such an election, the appreciation in the corporation's assets are now taxed to the corporation. The election results in a "step-up" in the basis in the assets of the acquired company to reflect the higher purchase price for the stock, so that the buyer can obtain larger depreciation deductions. However, to achieve this "step-up," the acquired company is treated as having sold its assets for the price paid for the stock.

This means that a corporate-level tax is imposed on the company and will be factored into the price the purchaser is willing to pay—reducing the purchase price.

Example

Acquirer, Inc. purchases all of the outstanding stock of Target Co. for $1 million. Target Co. has real estate assets with an adjusted basis of $100,000. Acquirer wishes to depreciate the real estate based on its $1 million purchase price for the stock. Accordingly, Acquirer makes an election (a *Section 338 election*) to treat its purchase price for the stock as the price paid for the assets of Target Co. The result is that Target Co. is taxed on the difference between its basis in the assets ($100,000) and the purchase price ($1 million). Accordingly, Acquirer can get its "step-up" in basis of the assets of Target Co., but it has to pay a price (in the form of a tax) for doing so. This tax can be paid by either the buyer or the Seller, but it obviously would affect the purchase price paid for the stock.

Q: APART FROM STOCK SALES AND REDEMPTIONS, IS THERE ANY OTHER WAY OF STRUCTURING A TAXABLE SALE?

A: Yes, a company can sell its assets. Mom & Pop, Inc. could sell all of its assets to the purchasing company. In fact, for non-tax reasons (as well as some tax reasons), acquiring companies often prefer to purchase assets rather than stock.

Q: WHY WOULD A COMPANY PREFER TO PURCHASE ASSETS RATHER THAN STOCK?

A: The state law reasons for this are simply that when a company purchases stock, it acquires all of the liabilities and obligations of the company. When it purchases the assets, however, it is still really acquiring a going business (at least if it purchases all of the assets used in the business), but it is not treated as acquiring the corporate entity in which the business was conducted. It therefore can normally escape many of the corporate liabilities that may be attached to the existing corporate entity. For this reason, a buyer most frequently approaches a business and offers to purchase assets rather than to purchase stock.

DJI Planning Guide

For nontax reasons, a buyer is almost always well advised to attempt to buy assets rather than stock. Even if the acquisition agreements contain extensive representations and warranties from the seller of stock that there are no unknown or undisclosed liabilities, it is still generally safer from the buyer's perspective to purchase assets.

Q: ARE THERE ANY TAX REASONS TO PREFER AN ASSETS PURCHASE?

A: Yes. A Buyer normally prefers to purchase assets in order to take advantage of a high purchase price "basis" in the assets with corresponding high depreciation deductions. Although it is possible for companies to buy stock in a target company and then make an election with the IRS to treat the stock purchase as an assets purchase (this is the so-called Section 338 election discussed above), there is some cost to doing so.

Q: HOW IS AN ASSET PURCHASE/SALE TAXED?

A: The corporation itself sells the assets, so it is taxable on any gain. The gain is measured by the difference between the price received for the assets and the corporation's adjusted basis in those assets. The corporation will normally then liquidate, distributing the sales proceeds to its shareholders.

Example

Smallco sells all of its assets to Conglomerate for $1 million. Smallco acquired its various assets (primarily machinery and equipment) over a number of years and has depreciated the assets to an adjusted basis of $200,000. Accordingly, Smallco realizes an $800,000 gain and must pay tax on this gain. Any resulting sales proceeds after paying the tax can be distributed to the shareholders of Smallco.

Q: ARE THE SALES PROCEEDS TAXED IN THE HANDS OF THE SHAREHOLDERS AS WELL?

A: Yes, and this makes for a true "double taxation." However, under the current rules governing corporate liquidations (which are discussed in Chapter 12), the same kind of double taxation results when a corporation merely distributes its assets to its shareholders. The corporation pays a tax based on the difference between the current market value of the assets and their adjusted basis, and the shareholders pay another tax on top of that.

Q: HOW IS THE SHAREHOLDER TAX CALCULATED?

A: The shareholders will always pay a tax based on the difference between the amount they receive and their basis in their shares.

Example

Sam purchased his stock in Corner News, Inc. for an investment of $10,000. The Corner News company has a basis in its assets (a newsstand and several contract rights to distribute newspapers) of $20,000. Corner News sells all of its assets to Big News, Inc. for $100,000. Corner News, Inc. has a gain of $80,000 and must pay tax on that gain. The remaining sales proceeds (let's assume $15,000 in tax is paid, so the remainder of the $100,000 sales price after taxes is $85,000) are distributed out to Sam. Sam has a taxable gain of $75,000 ($85,000 minus his $10,000 basis).

Q: WHEN ARE TAX-FREE REORGANIZATIONS CONSIDERED?

A: It should be obvious from the above discussion of stock sales and asset sales that tax-free reorganizations are resorted to primarily as a means of avoiding income taxes. The economic benefits of an acquisition to the owner of the business being acquired can rapidly be depleted by a large tax bill. That is why cases like the Mom & Pop, Inc. reorganization with Chain Drug, Inc. described earlier occur daily.

One big reason reorganizations occur is the available tax losses or "net operating losses" of a corporation that another corporation may wish to acquire. This topic is discussed extensively in Chapter 11.

Q: WHAT ARE THE TYPES OF TAX-FREE REORGANIZATIONS?

A: There are a number of types of tax-free reorganizations, the most important of which are listed below.

- A **statutory merger or consolidation** (a merger pursuant to the laws of any state under which two companies are combined into one).
- A **stock-for-stock acquisition** (in which one company uses part of its stock to exchange for the stock of the other company).
- A **stock-for-assets acquisition** (in which one company uses its stock to swap for the assets of another corporation).
- An **assets-for-stock acquisition** (in which one company uses all or part of its assets to swap for the stock of another corporation).
- A **recapitalization** (in which one company reorganizes itself by issuing different stock and debt instruments).

Q: WHAT IS A STOCK-FOR-STOCK ACQUISITION?

A: An example of a stock-for-stock acquisition is set forth below.

Example

Bernard's Bikes, Inc. is a corporation owned entirely by Bernard. Bigbikeco wishes to buy out Bernard's shop and makes the following proposition. Bigbikeco will swap a small percentage of its voting common stock for all of the outstanding stock of Bernard's Bikes, Inc. After the acquisition, Bigbikeco will operate Bernard's Bikes, Inc. as a wholly owned subsidiary, and Bernard will own a small percentage of the outstanding stock of Bigbikeco. This transaction qualifies as a "stock-for-stock" acquisition and is therefore tax-free.

A diagram of a stock-for-stock acquisition appears in Figure 9–2.

FIGURE 9–2

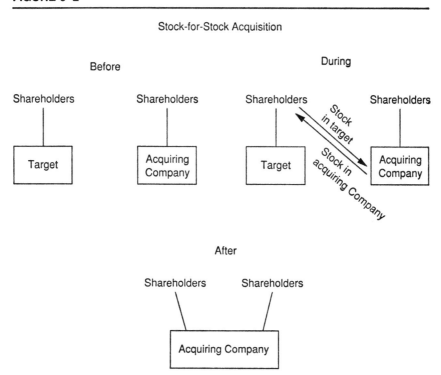

Stock-for-Stock Acquisition

Q: COULD THIS ALSO QUALIFY AS A STATUTORY MERGER?

A: No, not in this example. In this example, Bernard's Bikes, Inc. would still be operated as a wholly owned subsidiary. If as part of the transaction Bigbikeco merged Barnard's Bikes into itself so that Bernard's Bike disappeared, then the transaction would also qualify as a statutory merger. It could, in effect, have two different grounds upon which to support its tax-free treatment.

A stock-for-stock acquisition can frequently also qualify as a statutory merger. There is often overlap between the various reorganization provisions, although the IRS has a partial system of priority rules to handle such circumstances.

Q: WHAT IS A STOCK-FOR-ASSETS ACQUISITION?

A: A stock-for-assets acquisition takes place when the acquiring corporation offers stock for the assets of the target corporation. (The corporation to be acquired is often called a *target* in the context of acquisitions.) A stock-for-assets acquisition might look like the following example.

Example

Largeco wishes to acquire Smallco, which operates retail grocery stores. Largeco is concerned about the liabilities that Smallco may have (for labor law matters, toxic wastes, back taxes, slip and fall claims, etc.). Accordingly, Largeco proposes to use its voting common stock to "buy" all of the assets of Smallco. Smallco will then take this consideration it receives (voting common stock in Largeco) and distribute it out to its shareholders in liquidation. The result is that the Smallco shareholders end up owning shares in Largeco, and Largeco ends up owning the assets of Smallco.

A diagram of a stock-for-assets acquisition appears in Figure 9–3.

FIGURE 9–3

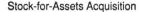

Stock-for-Assets Acquisition

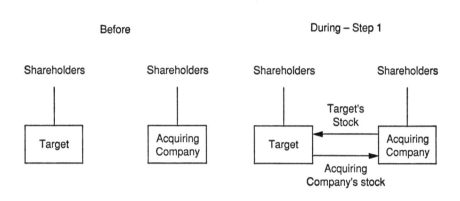

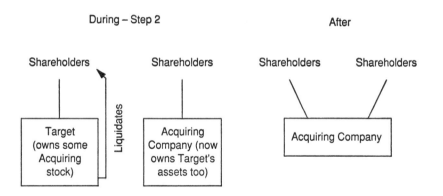

Q: WHAT IS AN ASSETS-FOR-STOCK ACQUISITION?

A: An assets-for-stock acquisition involves the transfer of assets to the target corporation in exchange for a controlling stock interest in the targct. The transaction might look like this:

Example

Largeco wishes to acquire Smallco. Largeco has several pieces of real property that are unneeded for its operations, and they are desirable to the owners of Smallco. Accordingly, Largeco transfers these pieces of real property to Smallco in exchange for stock. Once Largeco obtains control of Smallco, Largeco causes Smallco to distribute the stock of Smallco to Largeco.

A diagram of an assets-for-stock acquisition appears in Figure 9–4.

FIGURE 9–4

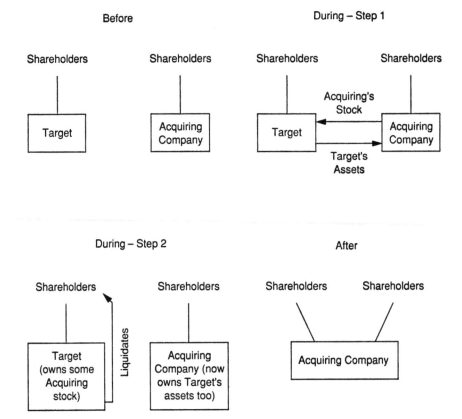

Stock-for-Assets Acquisition

Q: WHAT IS RECAPITALIZATION?

A: A recapitalization is not an acquisition technique but a type of tax-free reorganization. It is basically a reshuffling of the corporation's capital structure within the corporation's existing framework. For example, a "recapitalization" occurs when a corporation discharges its outstanding bond indebtedness by a transfer of its own preferred stock to its shareholders in exchange for the bonds.

Recapitalizations are most frequently accomplished with closely held corporations for estate planning reasons. With publicly held corporations, recapitalizations may be accomplished when a reshuffling of the debt and equity of the corporation is either necessary to improve the corporation's financial statement or would help the corporation meet its obligations.

Q: WHY WOULD A RECAPITALIZATION BE UNDERTAKEN FOR ESTATE PLANNING PURPOSES?

A: Traditionally, there have been very good reasons. A recapitalization in this context was often called an *estate freeze*. Basically, the traditional estate freeze transaction went something like the following example.

Example

Mom and Dad own 75 percent of the stock of Entrepreneur, Inc., with the other 25 percent being held by Junior. Getting on in years, Mom and Dad now want to transfer control of the business to Junior. They are also concerned that the business is going to continue to rise in value during their lifetimes, and they want to limit the value of the assets that will be included within their estate for federal estate tax purposes. They accordingly propose to "freeze" the value of their stock in the corporation.

How is this done? Instead of merely having one class of stock, the corporation issues two classes of stock: a class of preferred stock that Mom and Dad will own (they exchanged their common shares for the new preferred) and a class of common shares that Junior will own. The stock is structured so that all of the future appreciation in the value of the company will be accruing to the benefit of the common shares. Thus, the value of the stock that will be includable in the estate of Mom and Dad when they die is limited.

Q: DOES THIS PROCEDURE WORK?

A: Not any more. Except in rather limited circumstances, this technique was largely eliminated by the Revenue Act of 1987. Recapitalizations still do occur, but the most commonplace use of them, the so-called "estate freeze," has been all but eliminated.

Q: WHAT IS A LEVERAGED BUYOUT?

A: The popular name **leveraged buyout** (or LBO) refers simply to a purchase of a company using someone else's money. The "leverage" comes from borrowing, specifically borrowing against the assets and future cash flow of the business being acquired. The object of a leveraged buyout is obviously to gain control of the target company and typically to do so with as little cash investment as possible.

Q: HOW CAN A COMPANY BE ACQUIRED WITH FUNDS BORROWED AGAINST THAT SAME COMPANY'S ASSETS?

A: The leveraged buyout, when viewed from this perspective, does seem to defy logic. Basically, the lender lends against the strength of the assets of the company being purchased and against the future cash flow of the acquired business. It may seem that lenders would be unwilling to lend against this kind of security. But lenders are willing to do so because of the expected future income stream to be derived from the business.

In some respects, a leveraged buyout of a corporation can be compared to a real estate sale in which most of the purchase price comes in the form of mortgage financing. The leveraged buyout lender is really lending against the security of the business and its future cash flow in the same way that a real estate mortgage lender is lending against the security of (and in the case of commercial property, income from) the real estate.

Q: WHEN IS A LEVERAGED BUYOUT ATTRACTIVE?

A: The main appeal of a leveraged buyout is simply that it enables a buyer to purchase a corporation with a minimal cash investment. The cash investment may be as small as 5 percent, with the balance coming in the form of a loan or "leverage."

Q: WHAT ARE THE DISADVANTAGES OF A LEVERAGED BUYOUT?

A: The primary disadvantage is that the acquired company is instantly saddled with what may be an enormous debt. This is good in that it gives the management a tremendous incentive to operate efficiently in order that loan payments can be made on schedule. However, it is bad in the sense that sometimes the leverage is too great and the payments simply cannot be made. Even if the cash invested in the business is modest in relationship to the debt, this may be a bitter pill to swallow if the business goes under.

DJI Planning Guide

The debt on a leveraged buyout is often structured so that payments increase over time, the intent being to allow the company to stabilize without being burdened with large loan payments. However, the disadvantage of this method of debt structuring is that if the company's earnings do not accelerate at least as quickly as the loan payments, then the debt could become cancerous after the period of a few years. Still, some scaling of debt repayment is generally a good idea since it will give the company time to get back on its feet.

Q: ARE THERE ANY OTHER DISADVANTAGES TO LEVERAGED BUYOUTS?

A: Since LBOs allow a buyer to acquire a company with a minimal cash investment, an LBO may seem to be the perfect solution for any acquisition. However, LBOs work only when the cash flow from the target is likely to be sufficient to make the debt payments. This means that an LBO should not be considered when there are tremendous price fluctuations in the industry or when a steady and relatively certain cash flow cannot be expected.

A related disadvantage of leveraged buyouts is simply the degree of risk. Since one critical feature is that the buyer ends up owning the assets and business of the target directly, the buyer will by definition be liable for the loan payments as well. Consider the following example.

Example

Midgetco is an efficient microcomputer company with sales of $10 million annually. Its management team is top notch. It plans to acquire its biggest competitor, Smallco, which has sales of $50 million. Accordingly, with $45 million in loaned funds and $5 million in cash, it buys all of the assets of Smallco and begins operating the two companies together. Under the terms of the debt instruments, loan payments on the $45 million loan needed to purchase the assets of Smallco are payable monthly. If Midgetco cannot keep making payments, it will probably lose the assets it acquired plus perhaps its own (original) assets.

Q: WHAT ARE THE TAX IMPLICATIONS OF A LEVERAGED BUYOUT?

A: The success of a leveraged buyout depends on the fact that interest payments paid on the debt used to finance the acquisition are deductible. There is generally very little question about the deductibility of the interest payments since the loan or loans will be from an independent lender and will almost certainly be commercially negotiated.

Q: WHAT FORM CAN A LEVERAGED BUYOUT TAKE?

A: The three most common structures for an LBO are these:

• The buyer purchases the assets and all the business of the target.
• The buyer purchases the stock of the target and then merges with the target.
• The buyer and the target merge, but there is no purchase of stock or assets.

In each case, one basic goal is to ensure that the buyer ends up owning the assets and business of the target directly. The basic scenarios may also involve the use of holding companies and/or subsidiaries.

EMPLOYEE STOCK OWNERSHIP PLANS

Q: HOW CAN AN EMPLOYEE STOCK OWNERSHIP PLAN BE USED IN AN ACQUISITION?

A: The **employee stock ownership plan** (or ESOP) has become very popular in recent years in a limited class of acquisition circumstances. An ESOP is a type of pension plan that is designed to invest in securities of the employer that establishes the plan. An ESOP is specifically allowed to invest in employer stock. Other types of qualified pension plans are very restricted in the type and amount of the stock investments they may make under the Employee Retirement Income Security Act of 1974 ("ERISA").

An ESOP makes an attractive vehicle for buying a whole company.

Q: HOW DOES AN ESOP ACQUISITION WORK?

A: The transaction would go something like this:

Example

Merchandising, Inc. has five major shareholders who wish to sell out. Instead of selling to an outside company (an outside buyer may even be unavailable), Merchandising, Inc. establishes an ESOP to buy its own securities. The ESOP purchases the stock of the company from the five shareholders with borrowed funds. The ESOP is obligated to repay the borrowed cash over time. So that the ESOP can make these loan payments, the company makes dividend payments to the ESOP until the loan is paid off. The ESOP is then the real owner of the company, and the employees who are participants in the ESOP are the beneficial owners of the business.

Q: DOES THIS TYPE OF TRANSACTION REALLY WORK?

A: Yes, and it has become very popular in recent years. Many of the widely publicized "employee buyouts" are really ESOP buyouts.

Q: WHY DO THE SELLERS OF STOCK WANT TO SELL AN ESOP?

A: One obvious incentive is that when there is not another buyer immediately available, an ESOP serves as a ready purchaser. The second reason is that the existing management (which might include the selling stockholders) can remain in place following an ESOP stock purchase, whereas they would not typically remain in place if an independent buyer came in and bought the stock.

A third reason, and a very significant one, is the tax benefits that flow to the seller of stock who sells to an ESOP.

Q: WHAT ARE THE TAX BENEFITS TO THE SELLER IN AN ESOP SALE?

A: The seller who sells stock to an ESOP gets a tremendous tax advantage, provided that some technical requirements are met. Basically, the shareholder who sells stock to an ESOP is allowed to reinvest the sales proceeds in stock in publicly traded companies without incurring a tax on the sale to the ESOP. It works like this:

Example

Sam Senior sells all of his stock in Smallco to the ESOP he established for employees. Sam originally purchased the stock 25 years ago for $50,000, and the price paid by the ESOP is $2 million. Accordingly, Sam has almost a $2 million gain. If he meets certain requirements, however, Sam can purchase securities in public companies with the entire $2 million sales price and *defer* the recognition of gain on the sale.

Although he pays $2 million for the substitute securities, he will get only a $50,000 basis in them (the same basis he had in his Smallco stock). When Sam ultimately sells the securities in the public companies (which may be over time and in a variety of installments), he will recognize the gain at that time. Since his basis in these public company securities will be only $50,000, all of the gain will be inherent in those securities.

Q: WHAT REQUIREMENTS MUST BE MET IN ORDER FOR THIS REINVESTMENT TO BE AVAILABLE?

A: To begin with, the taxpayer must file an election with the IRS electing not to currently pay tax on the gain on the sale of the stock to the ESOP.

Secondly, the taxpayer must purchase **qualified replacement property** within a specified period. The period commences 3 months *before* the date of the sale of the ESOP and ends 12 months after the sale. Qualified replacement property includes any securities issues by a domestic corporation that meet certain tests.

Example

Sam sells his stock to an ESOP on March 31, 1988. The replacement period under which he may acquire stock in other companies and defer recognizing the gain on the sale of his stock to the ESOP commences on December 31, 1987, and ends on March 31, 1989. Thus, Sam could actually *anticipate* the sale of the ESOP by beginning to make purchases of qualified securities prior to the date the sale to the ESOP occurs.

Q: BUT WHAT CONSTITUTES A QUALIFIED SECURITY ELIGIBLE FOR REINVESTMENT?

A: Any security issued by a domestic corporation that qualifies as an "operating corporation" and that meets certain income tests.

The "operating corporation" portion of the definition requires that the corporation have more than 50 percent of its assets devoted to the active conduct of a trade or business. What the rules are trying to prevent here is the purchase of securities in a holding company that does not conduct an active business.

Q: WHAT ARE THE INCOME TESTS?

A: As to the income tests that the corporation must meet, the corporation that issues the securities cannot have more than 25 percent of its gross receipts from the previous taxable year attributable to passive investment income. Here again, the rules are designed to prevent investing in a mere holding company that produces primarily dividends, interest, and similar types of passive income.

Various technical rules apply to insure that securities issued by a corporation that appears to be an operating company are not really holding company securities in disguise. For example, in applying the active business assets tests and the income test referred to above, groups of controlled corporations are aggregated. They are all looked at together in order to determine whether more than 50 percent of their assets is used in the active conduct of a trade or business, and in order to determine whether more than 25 percent of their gross receipts is from passive investment income.

DJI Planning Guide _____

Aside from these technicalities, the qualified replacement property rule allows the seller of stock to an ESOP to go into the marketplace and purchase a portfolio of securities, thus shielding the gain on the ESOP sale from gain recognition. Most publicly traded companies will satisfy *both* the operating assets test and the noninvestment income test, so these limitations should simply not be a problem in the ordinary case.

Moreover, there is even a special exception under which the 50 percent active business assets rule does not apply to financial institutions. Thus, in addition to buying stock in public companies, the seller of stock to an ESOP can purchase stock in banks, savings and loans associations, and life insurance companies. All in all, the ESOP reinvestment rules are extremely favorable and certainly serve as an incentive to make an ESOP sale.

_____

Q: CAN ALL OF THE REINVESTMENT OCCUR PRIOR TO THE SALE TO THE ESOP?

A: Yes. Since the reinvestment period begins 3 months *before* the sale to the ESOP and ends 12 months after the sale to the ESOP, all of the replacement stock (into which the ESOP stock sale proceeds are deemed to apply) could be purchased prior to the sale of stock to the ESOP.

Q: ARE THERE ANY OTHER REQUIREMENTS THAT APPLY TO THIS KIND OF ESOP SALE?

A: Yes, there is one additional significant requirement. In order for the seller of stock to an ESOP to qualify for the kind of tax-free reinvestment described above, after the sale occurs the ESOP must hold at least 30 percent of the corporation's stock. Normally, this restriction is not a problem since sales to

ESOPs are most commonly made when a person or small group of people owns all or nearly all of the outstanding stock of the corporation.

Q: ARE THERE ANY DRAWBACKS TO THE ESOP BUYOUT METHOD?

A: Yes. One problem is the sensitivity of determining the purchase price for the stock. Since ESOP buyouts are used most frequently when there is no other ready source of a purchaser, it sometimes becomes difficult to determine what the "market value" of the stock is for purposes of determining sales price.

The market value is especially important since the ESOP is really for the benefit of employees, and the employer is a fiduciary of the employees. As a fiduciary, the employer is held to a high standard of care to make sure employees are treated fairly. This means that the employer must be very careful not to cause the shareholder to sell the stock to the ESOP for an inflated price. All valuations must generally be made by an independent appraiser unless the stock is publicly traded.

In an ESOP sale, there is also typically some loss of control for existing management. However, considering the alternative of a sale to an independent third party, the continued control aspects are normally better with an ESOP sale.

DJI Planning Guide _____

Sales to an ESOP are most frequently used when there is no other ready purchaser for the stock. However, they are certainly not limited to this context. Particularly with the owners of a closely held business who wish to take advantage of the favorable rules governing the reinvestment in public company securities of the sales proceeds they receive on the sale of stock to an ESOP, the possibility of an ESOP sale can be very attractive indeed.

CHAPTER 10

CORPORATE DIVISIONS AND PARTIAL LIQUIDATIONS

INTRODUCTION

Most of the focus in the merger and acquisition arena today is on combinations (rather than divestitures) of businesses. But this is certainly not the only area of substantial activity today. In fact, many companies today are becoming selective about the businesses they conduct. Companies that operate many businesses are evaluating which lines they run efficiently and profitably and which they do not. The trend of a few years ago toward increasingly large conglomerates conducting many businesses seems now to be reversed.

In a corporate division or so-called **divisive reorganization**, a business is divided into several parts, either entirely or partially on a tax-free basis. A corporate division may be desirable in a number of different circumstances. For example, a corporation may be divided to facilitate a planned disposition of one of two businesses being conducted through one corporation. After a division, one of the two businesses might be merged with another enterprise, tax-free.

A corporation division might also be desirable to shield the assets of one business from the risks and creditors of the other. There also may be legal reasons for a division. A corporation may be required by a court or government order to divide its businesses among different groups of shareholders pursuant to the antitrust laws, federal banking laws, or other regulatory schemes.

A corporate division may also be desirable to resolve differences among shareholders, employees, and other involved parties. A corporate division can leave one group of shareholders conducting one business and another group of shareholders conducting another.

The tax-free nature of these divisions is of critical importance. In most cases, if the distribution of stock in one of the entities (the manner in which a division is usually accomplished) is taxable, then the result will be disastrous: There will be large taxes to pay, perhaps with no cash to pay them.

Instead of dividing the business and operating both parts separately, it may be desirable to constrict the operations of the business and distribute cash and/or property to shareholders. This general procedure is known as a **partial liquidation**. A "complete liquidation," on the other hand, involves a total cessation of the business (at least in the corporate form) rather than a constriction of the business or contraction of product or service lines. (Complete liquidations are discussed in Chapter 12.)

There are two primary tax consequences of a partial liquidation, one at the corporate level, and one at the shareholder level. The goal of most partial liquidations from a business standpoint is to cease conducting a particular activity and to sell or distribute to shareholders the assets used in that activity.

From a tax standpoint, the goal is frequently to get as much cash in the hands of the shareholders with as little tax as possible. This has become more difficult since the 1986 Tax Reform Act.

CORPORATE DIVISIONS

Q: WHAT IS THE BASIC GOAL OF A CORPORATE DIVISION?

A: The basic goal is to separate a corporate business into two parts without tax consequences. The separation into two parts is quite simple, since one portion of the business could obviously be sold. It is accomplishing the division without incurring a large tax that is the tricky part.

Q: WHAT WOULD HAPPEN IF ONE OF THE BUSINESSES WERE SOLD?

A: If the assets of one business are sold, the corporate seller will pay a tax based on the difference between the sales price and its basis in the assets. Then, if the sales proceeds are paid out to shareholders, there will be a tax on the shareholders as well.

Example

Microslump conducts a microchip manufacturing business and a computer servicing business. In the face of sagging microchip sales, it sells its microchip division for $5 million. It has a basis of $1 million in its microchip assets, so it has a taxable gain of $4 million. Microslump then distributes the remainder of the sales proceeds (assume there is $3.7 million left of the $5 million after taxes) to the shareholders. They also pay a tax based on the difference between their basis in their shares and the amount of cash they receive.

Q: WHAT ARE THE BASIC REQUIREMENTS OF A TAX-FREE CORPORATE DIVISION?

A: The basic conditions are these:

• The corporation must own (or create) a subsidiary, of which it must own at least 80 percent, to hold the business to be separated; and it cannot have acquired control of the business to be separated within the five years prior to the distribution.

• The separation must be supported by a valid business reason and must not be a device to distribute earnings and profits (more about this important requirement later).

• Both the retained and the transferred business must have been actively conducted for at least five years prior to the separation, and it must be actively conducted immediately after the distribution (more later about this requirement, too).

• Stock and securities of the controlled corporation holding the business to be separated must be distributed to the shareholders.

• The shareholders must maintain an ongoing economic interest in the business enterprise.

These requirements are discussed in more detail below.

Q: WHAT ARE THE BASIC TYPES OF CORPORATE DIVISIONS?

A: There are three basic types of corporate divisions that are subject to these rules. They are commonly known as "spin-offs," "split-offs," and "split-ups." The basic distinctions are as follows.

• *Spin-off.* In a spin-off, the parent corporation distributes stock in its subsidiary to the parent's shareholders. The parent's shareholders need not surrender any stock in the parent. Before the transaction, the parent's shareholders hold stock in one company (the parent). The parent, in turn, holds stock in the subsidiary. After the transaction, the parent's shareholders own the shares of the subsidiary directly (in addition to owning shares in the parent).

• *Split-off.* In a split-off, the parent distributes its stock in a subsidiary to some or all of the shareholders of the parent. In exchange, the parent's shareholders surrender to the parent some or all of their shares in the parent corporation. Before the transaction, the shareholders of the parent own the stock in the parent, and the parent, in turn, owns stock in the subsidiary. After the transaction, the shareholders of the parent own shares of stock directly in the subsidiary, but the new subsidiary's shareholders may no longer own shares in the parent.

• *Split-up.* In a split-up, the parent corporation distributes stock in two or more of the parent's subsidiaries to its own shareholders. The parent corporation winds up its affairs and liquidates, distributing its stock in the subsidiaries. Before the transaction, the stock in the parent is held by the shareholders, and the parent owns the stock of two or more subsidiaries. After the transaction, the parent is liquidated completely, and the former parent shareholders will now own shares in the subsidiaries directly.

Q: ARE THESE THREE TRANSACTIONS REALLY DIFFERENT?

A: Yes, although they are obviously related. It is easier to see the variations in diagrams. Consult Figures 10–1, 10–2, and 10–3.

FIGURE 10–1

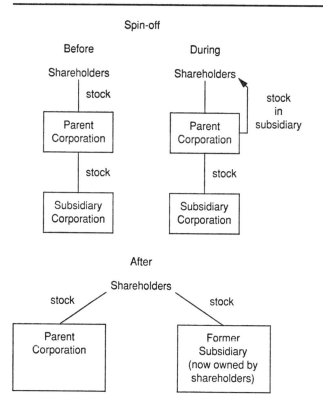

FIGURE 10–2

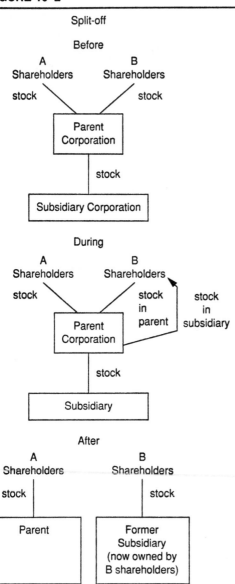

Split-off

Before

During

After

Q: HOW ARE THESE RULES USED IN BUSINESS?

A: Probably the most common division is the "split-off." Basically, when some of the shareholders of a corporation desire

FIGURE 10–3

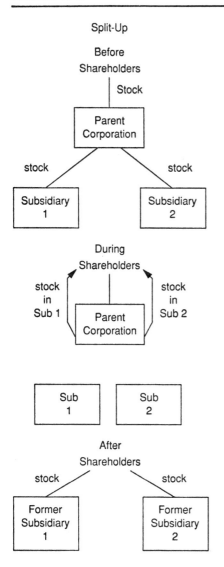

Split-Up

Before
Shareholders

to conduct one business, while others desire to conduct another business, the two corporations can be separated with the groups of shareholders going their separate ways. A spin-off transaction frequently goes something like this:

Example

Al, Burt, and Claude each hold one-third of the stock in Smallco. Smallco conducts two businesses, a construction business in Illinois and a construction business in Florida. Now Claude wishes to conduct the business in Florida only, and Al and Burt are amenable to dividing the business in this way.

Accordingly, Smallco incorporates its Florida construction business as a subsidiary (called Constructiflorida). Since Claude is the shareholder who wishes to conduct the Florida business, Smallco makes a distribution of its Constructiflorida stock to Claude. In exchange, Claude turns in his Smallco stock. Al and Burt now own the stock in Smallco, and Claude owns the stock in Constructiflorida. The result is a tax-free "divisive" reorganization.

Q: HOW IS A SPIN-OFF DIFFERENT?

A: In a spin-off, the shareholders of the corporation end up owning stock in two corporations.

Example

Al, Burt, and Claude each hold stock in their construction corporation. The corporation conducts two businesses, one in Florida and one in Illinois. In order to insulate each business from the potential claims of the other, they form a subsidiary into which they transfer one of the businesses. The parent distributes the stock in the subsidiary to Al, Burt, and Claude. Al, Burt, and Claude now hold stock in the subsidiary directly as well as continuing to hold stock in the parent.

Q: WHAT REQUIREMENTS APPLY TO TAX-FREE CORPORATE DIVISIONS?

A: For the three basic types of corporate divisions (spin-offs, split-offs, and split-ups), there are common requirements. One of the most important is the requirement that the two businesses be actively conducted for five years prior to the division.

Another requirement is that the division of the business must be motivated by a valid business purpose.

Q: IS IT NECESSARY FOR BOTH BUSINESSES TO BE ACTIVELY CONDUCTED FOR FIVE YEARS?

A: Yes, and this requirement cannot be waived. Even one day short of a full five years of active conduct of business for *either* of the businesses will cause the transaction *not* to qualify as tax-free.

Note

The "five-year active business" test first necessitates that there are *two* businesses. There must be two businesses, and both must be actively conducted for a period of at least five years.

Q: WHAT CONSTITUTES A "BUSINESS"?

A: Passive investments do not qualify as the active conduct of a trade or business. For example, holding stock and securities may generate income, but it is not an active trade or business. Even someone who actively trades in stock and securities and considers himself a dealer may have a hard time qualifying his activities as a trade or business, since a high standard has traditionally been applied to these activities.

With real estate, the mere holding of investment property also does not constitute the conduct of a trade or business. However, actively leasing property and managing it does constitute a trade or business.

Q: DOES REAL ESTATE LEASING ALWAYS QUALIFY AS AN ACTIVE BUSINESS?

A: No. It really depends on the degree and scope of the real estate activity. Since real estate activities are common in many types of business organizations, businesses frequently inquire whether they may separate their real estate activities from the rest of the business.

Consider the following example:

Example

A bank owns a two-story building. It occupies the ground floor and one-half of the second floor in its banking business and leases the balance of the second floor as storage space to a neighboring retail merchant. The bank now wishes to transfer the building to a new corporation and distribute the stock of the new corporation to the bank's shareholders (thus conducting a tax-free divisive reorganization). However, this real estate activity is not considered sufficient to be a separate trade or business (since it is merely incidental to its banking business). Consequently, the reorganization would not be tax-free.

Q: BUT DOES THIS MEAN THAT *NO* REAL ESTATE OPERATIONS CAN EVER BE CONSIDERED A SEPARATE TRADE OR BUSINESS?

A: No, it does not. It is simply a question of degree. Compare this example:

Example

A banks owns an 11-story office building. It operates only the ground floor in its banking business and leases the remaining 10 floors to various tenants. The bank's real estate department rents, manages, and maintains the 10 rented floors. The bank now wishes to transfer the building to a new corporation and distribute the stock of the corporation to its shareholders (thus establishing a tax-free corporate division).

The corporation's banking activities are one trade or business, and its real estate leasing activities constitute another. Consequently, as long as both businesses have been actively conducted for at least five years, the division will be tax-free.

DJI Planning Guide _____

Because of the desirability of a tax-free division and the difficulty with real estate activities constituting an active business, some corporations have actually beefed up their real estate activities to try to be closer to this example than the previous example!

Q: IS IT EVER POSSIBLE TO DIVIDE TWO ASPECTS OF *ONE* BUSINESS?

A: Yes, it is. Although the general requirement is that there must be *two* trades or businesses, each of which must be actively conducted for at least five years, it is possible in some cases to divide *one* business. The most common example is a business conducted in two separate areas.

Example

A corporation manufactures and sells ice cream in two separate states. It can divide its business into two corporations, each conducting the business in a different state. The areas need not necessarily be in two separate states, but they would have to be physically separated (for example, a Northern and a Southern California division) to qualify for such a division.

Q: IF TWO OPERATIONS ARE NOT PHYSICALLY SEPARATED AND ARE NOT DISTINCT TYPES OF BUSINESSES, IS IT STILL POSSIBLE THEY MIGHT BE DIVIDED TAX-FREE?

A: Yes. The IRS has allowed divisions of a *single* business based on separate "functional components." Basically, this means that a business that conducts several different functions can be divided into two or more businesses. The separate functions, of course, would each have to satisfy the five-year active trade or business requirement. However, these functional division rules give a business great flexibility.

Example

The following types of functional tax-free divisions illustrate permissible functional divisions:

- A meat processing and wholesaling company decides to separate its meat processing activities from its selling activities.
- A steel fabricator and seller decides to separate its fabrication activities from its selling activities.
- A car dealer determines to separate its financing activities from the other business assets of its dealership relating to sales and servicing.
- A furniture retailing business determines to separate its retail credit activities from its furniture selling activities.

Q: WHAT IS THE MAJOR REASON BUSINESSES CHOOSE TO DIVIDE?

A: There is no universal answer. However, probably the most common reason is the desire of some of the principals to conduct business in one location or conduct one line of business—with the desire of other principals to conduct another. Sometimes there are also differences of opinion—or even outright hostility.

Another common reason is to facilitate employees purchasing stock in one business without acquiring an interest in the other. That situation frequently looks something like this:

Example

Doctor Billco, Inc. operates two businesses, a professional medical practice and a fee billing service. Originally started as a billing division of the corporation for the physicians, the billing service quickly grew to the most profitable (and most employee intensive) portion of the corporation's business. A new doctor, Dr. Newly, now wishes to buy into the medical practice, and he has been offered a 10 percent share interest by the existing shareholders.

Because the business is conducted in one corporation and the company has a substantial net worth, Dr. Newly would have to pay $90,000 for 10 percent of the stock, most of that value being attributable to the billing service. Dr. Newly has no interest in the billing service or this kind of large investment. A tax-free division of the two businesses into two separate corporations, however, would enable Dr. Newly to buy into the medical practice alone for only $8,000 without also buying into the billing service.

Q: WHAT IS THE BUSINESS PURPOSE REQUIREMENT?

A: In order for any division of a business to qualify as tax-free, the IRS requires that there be a business purpose for the division. The purpose of this requirement is to prevent tax avoidance. Generally, the purpose must be a corporate purpose, not a personal shareholder purpose such as to facilitate estate planning.

DJI Planning Guide ⸻

Because of IRS concern over the issue, the corporation's business purpose should certainly be documented in the corporate records. Recitations in corporate minutes and other documents of the business reasons for the division should help justify the division if the IRS ever questions the transaction.

Q: WHAT TYPES OF BUSINESS PURPOSES WILL BE SUFFICIENT?

A: A common business purpose is the type of employee purchase described in the immediately preceding example (where an employee wants only to buy into one business). But there are many other valid business purposes to justify a division. Examples include the following:

- Division of two companies to permit dissident shareholders to separate.

- Division permitting shareholders to restrict their investment and activities to one business.
- Division enabling an employee to increase his interest in the business.
- Division to avoid labor problems.
- Division to eliminate customer friction and potential antitrust problems.
- Division to comply with foreign or domestic laws.
- Division to permit one company to use its stock in making acquisitions of other companies.
- Division so that one of the resulting two entities can participate in a tax-free reorganization.
- Even a division to reduce or avoid state and local taxes would be a valid business purpose.

Q: BUT ISN'T A PURPOSE TO AVOID TAXES *NOT* A VALID BUSINESS PURPOSE?

A: A purpose to reduce *state and/or local* taxes *is* a valid business purpose. A purpose to reduce *federal* income taxes would not be considered a valid business purpose for a division.

Note

Of course, it is perfectly permissible for a division to actually reduce the corporation's tax burden. It is only necessary that there be a valid business purpose for the division. Incidental tax benefits are certainly permissible, and indeed, virtually expected.

Q: ARE THERE ANY OTHER REQUIREMENTS OF A CORPORATE DIVISION?

A: Yes. The division cannot be a "device to distribute the corporation's earnings and profits."   Basically, this means that the corporation cannot use the corporate division to siphon off earnings and profits. Earnings and profits are the corporation's earnings from the current and previous years, maintained on the corporation's books on a rolling basis.

Earnings and profits are often referred to loosely as "retained earnings" on the corporation's balance sheet, but there are certain technical differences between retained earnings and earnings and profits. The amount of earnings and profits determines the amount of a distribution to shareholders that will be taxed as a dividend.

Example

Smallco has total earnings and profits from prior years of $500,000 and earns another $250,000 this year. Accordingly, its earnings and profits total $750,000. If Smallco distributes a $500,000 dividend to its shareholders, the entire amount will be taxable as a dividend (as ordinary income to the shareholders).

However, if the corporation had no earnings and profits and paid out a dividend, then this distribution would be taxable as a "return of capital." That means shareholders would pay tax only to the extent they got more cash than their basis in their stock.

For example, if Sam gets a $50,000 dividend distribution from a corporation with no earnings and profits, and his basis in this stock is $40,000, then he has only $10,000 in income, and that will be a capital gain. But if he receives a $50,000 dividend distribution from a corporation having plenty of earnings and profits, then he has $50,000 in ordinary income.

Q: HOW DO EARNINGS AND PROFITS AFFECT A CORPORATE DIVISION?

A: One of the requirements of a corporate division is that it not be used as a "device to distribute the corporation's earnings and profits." As is clear from the above example, the corporation's earnings and profits (or "retained earnings") account is used to determine the extent of dividend taxation to shareholders. A corporate division could have the effect of distributing earnings and profits, since shareholders will receive stock. Accordingly, corporate divisions are closely watched by the IRS.

Note

Where there are no earnings and profits in the corporation, by definition there can be no concern over distributing "earnings."

Q: HOW IS THIS "DEVICE" TEST MONITORED?

A: It is frustrating to tax planners, because it is not entirely clear. Even though a transaction satisfies all of the various technical Internal Revenue Code requirements for a tax-free corporate division, it may fail tax-free treatment based upon this "device" test.

Although there is no clear rule, here are some circumstances that may result in the division being treated as a device to distribute earnings and profits, thus knocking out tax-free treatment:

• *A prearranged sale of either company's stock after the corporate division.* Note that the prearrangement need not necessarily be a binding contract; mere preparations and oral agreements may be sufficient.

• *A sale of stock in either company after the division even without prearrangement.* Here the length of the waiting period between the distribution and the sale will be particularly relevant. The closer in time the sale occurs to the distribution, the more likely it is that the division was really a device to distribute earnings.

• *Gifts of stock in either company after the division, followed by a sale by the person who receives the gift.* This is merely a variation of the disposition rules mentioned earlier.

• *A pro rata distribution of the stock in the spun-off corporation.* This might be a device to distribute earnings, since it could enable shareholders individually to sell their stock in the spun-off corporation without touching their stock in the original company. But a pro rata distribution with no evidence of a prearranged sale is generally OK.

Q: DOES ANYTHING ELSE LOOK LIKE A DEVICE TO DISTRIBUTE EARNINGS?

A: Yes. Here are a few more circumstances that look like devices to distribute earnings:

• *A complete or partial liquidation of the spun-off corporation after the division, with shareholders receiving assets.* Here the distribution of earnings might come in the form of distributions of assets in kind to shareholders.

• *An arrangement to apportion certain types of assets in the two corporations after the division.* If one corporation ends up with a larger portion of investment assets than active business assets—the kind of assets that may spell dividend distributions—then the transaction may be a device to distribute earnings. Cash and other liquid assets are particularly suspect.

• *The termination of one of the two businesses after the division.* But the more time that elapses between the division and the termination of one of the businesses, the more likely it is that the transaction will *not* be treated as a device to distribute earnings.

Q: IS THE "DEVICE" REQUIREMENT FREQUENTLY INVOKED?

A: No, not terribly frequently. There are also some helpful case authorities that indicate the circumstances under which the transaction will not be treated as a device to distribute earnings and profits.

DJI Planning Guide ⎯⎯⎯⎯⎯⎯⎯⎯⎯⎯⎯⎯⎯⎯⎯⎯⎯⎯⎯

Because the stakes in the corporate division are usually high, and certain aspects of the law are murky—such as this "device" rule—it is customary to seek advance approval from the IRS before consummating a corporate division. Seeking this kind of advance ruling is clearly advisable. If the IRS is convinced the transaction is appropriate, it will issue a binding ruling that the transaction is tax-free. This IRS letter ruling is then attached to the tax returns for both corporations for the year.

PARTIAL LIQUIDATIONS

Q: WHY MIGHT A CORPORATION PLAN A PARTIAL LIQUIDATION?

A: The most classic case for a partial liquidation occurs when a corporation involved in several lines of business ceases operations in one line of business but continues in the other.

Example

> A corporation, Realnutco, engages in real estate rentals and also manufactures nuts and bolts. If the corporation discontinues its real estate activities, the corporation can either retain those real estate rental assets (presumably for no meaningful purpose if it will no longer engage in the business), or it can dispose of the assets by distributing them to shareholders or selling them and distributing the sales proceeds to shareholders.

Q: ARE THERE ANY OTHER REASONS TO CONDUCT A PARTIAL LIQUIDATION?

A: Yes. The type of "corporate contraction" described in the preceding example is probably the most common type of partial liquidation situation. However, it is certainly not the only one.

For example, as discussed previously in this chapter, when shareholders in a business decide to part company, they may split the business through a tax-free corporation division, or they may wish to distribute the assets to the departing shareholders.

Q: HOW IS A PARTIAL LIQUIDATION TAXED?

A: The corporation will not pay a tax on distributions of cash. It will pay a tax only to the extent it either sells assets and recognizes a gain or distributes appreciated assets. The corporation's distribution of appreciated assets is, for tax purposes, effectively treated as a sale.

Example

Diversified Widgets suspends its widget-making operations and prepares to dispose of its widget-making assets. It holds these assets with a basis of $200,000, and its plant is currently worth $700,000. If it sells the widget plant, it obviously will have a gain of $500,000 ($700,000 minus $200,000). If instead it distributes the widget plant to its shareholders, it will still have a gain of $500,000. Note that if it distributes the assets, it will have a tax liability but not necessarily any cash to pay the tax (that is, it will have to use other funds to pay the tax). Of course, if the distributed assets are not appreciated assets (for example, a plant with a market value of $500,000 and a basis of $500,000), they will not produce a taxable gain.

DJI Planning Guide

Distributing appreciated assets to shareholders must be carefully considered since it will result in tax at the corporate level. Only when there is sufficient cash in the corporation to pay the tax and there is some reason to distribute the assets themselves (e.g., the recipient shareholder wishes to use the assets himself) should the distribution be made.

Q: HOW IS A SHAREHOLDER TAXED ON A PARTIAL LIQUIDATION?

A: First, we need to define what qualifies as a partial liquidation. It really matters from the perspective of the shareholder. There are two current means of qualifying a distribution as one in partial liquidation.

- A distribution attributable to the termination of a "qualified trade or business."
- A distribution that is "not essentially equivalent to a dividend."

The first of these two avenues to partial liquidation treatment requires the same basic things required for a tax-free corporate division discussed earlier. In other words, one of the businesses conducted by the corporation must be terminated, and it must have been actively conducted for at least five years prior to the distribution. Certain other technical provisions apply. For example, the terminated trade or business must not have been acquired within a five-year period in another tax-free transaction.

Q: CAN ASSETS ATTRIBUTABLE TO ANY BUSINESS BE DISTRIBUTED IN THIS WAY?

A: Yes, although, just as in the area of tax-free corporate divisions discussed earlier, the question is, "What is a business?" Passive holding of real estate investments, for example, is not a business. However, actively managing real estate assets does constitute a business. It is really a question of degree. Service businesses are clearly active, so they do not generate much controversy.

Even if a partial liquidation does not satisfy the "termination of a qualified business" criterion of partial liquidation treatment, it can *still* qualify for partial liquidation treatment if it is not like a dividend. This "not like a dividend" standard is very difficult to apply with any assurance of success.

Q: WHY WOULD THE SHAREHOLDERS CARE IF A DISTRIBUTION IS IN PARTIAL LIQUIDATION?

A: Because if the distribution is *not* in partial liquidation, it is likely to be taxed as a dividend. As a dividend, of course, any amount distributed to the shareholders is taxable as ordinary income in full, with no amount being applied against their basis in their stock. In the case of a distribution in partial liquidation, as is described in the next scenario, the shareholders are taxed much more favorably.

Q: HOW IS A SHAREHOLDER TAXED IF THE TRANSACTION QUALIFIES AS A PARTIAL LIQUIDATION?

A: Whether the shareholders receive property in kind or in cash, their tax treatment will be the same. The shareholders will pay tax on the difference between the value of what they receive and their basis in their stock. Because the liquidation is only a partial liquidation, the shareholders will still own stock in the company.

Example

Slumpco, a major toxic waste clean-up company, discontinues its junk food manufacturing operations and sells the associated assets. It pays a tax on the appreciated assets and distributes the remaining cash. Rex, who paid $15,000 for his 100 shares of Slumpco stock seven years ago, receives a cash distribution of $21,000. Because the transaction qualifies as a partial liquidation, the first $15,000 of the distribution to Rex is treated as a return of capital and is therefore not taxable. The remaining $6,000 is taxed as a capital gain. Note that Rex *still* owns his 100 shares in Slumpco, but he now has a zero basis in his stock. Consequently, any further distribution on account of his shares will be taxable.

Q: DO SHAREHOLDERS CARE IF THEY ARE TAXED AS A CAPITAL GAIN OR AS ORDINARY INCOME?

A: Yes. Clearly the main reason to care—the favorable tax rate differential for capital gains—is gone. However, capital gains and capital losses still have to be separately netted every year. If the capital gains for the year exceed the capital losses, then the capital gains are taxed just like ordinary income.

But if the capital losses exceed capital gains, only $3,000 per year (for individuals) of ordinary income can be offset with the capital losses.

Example

Irving Investor sells some stock this year that generates a $30,000 capital loss. As the end of the year approaches, he has no capital gains to offset the loss, so his loss will be limited to $3,000 this year.

Q: CAN ONE PLAN AROUND THIS $3,000 LIMIT ON CAPITAL LOSSES?

A: Yes. In the preceding example, Irving may choose to sell one of his investments to produce a capital gain in an offsetting amount—such as stock that would bring a $27,000 capital gain. If he makes the sale before the end of the year, he will have avoided the excess capital loss problem. The remaining $3,000 loss can be deducted against his ordinary income.

DJI Planning Guide

It is advisable for all taxpayers to review any capital gains and losses generated during the year—and to do it *before* it is too late to make other sales. December 1 or so of each year would be a good benchmark for making this evaluation. If there are losses that need to be offset with capital gains, this will allow sufficient time to determine the amount of offsetting gain needed and, hopefully, time to sell the appropriate asset.

Q: WHAT IF THE CAPITAL GAINS RATE COMES BACK?

A: Then obviously the desire for capital gains treatment on a partial liquidation, and indeed in other contexts too, will be that much greater.

Note

On that note, it seems likely that the capital gains rate will be brought back into the law in the near future. Bills have already been introduced into Congress that do just that, and it is only a question of time before one of them is passed. Even if a return to capital gains rates comes in combination with increased ordinary income rates, as seems likely, all the old incentives to characterize gains as capital gains will be back.

CHAPTER 11

PLANNING FOR TROUBLED BUSINESSES

INTRODUCTION

It may seem odd to discuss taxes and tax planning in the context of a business that is not doing well financially, or perhaps even failing. Indeed, all of us are more likely to worry about taxes when a business is doing well and creating a large taxable income.

There are several reasons why this view is shortsighted, however, and why attention really does need to be paid to taxes even in the context of a troubled business. To be sure, the primary consideration will be getting the business back on its feet or, if that is no longer possible, selling it or liquidating it. But it is frequently very important to keep an eye on the tax man as well.

For one thing, taxation does not necessarily follow what we consider to be true economic income. Some situations that occur in the context of a failing business may give rise to taxable income even though the business may not receive any cash.

Moreover, in this climate of corporate takeovers and acquisitions (a topic addressed in Chapter 9), a declining business may have losses that make it an attractive target to another company. In this context, one of the valuable assets of the company may be its losses!

Knowing how to preserve these losses so that they might

be acquired can be a very critical tax planning step. It can lead to both saving taxes and producing a gain on the disposition of the business.

Q: FROM A TAX PERSPECTIVE, WHAT HAPPENS WHEN A BUSINESS FILES FOR BANKRUPTCY?

A: There is no immediate tax consequence.

Q: CAN THE IRS PERSIST IN TAX COLLECTION EFFORTS AGAINST A COMPANY IN BANKRUPTCY?

A: The corporation's tax liabilities are "stayed" (a stay is a legal order precluding further action) until it becomes clear how much money there is and who will get what. The IRS is treated like another creditor for this purpose. The "stay" in the bankruptcy proceeding will prevent the government from enforcing its tax claims, as by liens, etc. However, this stay does not prevent the government from trying to collect taxes that become due *during* the pendency of the bankruptcy.

Q: IS A CORPORATION'S LIABILITY FOR TAXES DISCHARGED IN BANKRUPTCY?

A: It depends. The main objectives of a bankruptcy proceeding, of course, are to marshall the assets of the bankrupt company; to keep creditors away during this process; then, in an orderly fashion, to pay creditors all or at least a portion of what they are due; to discharge (or remove) remaining liabilities; and, finally, to allow the corporation, in effect, to "start over."

However, liabilities for federal taxes are not necessarily discharged in the bankruptcy proceeding. In a case brought under Chapter 7 of the Bankruptcy Code (under which the debtor continues in operation and in possession of its assets), the corporation is *not* entitled to a discharge of tax liabilities, or, for that matter, other liabilities. In a case brought under Chapter 11 of the Bankruptcy Code (where there is a trustee appointed by the Bankruptcy Court who takes over the company's operations), the plan of reorganization that is ultimately approved may or may not discharge the taxes.

If the business as reorganized after the bankruptcy will continue, then the taxes may well be discharged either in whole or in part. But if the business is liquidated as a result of the bankruptcy, the tax liability will clearly not be discharged and the IRS may grab for as much as it can get.

As a practical matter, even in a Chapter 11 bankruptcy case where the business will be continued, large tax liabilities are not likely to be discharged. Usually, the government has a high enough priority in these cases to get paid most or all of what it is due.

Q: THEN DOES IT MAKE SENSE TO DECLARE BANKRUPTCY?

A: It seldom does for tax reasons. If the government is a creditor and seeks to collect a tax liability, and other creditors are breathing down the neck of the business, then the bankruptcy can be an effective means of staving off the creditors until the business can get back on its feet. Of course, there may be many disadvantages to a bankruptcy, such as unfavorable publicity and breakdowns in relationships with suppliers or customers.

Q: IF A BUSINESS IS REORGANIZED IN A BANKRUPTCY PROCEEDING, ARE THERE ANY TAX CONSEQUENCES?

A: A bankruptcy reorganization is one type of tax-free reorganization. If the transaction is properly planned, there should be no tax due because of the reorganization itself. In a bankruptcy reorganization, the assets of the bankrupt corporation will typically be transferred to another corporation, and stock or securities of the bankrupt corporation will be distributed to the new controlling corporation.

Q: WHAT OPTIONS ARE THERE APART FROM BANKRUPTCY?

A: There are many. One obvious solution is simply to work out arrangements with the creditors. This is where the tax planning really gets interesting. Consider the following example:

Example

On The Rocks, Ltd. owes $300,000 to Abe, $500,000 to Betty and $800,000 to Claude. Abe, Betty, and Claude know that On The Rocks may be going down the drain. Accordingly, they each agree to a $100,000 loan reduction, so that the amount On The Rocks will owe is $200,000 to Abe, $400,000 to Betty and $700,000 to Claude. Because this **discharge of indebtedness** represents money that On The Rocks will now not have to pay, it is considered taxable income to On The Rocks. On The Rocks will have to pay tax at up to the 34 percent corporate tax rate on the $300,000 it is "deemed" to have received.

Q: DOES THIS INCOME ARISE WHENEVER DEBT IS DISCHARGED?

A: Not when the debt is actually paid. For instance, if in the above example On The Rocks has used $300,000 if its cash to pay down the outstanding loan balances to Abe, Betty, and Claude, there would clearly be no income to On The Rocks. On The Rocks would have simply used cash to pay an obligation.

The other two circumstances in which there will not be discharge of indebtedness income are where the company is "insolvent" or where the discharge of indebtedness incurs in a Title 11 bankruptcy case.

Q: DOES THIS MEAN THAT IF THE CORPORATION IS INSOLVENT OR IN BANKRUPTCY, THE DEBT CAN BE FORGIVEN WITHOUT ANY TAX CONSEQUENCES?

A: No, that is not quite correct. Although in a Chapter 11 bankruptcy case or insolvency situation, the discharge of the company's debt will not create immediate taxable income, there may be a tax consequence down the road. The amount of the debt discharged will reduce the corporation's net operating losses, certain tax credits, and net capital losses.

If there are still additional discharges of indebtedness amounts after the discharge of debt is applied against these items, the balance will reduce the basis of the corporation's property. What this means is that when the property is later sold, this reduced amount will really be taxed.

Example

On The Rocks, Ltd. has a $1 million debt to N Bank. Pursuant to a bankruptcy or insolvency proceeding, this $1 million liability is discharged. Although On The Rocks will not pay any current tax on this $1 million of phantom "income," the $1 million will be applied to reduce any net operating loss that the company has. Thereafter, it will be applied against various tax credits and any capital loss of the company.

If there is still some balance of the $1 million remaining, it will be applied against the basis of assets the company owns. So if On The Rocks owns a building worth $2 million with a basis of $1 million, the entire $1 million basis could be wiped out. Obviously, if the building is later sold for $2 million, then the taxable gain on the sale would be the difference between the basis and the $2 million sales price, resulting in the discharge of indebtedness income coming home to roost at that point.

DJI Planning Guide _____

This so-called "discharge of indebtedness income" can obviously be very frustrating, since in many respects it does not seem to represent a true accretion to wealth justifying taxation. Since the only two avenues for avoiding current tax on a discharge of indebtedness are either to be insolvent or to undergo a bankruptcy reorganization, a few businesses have chosen to undergo a bankruptcy reorganization in order to take advantage of the exception from the ordinary income on discharge of indebtedness rule.

Q: WHAT TAX CONSIDERATIONS APPLY WHEN THE BUSINESS WILL NOT BE CONTINUED?

A: If a troubled business will not be continued but will either be liquidated or sold off, then the biggest tax planning goal will be to preserve the company's net operating losses and other tax benefits so that it may be attractive to a buyer. A **net operating loss** (or NOL) is simply the bottom line loss for tax purposes that a corporation has for a year.

A corporation is entitled to carry such a loss back to the three prior years, giving rise to tax refunds if tax was paid in the three prior years. It can also carry the losses forward 15 years into the future to reduce the potential tax liabilities for those future years. Thus, a net operating loss is an attractive asset for a corporation.

Example

Losing, Inc. had its first unprofitable year in 1988, with a net operating loss of $600,000. In 1987, it had a profit of $400,000, and in 1986 a profit of $600,000. It can carry the loss back to 1987 (up to the $400,000 of profit for that year) and back to 1986 (wiping out $200,000 of the $600,000 profit for 1986). A refund for the taxes previously paid for those years will be available. Alternatively, the company can carry the loss for 1988 into the future and recover it from income earned in 1989 through 2004.

Q: HOW CAN A NET OPERATING LOSS BE PRESERVED?

A: It depends on the manner in which the transaction is handled. Great attention has been focused on so-called "trafficking in net operating losses" over the past 10 years. Admittedly, there have been abuses of the net operating loss rule that have led to the "trafficking" metaphor.

Consider the following example:

Example

Lossco has assets of $3 million and a net operating loss of $60 million due to 10 years of dismal results in the fertilizer business. Profitco has embarrassingly large profits from its oil operations. Profitco pays $8 million for the stock of Lossco and begins using the $60 million NOL. Profitco's board is pleased as punch that for only $8 million, it has acquired $3 million in assets plus an NOL that will shield $60 million of its own profits from taxation. That makes an $8 million purchase price for approximately $23 million worth of value ($3 million in hard assets and $20 million plus in tax benefits).

As a result of such abusive transactions, Congress has changed the rules governing acquisitions of net operating losses a number of times, most recently in the Tax Reform Act of 1986 and again in the Revenue Act of 1987. Unfortunately, the current rules can only be described as Byzantine. Under them, a company's ability to acquire another company's net operating losses is now quite restricted.

Q: HOW CAN ANOTHER CORPORATION'S NET OPERATING LOSS BE ACQUIRED?

A: To begin with, you have to distinguish between a business that is merely "reorganized," as pursuant to a bankruptcy proceeding, and one that is actually acquired by someone else. In the case of a bankruptcy proceeding, a net operating loss can generally be used after the proceeding as long as there is no change in ownership, even if some of the creditors become shareholders following a capital restructuring resulting from a discharge of indebtedness. It is clear that a corporation's mere internal capital restructuring (for example, some shareholders exchanging common stock for preferred stock) will not affect its ability to use the net operating loss in the future.

In the case of an acquisition, very detailed rules apply. The new rules restrict the use of income to offset net operating losses only if there is an ownership change. An ownership change generally occurs if the percentage of stock of the new loss corporation owned by any one or more 5-percent shareholders has increased by more than 50 percentage points above the lowest percentage of stock of the old loss corporation owned by those 5-percent shareholders during the prior three years.

Q: HOW DOES THIS LIMITATION WORK?

A: This formula defining a change of ownership is complex. A change in ownership is deemed to occur whenever the percentage of stock (based on value) owned by one or more 5-percent (5%) shareholders increases by more than 50 percentage points over the lowest percentage of stock held by those stockholders at any time during a measurement period. The measurement period is the three-year period prior to the ownership shift.

Example

Miserable, Inc. is and has for many years been owned by three shareholders: Abner, owning 100 shares, Bobby, owning 50 shares, and Clyde, also owning 50 shares. Abner now sells Bobby 60 shares, increasing Bobby's percentage ownership in the company by 30 percentage points (from 50 to 100 shares). A year later, Abner buys Clyde's 50 shares. Abner's interest in Miserable has increased by 25 percentage points from a low point of 40 shares to a high point of 90 shares. Even though Abner and Clyde jointly increased their stock ownership interest by only 25 percentage points (between the two of them, they owned at least 75 percent of the company at all times), the total of the separate increases in their stock ownership compared to their lowest percentage ownership is 55 percentage points. Consequently, there is a "shift" in ownership that will restrict use of the NOL!

Q: WHAT IS AN OWNERSHIP SHIFT?

A: An ownership shift involving a 5-percent shareholder may arise in a variety of ways, including the following.

• A taxable purchase of stock by a person who owns at least 5 percent of the corporation's stock (either before or after the purchase!).
• The sale of stock by a person who holds at least 5 percent of the stock of the loss corporation either before or after the sale.
• A tax-free exchange of property for stock of the corporation resulting in a change of the percentage ownership of the 5-percent shareholder.
• A redemption (sale of stock to the corporation) resulting in a change in the ownership of a 5-percent shareholder.
• An exercise of a conversion privilege to a debt instrument, such as a bond converted to common stock.
• An issuance of stock by a corporation affecting the percentage of stock owned by a 5-percent shareholder.
• Even a granting of stock options!

Q: WHAT HAPPENS IF AN OWNERSHIP SHIFT OCCURS?

A: Making the complex determination of whether an ownership shift has occurred is only half the battle. Then it is necessary to determine the extent of the net operating loss that will be allowable in the future following the ownership shift.

Note that the fact that an ownership shift has occurred does not mean that net operating loss will not be allowable. Instead, the net operating loss in the future will be limited. This limit is designed to restrict corporations from acquiring other corporations with inherent net operating losses. The restrictions cut back on acquisitions for the specific purpose of using the acquired entity's net operating losses to offset the income from the acquiring company's profitable operations.

Q: IF AN OWNERSHIP SHIFT OCCURS, CAN AN NOL STILL BE USED?

A: If an ownership change does occur, there is an initial hurdle to be jumped in order to be able to use the net operating losses, even subject to limitations. A net operating loss carryforward will be disallowed entirely unless the "continuity of business enterprise" requirement is satisfied for two years following the ownership shift.

Basically, this requirement necessitates that the acquiring corporation fulfill one of these two criteria:

• It must continue at least one significant line of the acquired corporation's "historic business."
• Or it must use a significant portion of the acquired corporation's business assets.

The acquired corporation's historic business is generally the business it has been most recently conducting before the ownership shift.

Note

In essence, this continuity of business enterprise test is designed to prevent a corporation from "buying" loss corporations solely in order to use the net operating loss, without regard to the actual need for the business or its assets.

Example

Colonel Motors, Inc. manufactures and distributes automobiles throughout the United States. It consistently has had very profitable operations. In 1988, it acquires in a stock acquisition Sledgeco, Inc., a toxic chemical company that has a net operating loss of $5 million. In order to be entitled to use *any* of the net operating loss (we will discuss later what *limits* apply to the use of Sledgeco's net operating loss), Sledgeco would have to satisfy the continuity of business enterprise test.

This means that Colonel Motors would have to continue to operate the "historic business" of Sledgeco (toxic chemical production) *or* that Colonel Motors would have to use a significant portion of Sledgeco's assets in its own operations. If Sledgeco has primarily warehouse and factory assets, for example, Colonel Motors might be able to use these assets in its *own* operations without continuing the toxic chemical production and still satisfy the continuity of business enterprise test.

DJI Planning Guide

One possibility for a company with a burning desire to acquire another corporation and use its net operating loss is to intentionally satisfy this continuity of business enterprise test but to cease operating the business of the acquired company after the two-year period expires. Although this strategy would appear to satisfy the statutory test, there is another potential problem. As noted in the following discussion, the IRS has an independent power to disallow the use of an acquired net operating loss if it has been acquired with a principal purpose of tax avoidance.

Q: WHAT IF THIS CONTINUITY OF BUSINESS ENTERPRISE TEST IS SATISFIED?

A: Then one goes to the next step, which is determining the *extent* of the operating loss of the acquired company that can be used in the future. If an ownership change occurs and the continuity of business enterprise requirement is satisfied, then the amount of taxable income of the surviving corporation (in the case of a reorganization) or the original loss corporation (in the case of a purchase) cannot exceed a certain limit every year. This limit, called the **Section 382 limitation,** is defined by a formula.

The Section 382 limitation is the product of these two figures:

- The value of the old loss corporation immediately before the ownership change.
- And the applicable long-term tax-exempt rate (described below).

Q: HOW DOES THIS FORMULA WORK?

A: To figure the annual limit on the use of the net operating loss, multiply the loss corporation's value immediately before the ownership change by the federal long-term tax-exempt rate published by the IRS. Determining the valuation of the loss corporation immediately before the change should be fairly simple. Basically, the value of the company is the value of the stock of the corporation (including both preferred and common stock).

In certain cases, however, this stock value is subject to adjustments. For example, the value of the company must be reduced by the amount of any capital contributions made to the old corporation as part of a plan to avoid the net operating loss restrictions.

There are several other limitations on the value principle as well. Basically, they are designed to prevent a company from artificially increasing the value of its stock to make it more attractive to an acquiring company. Increasing the value of the loss corporation's stock would be attractive to an acquiring company because the acquiring company would then be able to use a higher amount of the old corporation's net operating loss after the acquisition.

Example

Lossco, having outstanding stock worth $800,000, has a $1 million net operating loss. Shortly before it is acquired, shareholders of Lossco make a $200,000 capital contribution to the corporation. Thereafter, the acquisition takes place and the stock of Lossco is purchased for $1.1 million.

Because of the recent capital contribution, the value of the Lossco stock that will be relevant for purposes of determining the limit on the use of its net operating loss in the hands of the acquiring company will be $800,000 rather than $1 million.

Q: HOW IS THIS MULTIPLICATION PERFORMED?

A: The value of the loss corporation's stock immediately before the ownership change is multiplied by the federal long-term tax-exempt rate published by the IRS to determine the *annual* limit on the use of the net operating loss in the future. This interest rate published by the IRS is released monthly, but the highest rate for the three-month period ending with the change is the one used in the formula. As an example, the interest rate for May, 1988 was 7.44 percent (the highest of the IRS announced rates for May and for the prior two months).

The operation of the annual limit on net operating losses is illustrated in this example.

Example

Lossco has outstanding stock with a value of $1 million and a net operating loss of $2 million. The loss was accumulated over the last 10 years. All of Lossco's outstanding stock is purchased by Profitco for $1.8 million in May of 1988, which clearly constitutes a change in ownership of the stock. Profitco plans to continue operating Lossco, thus satisfying the "continuity of business enterprise" requirement.

To determine the annual limit on the amount of the net operating loss Profitco will be able to use, multiply the $1 million value of the Lossco stock immediately before the transfer by 7.44 percent, the announced IRS rate for May. This means that Profitco can use $74,400 per year of the net operating loss.

Q: IF THIS NOL PERCENTAGE TEST IS SATISFIED, WILL THE NET OPERATING LOSS BE USABLE?

A: Not necessarily. There are other limitations on the acquisition of net operating losses as well. If one or more persons or companies acquire control of a corporation principally to avoid taxes (that is, principally to acquire the net operating loss), then the net operating loss will not be available.

This is an "evil intent" provision that might seem difficult to enforce. Questions of proof of intent can be difficult, but the IRS has invoked this restriction frequently in the context of acquisitions. Basically, the IRS can come in after an acquisition and evaluate whether the primary reason for the acquisition was the acquisition of the net operating loss.

DJI Planning Guide

The issue of principal purpose of tax avoidance can arise in any context. However, it is most likely to arise when there is no other sound business reason for the acquisition. If the acquiring and acquired company are both in the same line of business, have the same customers, or are competitors, then there will probably be business reasons that can be advanced for the acquisition—even if the net operating loss is awfully attractive.

The real rub comes when the acquired business is totally unrelated to the acquiring business. In this circumstance, some attempt should be made to discern—and document—why the acquisition took place.

Q: CAN A COMPANY WITH AN NOL ACQUIRE A PROFITABLE COMPANY TO OFFSET ITS OWN LOSS?

A: It depends. Under new restrictions imposed in 1987, loss corporations cannot use their losses to shelter the built-in gains of an acquired company that are recognized within five years of the acquisition. This means that a corporation with a loss will not generally be able to acquire a profitable corporation and immediately offset its loss against certain built-in gains.

Example

Lossco acquires all of the stock of Winco, which has a building with a basis of $1 million and a market value of $20 million. Lossco has a $20 million net operating loss. Lossco wants to cause

Winco to sell the building (at a $19 million gain) using Lossco's net operating loss to offset the gain so it is not taxable. The new rules disallow this procedure.

Note

This does not mean that the loss cannot be used, but only that it cannot be used for built-in gains. Lossco's loss could generally be offset against Winco's profits from its operations in the future.

DEDUCTIONS TO INVESTORS

Q: WHAT HAPPENS TO THE SHAREHOLDER'S INVESTMENT WHEN A CORPORATION GOES BANKRUPT?

A: A shareholder who receives nothing when a company goes out of existence is entitled to a **worthless stock loss**. In fact, it is not even necessary for the company to go bankrupt in order for the loss to be available. But there has to be some event that fixes the worthlessness of the stock.

Technically, this occurs whenever there is no reasonable expectation that the stock will have any value. This can occur where the company is insolvent, but if operations are continuing, then there may be some expectation that the company will turn around.

Note

Under IRS rules, if the investor takes the worthless stock loss deduction before the stock is really worthless, then the deduction will be denied. Moreover, if he does not claim the worthless stock deduction when the stock actually becomes worthless but claims it in the next year, then it will not be allowable in the second year. The deduction is allowable *only* in the year the stock becomes worthless, putting a premium on this determination!

Q: HOW MUCH IS THE DEDUCTION WORTH?

A: A worthless stock loss is a deduction in the amount the taxpayer paid for the stock, but it is allowable only as a capital loss.

Example

Irving Investor bought 100 shares in Speculative Co. for $50,000, and the company becomes worthless in 1989. Irving can claim a tax deduction for the full $50,000 invested. This will be a capital loss on his tax return, so it can offset only an equivalent capital gain or up to $3,000 per year of ordinary income. So if Irving has *no* capital gains in 1989, he can deduct only $3,000, carrying over the $47,000 balance to 1990 and subsequent years.

DJI Planning Guide

As is clear from this example, although ordinary income and capital gains are now taxed at the same rates, a capital loss is still less advantageous than an ordinary loss.

Q: WHY ARE CAPITAL LOSSES WORTH LESS THAN ORDINARY LOSSES?

A: Because capital gains and capital losses still have to be separately netted, and any excess capital loss is deductible (to an individual) only at the rate of $3,000 a year.

Example

Irving's $50,000 stock investment in Speculative Co. becomes worthless, so he writes the $50,000 off as a capital loss in 1989. If Irving has an offsetting $50,000 capital gain, then he can deduct the full $50,000 capital loss (by applying the capital loss against the capital gain). However, suppose Irving has only $10,000 in capital gains for 1989. In this case, Irving has a $40,000 *excess* capital loss. He can deduct only $3,000 against his ordinary ·ncome in 1989 (even if his ordinary income is $500,000!).

DJI Planning Guide _____

Irving can go out and make sales of capital assets before the end of the year to generate additional capital gains against which to offset his capital losses. He can selectively pick assets (stock, real estate, or what have you) that will produce enough taxable gain to offset any capital loss.

If this kind of planning is not engaged in, then the excess capital loss will obviously remain available for future years. But one can view capital loss carryovers as tax losses that are not earning interest. The way to make them work currently is to generate current offsetting capital gains.

Q: IS IT POSSIBLE FOR A WORTHLESS STOCK LOSS TO PRODUCE ORDINARY LOSS RATHER THAN CAPITAL LOSS?

A: Yes, in two circumstances. When the stock constitutes an ordinary income (inventory type) asset to the holder, a worthless stock loss may produce ordinary loss treatment. A dealer in securities might qualify for ordinary loss treatment, but virtually no one else would.

The second possibility for ordinary loss treatment on a worthless security loss is if the stock constitutes **Section 1244 stock**.

Q: WHAT IS SECTION 1244 STOCK?

A: Section 1244 stock, also sometimes called "small business stock," can only be issued by a "qualifying small business corporation." A corporation is a qualifying small business corporation only if the amount of money and other property it receives as capital is $1 million or less.

Various other requirements apply to this definition, including the requirement that the corporation issuing the stock must be an operating company as opposed to a company that merely holds investments. If these various requirements are met, then in the event the stock becomes worthless, the holder can take an ordinary loss deduction rather than a capital loss deduction. The ordinary loss deduction is subject to an overall limit of $50,000 per year ($100,000 for husband and wife filing a joint return).

Q: WHAT IF A SHAREHOLDER ALSO HOLDS SECURITIES IN THE CORPORATION? DOES THE WORTHLESS SECURITY LOSS RULE APPLY?

A: Yes, the worthless items may be either stock or securities, such as bonds, debentures, notes, and other debt instruments. The rules discussed earlier will generally apply.

Q: WHAT ABOUT LOANS TO THE CORPORATION THAT ARE NOT PAID?

A: Here, a bad debt deduction is allowable. The question is whether the debt would be deductible as a **business bad debt** or a **nonbusiness bad debt**. As these names suggest, a business bad debt is a debt that becomes uncollectible that was made in connection with a taxpayer's trade or business and for business reasons. A nonbusiness bad debt is a debt made in a nonbusiness context that becomes uncollectible.

Q: WHAT IS THE DIFFERENCE BETWEEN BUSINESS AND NONBUSINESS BAD DEBTS?

A: Plenty. Business bad debts are deductible as ordinary losses. Nonbusiness bad debts are deductible only as capital losses. Hence, nonbusiness bad debts are subject to all of the limitations on capital losses discussed previously.

In addition, nonbusiness bad debts can be deducted only when they are totally worthless. Business bad debts can be deducted to the extent they become worthless in whole in or in part.

Example

Red loans Ted $80,000. A year later when the first $20,000 installment of principal is due, it is clear Ted cannot pay it, so it is worthless to the extent of that $20,000. If the loan is a business loan, Red can immediately deduct the $20,000 (against ordinary income). If the loan is a nonbusiness loan, however, nothing can be deducted until the whole debt is worthless, and then only as a capital loss.

Q: WHAT IF THE *COMPANY* IS OWED MONEY THAT IS NOT PAID?

A: The corporation would then be entitled to a bad debt deduction. And in the case of a corporation, the debts are presumed to be business rather than nonbusiness debts. A debt is deductible in the year it becomes worthless, regardless of whether it is written off on the corporation's books.

A partially worthless debt, however, is deductible by a corporation only if and to the extent that it has been "charged off" during the year. The "charge off" is basically a bookkeeping entry recording the total or partial worthlessness of the debt.

DJI Planning Guide ————————————————————

Charging off the debts as they become partially worthless is generally advisable in that it generates current tax deductions. At least where the tax deductions are needed to offset any taxable income, current charge-offs are appropriate and advisable. If for some reason the debt later becomes collectible (for example, if the debtor becomes solvent again), then the amount charged off would be taken back into income at that time.

CHAPTER 12

DISSOLVING
THE BUSINESS

INTRODUCTION

The owners of a business may dissolve it for any one of many reasons. The most straightforward reason is the simple desire to cease business and either sell off the assets or distribute them in kind to the owners. Yet the desire to liquidate may be for many other reasons as well.

A dissolution or liquidation may be prompted by the death or retirement of some or all of the owners, disagreements among owners, the desire to sell all or part of the business, or even a preference (based upon tax or other reasons) to continue business in another form. There may also be a variety of tax reasons that necessitate a dissolution. Several of the tax problems that may make a dissolution desirable are the accumulated earnings tax, the personal holding company tax, and the unreasonable compensation doctrine. (On these topics, see Chapters 2 and 6.)

Ultimately, the *reason* to dissolve is the easy part. To a far greater extent than ever before, the taxation involved in going *out* of business is materially more complex and costly than that of going *into* business. This is particularly the case in the context of corporations as a result of the Tax Reform Act of 1986. Every business should be aware of the new rules.

PROPRIETORSHIPS

Q: HOW IS A PROPRIETORSHIP TAXED UPON DISSOLUTION?

A: A proprietorship is not an entity at all, but merely a manner in which one person (or one person and his or her spouse) can conduct a business. Consequently, the taxation of the dissolution of the business is quite straightforward. Normally, the discontinuation of a proprietorship has few tax consequences.

It is actually more appropriate to characterize the demise of a proprietorship as a cessation of business activity rather than a dissolution, since there is no legal entity to dissolve. If a proprietor stops conducting business and sells the business assets, then any gain or loss on the sale will pass through and be included in the proprietor's tax return.

Example

Vivian ceases conducting her video store (ViviVideo) as a sole proprietor, selling off her remaining stock. The sales of inventory, plus any sales of capital assets used in the business (display cabinets, video recorders, etc.), are treated as ordinary sales to her, increasing the income on her individual tax return. By the same token, if she sells any assets at a loss (for example, a new recorder she sells for $500 that she bought for $800), then she also takes the loss individually.

PARTNERSHIPS

Q: WHEN A PARTNERSHIP DISSOLVES, DOES THE PARTNERSHIP RECOGNIZE GAIN OR LOSS?

A: Because a partnership is a flow-through entity, it does not pay tax itself. Instead, all of the partnership income and/or loss passes through and is taxed to the partners in accordance with their respective partnership interests. From a tax perspective, therefore, the dissolution of a partnership is usually not painful.

Q: HOW ARE PARTNERS TAXED
UPON DISSOLUTION?

A: Individual partners will recognize income based on the difference between what they paid for their partnership interest and the amount of cash they receive. Depending on the timing of the dissolution, the partners may have taxable income (based on a sale of partnership assets) even before the distribution.

Example

Sam purchased his interest in the XYZ Partnership five years ago for $50,000. His basis in his partnership interest has been adjusted because of various distributions and other items, and it is now $30,000. Upon dissolution of the partnership in 1989, Sam receives $100,000 in cash. Sam computes his gain by subtracting his $30,000 adjusted basis from the $100,000 amount received, so he is taxable at his individual income tax rates (up to 28 percent) on $70,000.

When a partner receives property instead of cash in a distribution from the partnership, no gain will be recognized to a partner on the liquidating distribution of the noncash property. When property is distributed in some other context, as in ongoing partnership operations, again the partner recognizes no gain and will take a basis in the asset equal to the basis that the asset had in the partnership's hands immediately prior to the distribution.

Q: BUT ISN'T THE TERMINATION
OF THE PARTNERSHIP'S TAX YEAR
A DISADVANTAGE?

A: It depends. The termination of the partnership's tax year is generally bad if the partnership will be continued. For tax purposes, a partnership may be treated as terminating, with a new partnership starting thereafter, even though the business is not interrupted at all. The most common situation in which this termination treatment occurs is when there is a transfer of 50 percent or more of the total capital and profits interest in the partnership during any 12-month period. When this occurs, the partnership is treated as terminating, and a new partnership is treated as commencing on the following day.

Example

The XYZ partnership has 20 partners, each of whom own equal interests (they each own 5 percent of the total interest in the partnership). Because of a variety of disagreements amongst the partners, six of the partners (holding a total of 30 percent) sell their interests to outsiders in May. After continuing disagreements, four additional partners sell their interest the following March. A total of 10 partners (50 percent of the partnership) have transferred their interests within a 12-month period.

Accordingly, the partnership is treated as "terminating" for federal tax purposes, even though the business was never interrupted and the partnership maintains the same name. Note that even though the May and March transfers were in two separate tax years of the partnership, they occurred within a 12-month period and consequently are aggregated for purposes of determining whether 50 percent or more of the total partnership interests have changed hands.

Q: WHY IS THIS PARTNERSHIP TERMINATION A BAD THING WHEN THE BUSINESS WILL BE CONTINUED?

A: The termination of the partnership has no negative effects when the partnership will actually be dissolved. It is the continuation of a partnership thereafter, as in the preceding example concerning transfers of interests, that is disadvantageous. The partnership must begin anew with depreciation methods for property, tax elections, and so on.

The partnership's tax year will also be split into two: one portion of the year leading up to the terminating event and a separate tax year thereafter. This separation can create artificially high income to individual partners because more than one partnership year will be included in the individual partner's tax year.

On combinations of partnerships, see Chapter 9.

DJI Planning Guide _____

Although in the dissolution context, concern over the termination of the partnership is normally minimal, it is always a good idea to maintain an accurate log of transfers of partnership interests so that unintentional terminations can be avoided.

CORPORATIONS

Q: HOW IS A CORPORATION TAXED UPON DISSOLUTION?

A: This procedure is highly complex and has changed substantially in recent years. There are two incidences of taxation: one at the corporate level and one at the shareholder level. If a corporation dissolves and distributes its assets to shareholders, then the corporation will have to pay a tax based on the difference between its basis in the assets and the market value of those assets.

Example

Slumpco, Inc. has one major asset: a chemical production plant in which it has an adjusted basis of $1 million. (It originally purchased the plant for $1.5 million, and this figure has been reduced by $500,000 in depreciation deductions taken over the last few years, leading to an adjusted basis of $1 million.) The market value of the plant is $3 million.

Slumpco distributes the plant to its sole shareholder, who plans to conduct the business in the future as a proprietorship rather than in the corporate form. Slumpco must pay a tax on this liquidating distribution on the difference between the $3 million market value and its $1 million adjusted basis. This $2 million gain is taxed at the corporate level between the graduated corporate rates of 15 and 34 percent.

Under the corporate rate structure, the first $50,000 in corporate income is taxed at the 15 percent rate. The next $25,000 in corporate income (between $50,000 and $75,000) is taxed at the 25 percent rate, and anything over $75,000 is taxed at the 34 percent rate. Consequently, nearly all of the $2 million gain Slumpco has on its liquidating distribution would be taxed at the 34 percent corporate rate. The tax is a whopping $668,250!

Q: DOES THE CORPORATION PAY THE TAX EVEN IF THE ASSETS ARE NOT SOLD?

A: Yes. Even if the corporation does not sell its assets but only distributes them, it will pay a tax. Note, though, that the corporation pays a tax only to the extent the assets have appreciated. For example, if the corporation distributes cash, then it does not pay a tax on the cash distribution. If the corporation distributes property, then only the appreciation in the property is taxed.

Example

Liquid Co. is in the process of liquidating. It sells its major asset, a commercial building, for $5 million. It has an adjusted basis in the building of $1 million. The company also has various machinery and personal property that it plans to distribute in kind to several of the major shareholders. What will the tax be on the distribution?

The corporation will pay a tax on the $4 million of appreciation on the building. Moreover, the corporation will also pay a tax based on the appreciation in any of its personal property. Any cash distributed will not itself result in taxes at the corporate level.

Q: WHY DOES THE CORPORATION PAY A TAX EVEN IF IT DOES NOT SELL ITS ASSETS?

A: As a result of amendments made in the Tax Reform Act of 1986, a corporation is required to pay tax on any appreciation in its assets on liquidation even if the assets are not sold. In effect, the distribution of the assets is treated as a sale at the market value of the property.

Q: DOES THIS NEW GAIN RECOGNITION REQUIREMENT APPLY TO ALL CORPORATIONS?

A: When the 1986 Tax Reform Act was passed, the new rules applied to most corporations that were not liquidated before the end of 1986. However, limited classes of corporations were given until the end of 1988 to liquidate without being subject to the new rules. The classes of corporations that were entitled to liquidate and not to recognize gain based on appreciation in the corporation's assets had to satisfy the following requirements:

• More than 50 percent of the value of the corporation's stock must be held by 10 or fewer persons.
• These 10 or fewer shareholders must be individuals, estates, or certain types of trusts (but not corporations).
• The total value of the stock cannot exceed $10 million.

Q: DOES THIS MEAN THAT CORPORATIONS FALLING WITHIN THIS $10 MILLION RULE CAN LIQUIDATE ANY TIME BEFORE JANUARY 1, 1989, AND NOT PAY ANY TAX?

A: Not quite. There are a number of limitations to this favorable "grandfathering" treatment. (The rule is sometimes referred to as a grandfather rule because it allows old law treatment.)

One of the limitations is the value of the corporation. Although corporations with a value of up to $10 million can qualify for this relief rule, the value of the corporation actually has to be $5 million or less in order to be entitled to complete relief from the new tax. If the value of the corporation is between $5 million and $10 million, then only partial relief from the new rules is available, with some new tax applying.

Consider the following example.

Example

Pentangle Corporation has five individual shareholders who own 100 percent of the stock (hence the stock ownership requirement is satisfied). The corporation has a value of $7 million, and it is liquidated in November of 1988. Is a double tax payable on the distribution of the corporation's assets?

The answer here is yes and no. Under the relief provision granted to corporations having a value of $10 million or less on liquidations occurring before 1989, the first $5 million in value can be distributed generally under the old (pre-1986 Tax Reform Act) rules governing corporate liquidations. The balance between $5 million and $7 million receives partial old law treatment and partial new law treatment. The result is that, overall, 40 percent of the gains on the liquidation will be taxed under the new rules and 60 percent will not.

Q: HOW CAN THE PERCENTAGE OF OLD AND NEW LAW TREATMENT BE DETERMINED?

A: It can be determined by a formula, or, as shown here, it can be summarized in tabular form.

Value of Corporation	Percentage of Gain Taxed under New Rules
$10,000,000	100%
9,500,000	90
9,000,000	80
8,500,000	70
8,000,000	60
7,500,000	50
7,000,000	40
6,500,000	30
6,000,000	20
5,500,000	10
5,000,000	0

Q: SO IF THE VALUE OF THE CORPORATION IS $5 MILLION OR LESS AND THE SHAREHOLDER REQUIREMENT IS MET, THERE IS NO GAIN ON A LIQUIDATION BEFORE 1989?

A: Even this is not quite accurate. Although this is generally the case, there are several exceptions that make this tax treatment slightly less favorable than it would have been prior to the enactment of the 1986 Tax Reform Act. So it does not provide "complete relief" from the operation of the new tax rules.

These exceptions require gain recognition in the case of ordinary income assets (inventory and the like), short-term capital assets (capital assets held for less than the requisite one year holding period), and dispositions of installment obligations.

Example

Slumpco has five individual shareholders who own 100 percent of the stock, and the value of the company is $5 million. Slumpco liquidates in December of 1988 in order to take advantage of the favorable transitional rules governing liquidations. The corporation has appreciated factory assets, a small amount of appreciated inventory, and cash. The transitional rule provisions will enable it to liquidate without recognizing the gain upon the appreciation in the factory. However, because the inventory is an ordinary income asset, Slumpco will recognize gain on the distribution of the inventory.

Q: IF A CORPORATION DOES NOT USE THIS PROVISION BEFORE THE END OF 1988, IS THE BENEFIT OF THE RULE LOST?

A: Generally speaking, yes. At this writing, there is still enough time left in 1988 to take advantage of these favorable liquidation rules for small corporations. The alternative, also available through the end of 1988, is to file an election to be treated as a subchapter S corporation. S corporations, discussed in Chapters 1 and 2, are flow-through entities that are generally not taxed themselves.

If neither a liquidation nor an S election is made before 1989, the new—and more expensive—tax rules will apply when and if the corporation is liquidated.

DJI Planning Guide

For the corporations that qualify, either a liquidation or an S election prior to 1989 is generally available. Although many factors go into the decision, in most cases a liquidation or S election for these small corporations represents a last window of opportunity—now a brief one with the end of 1988 drawing near.

Q: WHY WOULD THESE SMALL CORPORATIONS ELECT TO BE S CORPORATIONS?

A: As an alternative to undergoing a complete liquidation, corporations meeting the above requirements (and otherwise satisfying the S election requirements discussed in Chapter 1) can make an S election. The objective of the S election would be to avoid the corporate level gain recognition that ultimately would be incurred on a liquidation of the corporation. The S election in some cases can obviate the need for a liquidation because, under the S corporation rules, individual shareholders would be taxed on each individual item of income, gain, loss, deduction, and credit of the S corporation.

When the S corporation ultimately does liquidate, it will be treated under the old corporate liquidation rules so that the corporation will not generally recognize a gain itself (i.e., only the shareholders will pay a tax, so there will be a single rather than a double tax).

Q: WHAT IF A CORPORATION THAT DOES NOT QUALIFY FOR THIS TRANSITIONAL RELIEF MAKES AN S ELECTION?

A: Even if the corporation does not qualify for the transitional relief described above, it can make an S election and will be treated as an S corporation. The problem lies in what happens if a corporation disposes of some of its assets after its election goes into effect. Since an S corporation does not generally pay a separate tax at the corporate level, and there is only a single-level tax payable by the shareholder, there is a great incentive for all the corporations that are eligible (regarding eligibility for S elections, see Chapter 1) to elect S treatment to avoid the corporate level tax on a liquidation.

In order to curb this incentive, Congress enacted a new tax in 1986 called the "built-in gain tax" which is imposed on S corporations that converted from C corporations. This built-in gain tax is designed to tax any appreciation in the value of a corporation's assets that occurred *before* it converted to S status (i.e., before its S election became effective).

Q: HOW DOES THIS BUILT-IN GAIN TAX WORK?

A: The built-in gain tax is not imposed at the time the election is made but rather when the assets are later disposed of if the disposition occurs within 10 years.

Example

Corporation XYZ has $15 million worth of assets and 25 shareholders. All the shareholders are individuals, and there are no nonresident aliens. Further, the corporation has only one class of stock. The corporation therefore qualifies to make an S election. The corporation makes the S election, and the shareholders consent.

Five years later, the corporation disposes of assets that had already appreciated in the corporation's hands before the S election was filed. A "built-in gain tax" is imposed on the S corporation based on the appreciation in the transferred assets that occurred before the S election became effective. Note that subsequent appreciation in the assets *after* the S election and before the sale is not counted in determining the amount of the built-in gain tax.

To take an example, if a corporation converts to S status at a time when it has assets having a basis of $5 million and a market value of $10 million, the maximum built-in gain tax that could be imposed later on would be based on $5 million. At the 34 percent tax rate that applies to built-in gains, this would mean a tax of $1.7 million.

Even if the assets increased in value by another $20 million or $30 million dollars between the effective date of the S election and the time the assets were disposed of, the built-in gain tax could still be imposed *only* on the $5 million gain that occurred before the S election became effective. This is because the built-in gain tax is designed to tax only "built-in" gain—that is, gain that arose and was built in when a corporation converted from regular C corporation status to S corporation status.

DJI Planning Guide

The taxpayer has the burden of proving the amount of *post*-S election appreciation. (The IRS has an incentive to maximize the *pre*–S election appreciation.) Consequently, it is a good idea to get appraisals of assets as of the date the S election becomes effective as a means of anticipating any dispute on the issue.

Q: IF A CORPORATION DOES NOT QUALIFY FOR THESE TRANSITIONAL RELIEF PROVISIONS AND IS NOT AN S CORPORATION, WHAT HAPPENS UPON LIQUIDATION?

A: As described above, the general rule is that the corporation must pay a tax upon liquidation whether it sells its assets or distributes them in kind to its shareholders. The corporation pays a tax on any appreciation in its assets, and then the shareholders pay a second tax on distribution.

Q: HOW IS THE SHAREHOLDER TAX COMPUTED?

A: The shareholders pay a tax on whatever they receive, less their basis in their stock.

Example

Shareholder S receives $50,000 in liquidation of the corporation of which he is a shareholder. He originally paid $20,000 for the stock, so he has a $30,000 gain. Since stock normally is classified as a capital asset, the gain will be a capital gain. If S has held the stock for more than a year, then it will be a long-term capital gain.

Note

Although the capital gain/ordinary income distinction has no current tax rate significance, capital gains and losses must still be separately netted, and excess capital losses are subject to strict deduction limits ($3,000 per year for individuals). See Chapter 10 for discussion.

Q: IS THERE ANY WAY TO AVOID THIS GAIN RECOGNITION ON LIQUIDATION?

A: Not directly, but it can be offset with corporate-level losses. Because of the incentives to artificially create losses at the corporate level to offset this corporate-level gain, the law now includes restrictions on the allowability of losses. Specifically, a liquidating corporation may not recognize a loss on the distribution of any property to a related person in certain circumstances. Additionally, a liquidating corporation may not recognize losses on property that was acquired for "loss recognition" purposes.

Q: WHAT DO THESE LOSS NONRECOGNITION RULES MEAN?

A: These loss nonrecognition rules mean that the corporation may have difficulty deducting losses even though it will be taxed on its gains. If this seems unfair, the tax avoidance intent that Congress was trying to single out should be mentioned.

Since the new scheme of taxing corporations on appreciation in their assets upon liquidation was new beginning in 1987, Congress was concerned that corporations would try to artificially create losses to offset these new corporate-level gains. The loss nonrecognition rules are designed to prevent this behavior.

The first restriction on losses prevents a deduction for a loss on a distribution to a related person unless the property is distributed to shareholders pro rata. It is designed to prevent a corporation from taking a loss when the assets are not really disposed of (i.e., are not sold to an unrelated party). The idea is that the asset upon which there is an inherent loss (meaning that the market value of the asset is *less* than its adjusted basis) will really stay in the family, so to speak, and that it is not appropriate in this situation to allow a loss deduction.

In fact, even if the property is distributed pro rata, certain types of property (basically property acquired in certain tax-free transactions within the last five years) will not generate a deductible loss.

Q: WHAT IS AN ASSET ACQUIRED FOR LOSS RECOGNITION PURPOSES?

A: It is not entirely clear how far the second restriction—namely preventing a deduction for losses when the property was acquired for loss recognition purposes—will go. Basically, however, what the rule was designed to prevent is a contribution of property on a tax-free basis to a corporation that will produce a loss, if the contribution is made within two years of a liquidation.

The idea is that if the liquidation occurs this soon (within two years) after the contribution of this "loss" property, then the IRS will assume that the reason for the contribution was to generate a loss. Notably, this rule generally does not apply to properties that are logically connected to the trade or business of the corporation.

Example

Furnimaker, Inc. produces home furnishings and, shortly prior to liquidating, acquires several oil wells on a tax-free basis that have a much higher basis than fair market value. The corporation liquidates and uses the loss on the oil wells to offset its gain on its furniture and other assets.

The loss on the oil wells here would probably not be allowed because there is no connection between the oil wells and the furniture, and it looks as though the oil wells have been acquired for the principal purpose of loss recognition. But if the loss assets were furniture or other assets that could be used in Furnimaker's business, the result would be different.

Q: ARE ANY LIQUIDATIONS TAX-FREE NOW?

A: Yes. As recently as 1986, most liquidations were tax-free at least to the corporation. The shareholders paid a tax based on what they received, but at least the corporation did not. Now, apart from the transitional rules discussed earlier for liquidations before 1989, liquidations will generally be expensive from a tax standpoint.

But there is at least one context in which tax-free liquidations will still be possible even after 1988, and that is for parent-subsidiary liquidations. A parent corporation that owns at least 80 percent of the stock of another corporation (its subsidiary) can liquidate the subsidiary tax-free. This tax-free treatment applies only to the extent the assets of the liquidating company are distributed to the parent. If appreciated assets are distributed to any minority shareholders, there will be a tax to the liquidating corporation.

Example

Dull Corporation is owned 90 percent by Boring Corporation and 10 percent by Smith. Dull distributes its assets 90 percent to Boring and 10 percent to Smith, with Smith receiving assets having a basis to Dull of $50,000 and a market value of $200,000. Dull must pay a tax on the $150,000 of appreciation on these assets. (Of course, Smith must also pay a tax on the value of what he received, $200,000, less his basis in his stock.) Dull is not required to pay a tax on the distribution to Boring.

DJI Planning Guide _____

Because the tax on distributions to minority shareholders is only on the appreciation in the liquidating subsidiary's assets, it may be wise to try to distribute unappreciated assets or cash to the minority shareholders in this situation. This will not alter the taxes payable by the shareholders—Smith in the above example. But it can reduce or eliminate the tax payable by the liquidating corporation.

GLOSSARY

INTRODUCTION

This glossary provides brief definitions of many of the technical and quasi-technical terms used in this book.

Accelerated Cost Recovery System Also called ACRS, this is a depreciation system applying to property placed in service between 1981 and 1987.

accelerated depreciation A faster method of depreciation than straight line depreciation. Under straight line depreciation, the cost of an asset is recovered in equal installments over a number of years. With accelerated depreciation, larger depreciation deductions are taken in the earlier years, with smaller deductions later on.

accrual method of accounting The method of accounting that determines income by when the right to receive income matures even though it might be paid at a later date.

accumulated adjustments account An S corporation's post-1982 accumulated gross income, less its deductible expenses. This account determines the amount of tax-free distributions that may be made by an S corporation.

accumulated earnings tax A special tax imposed on the earnings of a corporation to the extent they are in excess of the corporation's "reasonable needs." The accumulated earnings tax is imposed at the rate of 27.5 percent on the first $100,000 of accumulated taxable income and 38.5 percent on any excess.

affiliated group A group of corporations connected through 80 percent or more common ownership.

amortization A tax treatment similar to depreciation that results in deductions for an item over a period of time. For example, organizational expenditures of a corporation cannot be deducted immediately, but must be amortized over 60 months.

applicable federal rates The interest rates announced by the IRS that determine the amount of imputed interest that will be treated as paid and received where an obligation does not mean adequate stated interest.

association taxable as a corporation A partnership that has corporate characteristics (such as centralized management, continuity of life, free transferability of interests, and limited liability) and therefore is taxed like a corporation.

at risk The amount a person stands to lose in an investment.

basis The amount paid for something that establishes its cost for tax purposes. Basis can be adjusted upward through additional investment or downward by depreciation and certain other adjustments.

built-in gain A measurement applying to S corporations that were previously C corporations. The built-in gain is the amount of appreciation in the assets of the corporation that occurred prior to the effective date of the S election. The measurement is used to impose a "built-in gain tax" on any disposition of the assets by the S corporation within 10 years of its conversion from C status.

business bad debt A debt that becomes uncollectible made in connection with the taxpayer's trade or business and for business reasons. Business bad debts are deductible as ordinary losses.

C corporation An entity that is treated as a separate taxable entity from that of its shareholders. In most cases, unless a corporation is specifically described as an S corporation, it is a C corporation.

capital account The bookkeeping account that every partnership maintains showing the amount contributed by a partner. A partner's capital account is increased by his contributions to the partnership and decreased by distributions made to him.

capital gain The gain produced upon the disposition of a capital asset. Under earlier law, capital gains were treated more favorably than ordinary income and taxed at a lesser rate. Today, the tax rates on capital gain and ordinary income are the same.

capitalize To treat an asset as a capital asset or Section 1231 asset and depreciate over time.

carryback The practice of carrying back to prior years a tax loss so that income tax paid in prior years can be refunded.

carryover The practice of carrying an excess loss into the future so that it can be offset against future income.

cash method of accounting The accounting system that measures income by actual cash received.

constructive receipt The doctrine under which income may be treated as received even though the taxpayer does not take physical possession of it. The idea is that the taxpayer has the right to get it but does not exercise that right as a way of attempting to defer receipt of the income.

debt-financed portfolio stock A type of stock purchased with borrowed funds that results in a restriction on the dividends received deduction when dividends are paid on such stock.

defined benefit plan A type of qualified retirement plan under which participants are promised a particular benefit (such as 50 percent of salary) on retirement.

defined contribution plan A type of qualified retirement plan under which the participants are promised a certain contribution to the plan (such as 7 percent of salary or a percent of profits to be allocated to compensation) but no particular benefit on retirement.

delayed exchange A tax-free exchange under which the swap of the like-kind property is not simultaneous. It often involves a third party.

de minimus fringe benefits Small fringe benefits such as employer provided coffee and personal use of employer's coffee machines that are not taxable to employees.

depreciation Deductions that allow a taxpayer to recover the cost of an item over its useful life.

depreciation recapture Taxation at ordinary income rates on a sale or other disposition of depreciable property. Recapture applies to all depreciation taken on personal property but only the excess depreciation over straight line depreciation taken on real property.

discharge of indebtedness A circumstance that occurs and creates taxable income when the debtor is relieved of paying a debt. The two cases in which taxable income does not arise on a discharge of indebtedness are when the debtor is insolvent or when the discharge of indebtedness occurs in a bankruptcy case under Title 11 of the Bankruptcy Code.

dividends received deduction A series of deductions to which a corporation may be entitled upon receipt of dividends from other corporations. Depending on the amount of stock in the dividend-paying company that the receiving corporation holds, the deduction from dividends received may be 20 percent of the dividends, 70 percent of the dividends, or even 100 percent of the dividends.

divisive reorganization A wholly or partially tax-free division of a business into several different corporations.

earnings and profits The cumulative book earnings (adjusted by certain Internal Revenue Code provisions) of the corporation from prior years as well as the current year. They control the extent to which distributions from a corporation are treated as dividends and are also relevant for computing passive investment income of S corporations.

Employee Stock Ownership Plan Also called an ESOP, this is a type of qualified retirement plan designed to invest in employer securities.

expense Used as a verb, meaning to deduct the cost of an item entirely in one year.

First In First Out Also called FIFO, this is an inventory method that assumes the first inventory acquired (the oldest) is the first inventory sold.

fiscal year A tax year other than a calendar year.

401(k) plan Also called a "Cash or Deferred" plan or a "Cafeteria Plan," this is a type of plan that allows participants to elect whether to receive contributions in cash or to have them go into the plan.

imputed interest The interest that is treated as paid by a payor and received by a recipient, even though not stated to be "interest," when property is sold or an obligation is issued for less than an adequate stated interest rate. The IRS announces monthly what it considers adequate interest.

incentive stock options A type of stock option qualifying for special tax rules.

independent contractor Someone who renders services other than as an employee and is therefore not subject to withholding on his wages.

Individual Retirement Account Also called an IRA, this is the most popular retirement vehicle ever.

installment sale A sale under which a portion of the gain on the sale is taxable with each installment, instead of all of the tax being due up front.

inventory Assets held by a business that will produce ordinary income on sale.

involuntary conversion An event, such as destruction of property by fire, flood, earthquake, or government taking, that entitles a taxpayer to reinvest the proceeds (i.e., proceeds received from insurance or from a condemning governmental authority) tax-free.

Keogh plan A type of qualified retirement plan that may be set up only by partnerships and proprietorships. Corporations are not eligible. Rules governing Keogh plans are roughly parallel to those governing corporate plans.

Last In First Out Also called LIFO, this is an inventory method that assumes the most recently acquired inventory is the first inventory sold.

Leveraged Buyout Also called an LBO, this is an acquisition of a company using someone else's money. The lender lends against the strength of the assets of the company being purchased and the future cash flow of the acquired business.

like-kind Property that qualifies for a tax-free swap. It generally must be business property or property held for investment.

like-kind exchange A nontaxable exchange of property that must be either trade or business property or property held for investment.

listed property Property that is restricted as to depreciation and other deductions. Listed property includes automobiles, airplanes, trucks, and boats. It also includes certain entertainment, recreational, and amusement property, and computers and peripheral equipment.

long-term capital gain A gain produced upon the disposition of a capital asset held for more than one year. Such gains are no longer subject to a more favorable rate than ordinary income.

lump-sum distribution A type of distribution from a qualified retirement plan on the retirement of a participant that qualifies for favorable tax rules.

miscellaneous deductions The type of deductions that are now restricted in deductibility and are deductible to an individual only to the extent they exceed 2 percent of the individual's adjusted gross income. Most employee business expenses now fall into this category.

Modified Accelerated Cost Recovery System Also called MACRS, this is a system of depreciation applicable to property placed in service after 1987.

Net Operating Losses Also called an NOL, these are accumulated losses of a corporation that may be carried over into the future or carried back.

nonbusiness bad debt A debt made in a nonbusiness context that becomes collectible. It is deductible only as a capital loss.

nonqualified stock options A type of stock option not qualifying for special tax treatment.

nonrecourse liabilities A liability not extending beyond particular property, such as a real estate loan, where foreclosure on the property represents the maximum remedy the lender can pursue.

ordinary income Any type of income other than capital gain. Ordinary income includes salary, dividends, interest, and so on.

partial liquidation A cessation of part of a corporation's business, frequently accompanied by a sale of part of the corporation's assets.

passive investment income The type of income, consisting of dividends, interest, royalties, etc., that may result in an S corporation losing its status as an S corporation and reverting to C corporation status.

passive investment income tax A tax applicable only to S corporations on passive investment income such as dividends, interest, and royalties. The tax is imposed only on S corporations that have earnings and profits from years during which the corporation was a C corporation, and then only on passive investment income totaling more than 25 percent of the corporation's gross receipts.

personal holding company income   The type of income that subjects personal holding companies to the personal holding company tax. Basically, personal holding company income includes dividends, interest, royalties, and annuities. It also includes rents, mineral, oil and gas royalties, copyright royalties, and a variety of other items if certain percentage tests are met.

personal holding company tax   A tax imposed on certain closely held corporations, principally on investment income. The tax is imposed at the rate of 38.5 percent on the undistributed personal holding company income. The tax can be avoided by distributing money out to shareholders as a dividend.

personal interest   Interest that is not related to a trade or business or investment and therefore restricted as to deductibility. Forty percent of personal interest is deductible in 1988, 20 percent in 1989, 10 percent in 1990, and personal interest is not deductible at all thereafter.

personal service corporation   A corporation that engages in activities involving the performance of services in the fields of health, law, engineering, architecture, actuarial science, performing arts, or consulting. Such corporations are not eligible for the graduated corporate income tax rates and are instead taxed at a flat 34 percent rate.

phantom stock   A plan involving the creation of artificial shares that are treated economically as shares in the company for purposes of employee awards but do not entail any voting rights.

production of income   An activity that, even though not rising to the level of a "business," nevertheless is undertaken for profit. An example is investment activity such as investing in the stock market.

publicly traded partnerships   A partnership that meets certain tests as to interests being traded on an established securities market (or an equivalent) and that is therefore taxed like a corporation rather than a partnership.

qualified replacement property   The type of securities that a seller may reacquire tax-free after a sale of stock to an employee stock ownership plan (ESOP).

qualified subchapter S trust   A trust with individual beneficiaries that elects to be treated as the owner of S corporation stock and can therefore qualify to be a shareholder of an S corporation. Generally, other types of trusts are not eligible to be S corporation shareholders.

rabbi trust   A type of deferral agreement between employer and employee involving a trust arrangement that can defer the receipt of income and its taxability into the future.

reasonable compensation   The amount of compensation that may be deducted as a business expense. Compensation in excess of this amorphous limit would be unreasonable compensation and therefore not deductible even though paid.

recapitalization   A tax-free reorganization of one company involving the issuance of different stock and/or debt instruments.

recourse liability   A liability for which a taxpayer such as a partnership may be pursued and individually held liable.

restricted stock   Stock issued to employees under a plan that restricts the ability of the employee to dispose of the stock. Such plans are generally structured so that the employee is not currently taxable on the stock.

retained earnings   The entry on a corporation's balance sheet that is a rough guide to the corporation's earnings and profits. Although earnings and profits and retained earnings are not identical, there is a rough correlation between them.

rollover   A reinvestment of funds distributed from a qualified retirement plan, typically into an IRA. If made within 60 days after the plan distribution, and if certain requirements are met, the distribution will not be taxed until it ultimately comes out of the IRA.

S corporation   A corporation that has filed an election to be treated basically as a partnership, so that items of income, loss, deduction, and credit flow through to the shareholders and are not separately taxable to the corporation. To be able to make such an election, the corporation must have no more than 35 shareholders, no corporate shareholders, and no nonresident aliens as shareholders. Also, it can have only one class of stock.

schedule K-1   A portion of a partnership tax return that shows the amount of income or loss of a partner in the partnership. The K-1 is attached to the partner's individual tax return.

Section 338 election An election made by the acquirer of stock in a corporation to have the acquisition treated as an assets acquisition rather than a stock acquisition.

Section 382 limitation The formula limitation applying to the use of a net operating loss by a buyer after the acquisition of a company having a net operating loss.

Section 1231 assets Assets that are treated just like capital assets for nearly all purposes except for determining the limits on the deduction for losses from their sale. Depreciable business property and real property used in a taxpayer's trade or business are technically not capital assets but are instead Section 1231 assets.

Section 1244 stock Stock issued by certain small corporations that have capital of $1 million or less. If Section 1244 stock becomes worthless, then the holder of the stock can take an ordinary loss deduction instead of a capital loss deduction. The ordinary loss deduction is subject to an overall limit of $50,000 per year.

short-term capital gain The gain produced on the disposition of a capital asset held for one year or less.

stock-for-assets acquisition A tax-free acquisition by one company using its stock to acquire the assets of another corporation.

stock-for-stock acquisition A tax-free acquisition by one company using its stock to acquire another.

straight line depreciation Depreciation taken ratably over the life of an asset.

withholding An act required by an employer of all income taxes, Social Security taxes ("FICA"), and unemployment taxes ("FUTA"). Withholding is required on "wages," which includes all remuneration for services whether paid in cash or not.

worthless stock loss The tax loss to which the taxpayer is entitled when stock becomes valueless. It is deductible only as a capital loss.

INDEX

About the Author

Robert W. Wood, of the California and Arizona Bars, is a partner with the law firm of Steefel, Levitt & Weiss in San Francisco. A graduate of the University of Chicago Law School, he is Certified as a Specialist in Taxation by the California Board of Legal Specialization.

In addition to maintaining an active practice that emphasizes business and tax planning matters, Mr. Wood has written several other books in the tax field and more than 50 articles in a variety of legal, business, and trade publications. He also serves on the editorial boards of a half-dozen leading tax magazines and speaks regularly to trade and professional groups.